YOUTH PARTICIPATION IN EUROPE

Beyond discourses, practices and realities

Edited by Patricia Loncle, Morena Cuconato,
Virginie Muniglia and Andreas Walther

First published in Great Britain in 2012 by

The Policy Press
University of Bristol
Fourth Floor
Beacon House
Queen's Road
Bristol BS8 1QU
UK
t: +44 (0)117 331 4054
f: +44 (0)117 331 4093
tpp-info@bristol.ac.uk
www.policypress.co.uk

North America office:
The Policy Press
c/o The University of Chicago Press
1427 East 60th Street
Chicago, IL 60637, USA
t: +1 773 702 7700
f: +1 773-702-9756
sales@press.uchicago.edu
www.press.uchicago.edu

British Library Cataloguing in Publication Data
A catalogue record for this book is available from the British Library.

Library of Congress Cataloging-in-Publication Data
A catalog record for this book has been requested.

ISBN 978 1 44730 018 2 hardcover

The right of Patricia Loncle, Morena Cuconato, Virginie Muniglia and
Andreas Walther to be identified as editors of this work has been asserted by them
in accordance with the Copyright, Designs and Patents Act 1988.

The statements and opinions contained within this publication are solely those
of the editors and contributors and not of the University of Bristol or The Policy
Press. The University of Bristol and The Policy Press disclaim responsibility for
any injury to persons or property resulting from any material published in this
publication.

The Policy Press works to counter discrimination on grounds of
gender, race, disability, age and sexuality.

Cover design by The Policy Press.
Front cover: image kindly supplied by istock
Printed and bound in Great Britain by MPG Book Group
The Policy Press uses environmentally responsible print partners

Contents

List of figures and tables

Figures

Tables

About the contributors

Shakuntala Banaji is lecturer in media and communications at the London School of Economics and Political Science, UK. She lectures in film theory, world cinema, youth media, communication and development and has published widely on cinema, audiences, gender, ethnicity and politics, creativity and online civic participation. Her recent books include: *Reading Bollywood: The Young Audience and Hindi Film* (2006/2011); *South Asian Media Cultures: Audiences, Representations, Contexts* (2010/2011); *The Civic Web: Young People, Civic Participation and the Internet in Europe* (co-authored with David Buckingham and due out from MIT Press in 2012).

Valérie Becquet is a lecturer in sociology at the University of Cergy-Pontoise, France. Her research focuses on youth citizenship, dealing with youth participative practices in school and out of school and public policies aimed to develop political integration and youth involvement. She recently published: (ed) *L'expérience du service civil volontaire à Unis-Cité: quels enseignements pour le service civique?*, INJEP (2011); 'Le service civil volontaire en France: un dispositif public de socialisation politique des jeunes?', in S. Pickard, C. Nativel, and F. Portier (eds), *Jeunesse et Politique(s) en France et au Royaume-Uni aujourd'hui*, PSN (2011); 'L'engagement des jeunes dans l'espace public', in B. Roudet (ed), *Regard sur les jeunes en France*, Presses de l'université Laval, INJEP (2009).

David Buckingham is professor of media and communications at Loughborough University, UK. His research focuses on children and young people's interactions with electronic media, and on media education. His recent books include: *Beyond Technology: Children's Learning in the Age of Digital Culture* (2007); *Video Cultures: Media Technology and Everyday Creativity* (2009); *The Material Child: Growing Up in Consumer Culture* (2011).

Paul Burgess is senior lecturer/director youth and community work in the Department of Applied Social Studies, University College Cork, Ireland. His main research and teaching interests are community and youth development, community relations, cultural identity, European social policy, conflict resolution and educational issues. His main publications include: *Highways, Crossroads and Cul de Sacs: Journeys into Irish Youth and Community Work*, with P. Herrmann, Bremen:

Europäische Hochschulschriften (2010): *The Reconciliation Industry: Community Relations, Community Identity and Social Policy in Northern Ireland*, Edwin Mellen Press (2002); *A Crisis of Conscience: Moral Ambivalence and Education in Northern Ireland*, Avebury/Ashgate (1993).

Filip Coussée is a social pedagogue. He works as a researcher at Ghent University, Belgium. His focus is on social pedagogy as a perspective on social work and youth and community work. He studied the history of youth work in Flanders and its connections to developments in the other social professions and in other European countries. He works part time for Uit De Marge, the umbrella organisation of youth work initiatives working with socially excluded children and young people. His publications include: 'Empowering the powerful: challenging hidden processes of marginalization in youth work policy and practice in Belgium', *Critical Social Policy*, vol 29, no 3, pp 421–42 (with G. Roets and M. De Bie, 2009); 'The emerging social pedagogical paradigm in UK child and youth care: deus ex machina or walking the beaten path?', *British Journal of Social Work*, vol 40, no 1, pp 789–805 (with L. Bradt, R. Roose and M. De Bie, 2010); *The History of Youth Work in Europe and its Relevance for Youth Policy Today*, vol 2, Strasbourg: Council of Europe Publishing (with G. Verschelden, T. Van de Walle, M. Medlinska, and H. Williamson, 2010).

Morena Cuconato is associate professor for general and social pedagogy at the Department of Educational Sciences at the University of Bologna, Italy. She teaches and carries out research in the areas of youth policies, transitions in the life course, youth welfare and European school systems in comparative perspective. Her main publications include: *Politiche giovanili in Europa. Germania e Italia tra innovazione e continuità*, Bergamo: Edzioni Junior (with G. Lenzi, 1999); *Educazione comparata. L'internazionalizzazione dei sistemi formativi*, Bologna: Pitagora (2002); *La mia vita é uno yo-yo. Diventare adulti in Europa tra opportunità e rischi*, Roma: Carocci (2011).

Nicola De Luigi is tenured assistant professor at the Achille Ardigò Department of Sociology and the R. Ruffilli Faculty of Political Science (Forlì) of the University of Bologna, Italy. The main focus of his research has dealt with the relationship between youth, education and the labour market and the gender differences in transition to adulthood with a focus on work–family reconciliation issues. He has also focused his research on the analysis of the precariousness of social life connected with transformations in employment trends. His publications include: 'Les jeunes et le marché du travail en Italie, entre continuité et signaux de changement', in M. Vultur and D. Mercure (eds), *Perspectives internationales sur le travail des jeunes*, Montreal: Presses de l'Université Laval (2011); *Giovani e genere. L'immaginario degli studenti sammarinesi*, Roma: Carocci (with L. Gobbi (a cura di), 2010); 'Learning about children's participation in practice. Commentary' in B. Percy Smith, N. Thomas (eds), *A Handbook of Children and Young People's Participation. Perspectives from theory and practice*, London and New York: Routledge (with R. Bertozzi, A. Martelli and A. Mathew, 2009).

Lourdes Gaitán is lecturer doctor in the Faculty of Social and Human Sciences in Universidad Pontificia Comillas, Spain. Her fields of research are sociology of childhood, social policies of childhood, children's wellbeing and children's rights. Her main publications include: *Sociología de la infancia* (*Sociology of Childhood*), Madrid: Editorial Sintesis (2006); 'Childhood welfare and the rights of children' in S. Andresen, I. Diehm, U. Sander and H. Ziegler (eds), *Children and the Good Life: New Challenges for Research on Children. Dordrecht*, Heidelberg: Springer (2010); *Participación y ciudadanía de los niños ¿Derechos otorgados o derechos conquistados?* (*Participation and children's citizenship. Rights granted or rights won?*), Madrid: Editorial Sintesis (forthcoming).

Camilla Granholm is a PhD student in social work in the Swedish School of Social Science at the University of Helsinki, Finland. Her main research focus is Internet as a source of support and help for young people dealing with difficulties with mental health and life management issues. She recently published: 'Virtuaalinen auttamisympäristö voimaannuttavan vuorovaikutuksen ja sosiaalisen tuen tarjoajana' (Social support and empowering bonding in supporting online environments), in A. Pohjola, A. Kääriäinen, and S. Kuusisto-Niemi, S. (eds), *Sosiaalityö, tieto ja teknologia*, Jyväskylä: PS-kustannus, pp 157–81 (2010).

Tony Jeffs teaches at Durham University and is a member of the Institute of Social Sciences, University of Bedfordshire, UK. He is a member of the editorial board of the journal *Youth and Policy*. His recent publications include: *Youth Work and Practice* (2009) (with Mark Smith); *Reflecting on the Past: Essays in the History of Youth and Community Work* (2011) (with Ruth Gilchrist and Jean Spence); *Informal Education: Conversation, Democracy and Learning* (third edition: 2005) (with Mark Smith).

Gill Jones is professor emerita of sociology at Keele University, UK. Her fields of research are young people's transitions to adulthood, inequalities in youth, and family and state support for young people. Her main publications include: *Youth,* Cambridge: Polity Press (2009); *Leaving Home,* Buckingham: Open University Press (1995); *Youth, Family and Citizenship* (with C. Wallace), Buckingham: Open University Press (1992).

Pat Leahy is a lecturer in the School of Applied Social Studies at University College Cork. He is also a professionally qualified youth worker with extensive practice experience and is a director of Youth Work Ireland, the foremost youth work organisation in Ireland. His core research interests are young people in society, youth work, young people and drug use. His most recent publications are: *Youthwork as a Response to Drugs Issues in the Community, A report on the Gurranabraher-Churchfield Drugs Outreach Project*; *Profile, Evaluation, and Future Development*, Cork City: Youth Work Ireland Cork (2011); *Youth Participation in the Republic of Ireland* (with P. Burgess), Cork: Youth Work Ireland Cork (2011); 'Key aspects of the European dimension of youth and youth work' in P. Burgess, P. and Herrmann (eds), *Highways, Crossroads and Cul de Sacs, Journeys into Irish Youth and Community Work*, Bremen: GmbH & Co (2010).

Patricia Loncle is a senior lecturer at EHESP (School for Advanced Studies in Public Health), Rennes, France. Both a political scientist and a sociologist, her fields of research are youth policy; youth participation; history of youth care; and local implementation and local regimes in the fields of youth, social and health policies. She has recently published: 'La jeunesse au local: sociologie des systèmes locaux d'action publique', *Sociologie* [online], no 2, vol 2, http://sociologie.revues.org/947 (2011); *Politiques de jeunesse, les enjeux majeurs d'intégration*, Rennes: Presses universitaires de Rennes (2010); 'Les catégorisations de la jeunesse en Europe au regard de l'action publique', *Politiques sociales et familiales*, no 102, pp 9–19 (with Virginie Muniglia, 2010).

Alessandro Martelli is tenured assistant professor at the Achille Ardigò Department of Sociology and the R. Ruffilli Faculty of Political Science (Forlì) of the University of Bologna, Italy. Since 2004/05 he has also been an adjunct professor of sociology and local welfare. He has been a member of the editorial board for the *Journal Autonomie locali e servizi sociali*, published by il Mulino in Bologna, since 1996. His research activity is essentially focused on the relationship between young people, citizenship and social changes, as well as the development of welfare systems and the local organisation of social protection policies. His recent publications are: 'The debate on young people and participatory citizenship: questions and research prospects', *International Review of Sociology* (forthcoming); 'Learning about children's participation in practice. Commentary', in B. Percy Smith and N. Thomas (eds), *A Handbook of Children and Young People's Participation. Perspectives from theory and practice*, London and New York: Routledge (with R. Bertozzi, N. De Luigi and A. Mathew, 2009); 'La sociologia, l'Europa e l'Unione Europea: quale relazione? Una esemplificazione sulle traiettorie del welfare', in M. Borraccetti, G. Laschi and R. Lizzi (a cura di), *Gli Studi Europei nelle Facoltà di Scienze Politiche. L'integrazione e i primi 50 anni dai Trattati di Roma*, Bologna: Clueb (2008); *La regolazione locale delle politiche sociali. Un percorso d'analisi*, Milano: Angeli (2006).

Virginie Muniglia is research engineer at the EHESP (School for Advanced Studies in Public Health), Rennes, France. She is currently pursuing a PhD in sociology on vulnerable young people and their use of social and health policies at the EHESS (School for Advanced Studies in Social Sciences). Her fields of research are focused on young adults' life courses, social work and social policies. Her recent publications are: 'Les catégorisations de la jeunesse en Europe au regard de l'action publique', *Politiques Sociales et Familiales, Dispositifs Publics et Constructions de la Jeunesse en Europe*, no 102, pp 9–19 (with P. Loncle, 2010); 'Le Revenu de solidarité active: changements et continuités institutionnelles en phase d'expérimentation', *Politiques et Management Public*, vol. 28, no 2, pp 37–56 (with P. Loncle and T. Rivard, 2010); 'Les inégalités territoriales dans la décentralisation du fonds d'aide aux jeunes', *Revue française des affaires sociales*, no 1, pp 229–49 (with P. Loncle, T. Rivard and C. Rothé, 2008).

Lasse Siurala is director, docent (Aalto University, PhD) in the Youth Department, City of Helsinki, Finland. His main research interests are changing conditions of youth agency and active citizenship; agonistic pluralism as an approach to youth involvement; youth policy development; and non-formal learning as an educational approach in the youth field. He recently published: 'Non-formal education in Finland', in R. Clarijs (ed) *Leisure and non-formal education, A European Overview of After- and Out-of-School Education*, Prague: EAICY (2008); *Chasing Policy Objectives, Structures and Resources – US and European practices*, Publications 1/2011, Youth department, City of Helsinki (2011); 'History of European youth policies and questions for the future', in F. Coussée, H. Williamson and G. Verschelden (eds) *The History of Youth Work in Europe: Relevance for youth policy today*, Vol 3, Council of Europe Publishing (2011).

Reingard Spannring is a lecturer and researcher at the Institute for Educational Science, University of Innsbruck, Austria. Her fields of research are focused on political participation, transitions from school to work, workplace learning, non-formal and informal learning, transformative learning, critical pedagogy and ecopedagogy. Her main publications are: *Bildung – macht – unterschiede. 3. Innsbrucker Bildungstage* (Education – Power – Difference. 3rd Innsbruck Education Days), Innsbruck: Innsbruck University Press (with S. Arens and P. Mecheril, 2011); *Youth and Political Participation in Europe Results of the Comparative Study EUYOUPART*, Leverkusen: Barbara Budrich (with G. Ogris and W. Gaiser, 2008); 'Jugend und Schule. Entgrenzt arbeiten, entgrenzt lernen im Übergang von der Schule in den Arbeitsmarkt' (Youth and Schooling: Working and Learning without Boundaries in the Transition from School to Work), in G. Knapp and K. Lauermann (eds), *Schule und Soziale Arbeit. Zur Reform der öffentlichen Erziehung und Bildung in Österreich,* Klagenfurt: Hermagoras, pp 356–86 (2007).

Heini Turkia is project planner (M.Soc.Sc.) in the Youth Department, City of Helsinki. Her main research interest is developing new formats of youth engagement in local level. She recently published 'Nuorten kuulemisesta kohti nuorten toimijuutta' (From consultation to agency), *Nuorisotutkimus (Youth Research*, a scientific journal published by the Finnish Youth Research Network), vol 3, no 28, pp 51–6 (2010).

Natalia Waechter is senior researcher at the Institute for Advanced Studies, Vienna, Austria. Her fields of research are focused on youth research (identities, participation, transitions, generations, youth culture, online communication and communities), sociology of migration and ethnic minorities, and comparative European research. Among other publications, she has written: *Wunderbare Jahre? Jugendkultur in Wien. Geschichte und Gegenwart (Wonder Years? Youth Culture in Vienna. History and Contemporary Characteristics)*, Weitra: Bibliothek der Provinz (2006); 'Online and offline social networks: use of social networking sites by emerging adults', *Journal of Applied Developmental Psychology*, vol 29, no 6, pp 420–33 (with K. Subrahmanyam, S.M. Reich and G. Espinoza, 2008); 'Moved peoples and moved borders. Research on the interplay of ethnic, national, and regional identities in Central and Eastern Europe' (with A. Chovorostov), *Slovak Journal of Political Sciences*, vol 11, no 3, pp 179–86 (2011).

Andreas Walther is professor of education, social pedagogy and youth welfare at the University of Frankfurt am Main, Germany, where he is director of the Research Centre Education and Coping in the Life Course. He has been coordinating several EU-funded research projects on young people's transitions from youth to adulthood among which is the project Youth – Actor of Social Change (UP2YOUTH). A current project deals with the governance of educational trajcetories in Europe (see www.goete.eu). His main research areas are youth, youth policy and youth welfare, transitions in the life course, participation, and international comparison. His recent publications include: *Regimes der Unterstützung im Lebenslauf* (Regimes of support in the life course), Opladen and Farmington Hill: Budrich (2011); '"It wasn't my choice, you know?" Young people's subjective views and decision-making processes in biographical transitions', in I. Schoon and R. K. Silbereisen (eds), *Transitions from School to Work*, Cambridge: Cambridge University Press, pp 121–45 (2009); 'Activating the disadvantaged? Variations in addressing youth transitions across Europe', *International Journal of Lifelong Education*, vol 26, no 5, pp 533–53 (with A. Pohl; 2007).

ONE

The analysis of youth participation in contemporary literature: a European perspective

*Virginie Muniglia, Morena Cuconato, Patricia Loncle
and Andreas Walther*

'No democracy without participation' is one heading in the European Commission's White Paper on Youth in 2001 (European Commission, 2001, p 23). Since then, the issue of young people's participation has been on the top of European youth policy agenda; an issue which has also been evidenced by the Council of Europe's European Charter 'On the Participation of Young People in Local and Regional Life', revised by the Council of Europe in 2003. (Council of Europe, 2003a)

Today in Europe, the participation of young people in the decision-making process appears crucial to public authorities for a number of reasons. The crisis of trust and confidence towards traditional forms of representation (as shown both by the growth of abstention but also by the change or even the disengagement from the classical forms of associative and union mobilisation), the growth of individualisation, the building of more varied and uncertain biographical trajectories, and the appearance of an unsettled and weakened sense of belonging to the national and local communities, are factors that encourage public authorities to rally specifically round the young generations. However, the participation of young people remains an ambivalent political concern.

The participation of young people: a general but ambivalent political concern

References to participation can be interpreted as a key concept for an understanding of social integration in modern and late modern societies in which the actions and choices of the individuals – in their role as citizens – play an essential role in terms of influence, involvement and active citizenship. According to the White Paper, 'Young people want the right to give their opinion on all aspects of their daily lives, such as family, school, work, group activities, their local area, etc. However, in doing so, they are also involved in broader economic, social and political issues' (European Commission, 2001, p 24). This quotation reflects the awareness of a change in the way social integration has become politically institutionalised in terms of citizenship status; from members of society based on formally assigned rights and responsibilities towards a diversification of involvement possibilities and influence in late modern societies. One may also speak of an individualisation of governance. Consequently, participation in the White Paper is defined as 'ensuring young people are consulted and more involved in the decisions which concern them and, in general, the life of their communities' (European Commission, 2001, p 8).

This volume aims at investigating the meaning and the forms, the extent and conditionality of young people's active citizenship. What conditions are imposed on young people's citizenship? How are young people treated in a society that promotes citizenship in this sense?

The varied definitions of participation and the implications of differing forms of participation will therefore require exploration. Thus, the issue of participation itself represents an intellectual challenge, particularly in relation to the multiplicity of meanings this concept has acquired at regional, national and European levels. As Percy-Smith and Thomas underline in the introduction of their *Handbook of Children and Young People's Participation* (2010), the concept of participation is still 'in search of definition'; therefore, a core objective of this book is to analyse the relationships and tensions between institutionalised and newly emerging forms of participation.

This becomes more important as, even on the European policy level, we find not only different but contradicting statements on the relevance and meaning of participation. On the one hand, the 2001 White Paper to some extent accepts that participation means to accept social change towards new and unknown forms of society – which implies accepting uncertainty: 'We are expecting them [young people] to create new forms of social relations, different ways of expressing solidarity or of coping with differences and finding enrichment in them, while new uncertainties appear' (European Commission, 2001, p 4).

On the other hand, in the follow-up process of the White Paper and especially in the framework of the European Youth Pact, participation is much more related to the existing societal structures and institutions:

> Empowering young people and creating favourable conditions for them to develop their skills, to work and to participate actively in society is essential for the sound economic and social development of the European Union, particularly in the context of globalisation, knowledge-based economies and ageing societies where it is crucial that every young person is given the possibility to fulfil his or her potential ... Youth participation in democratic institutions and in a continuous dialogue with policy makers is essential to the sound functioning of our democracies and the sustainability of policies which impact on young people's lives (European Commission, 2007, pp 2–9)

The question of participation also represents a political challenge. If young people do not behave as active citizens in these areas, it damages the political legitimacy of these institutions (Giddens, 1994). This question is all the more pressing because young people are also users of all manner of public services: not only educational institutions but also public transport, libraries, public spaces, community centres, healthcare, career and employment services and so forth. It follows that their opinions about of these services are important and must not be neglected by local and national politicians.

Defining participation implies distinguishing degrees of participation. Most prominent with regard to the participation of children and young people is the ladder of participation, first introduced by Sherry Arnstein (1969) and further developed by Roger Hart (1992). It classifies models of participation according to whether children and young people are merely consulted or are actually involved in decision making according to who (adults or young people) initiates participatory processes, adults or the young people themselves. A concurrent theme in the discourse on youth participation is the distinction between 'real' participation and superficial or tokenistic action such as consultations without a transparent follow-up and involvement in decision-making processes. Such classifications of participation are on the one hand useful in order to distinguish and criticise existing practice. On the other hand, they tend to be misleading inasmuch as they imply an objective or essentialist understanding of participation. In fact, the participation discourse is also a struggle about the meaning of 'real' participation as much as measuring more or less participation on such a scale. It was clearly underlined in the European Commission's White Paper (2001, p 27) – as much as in many other official documents and declaration about young people – that: 'helping young people to participate has to be not restricted to asking their opinions'. It appears that this concern crosses many official documents and declarations about young people. The Declaration of the Youth Event under the Austrian EU-presidency is an example of how such official claims are contested:

> Young people want a two way process, consultation alone is not enough. We want to create a real dialogue. Therefore a structured dialogue needs to be established on an equal basis between youth representatives and decision-makers. This should be implemented from a local to a European level through all political structures. Furthermore, young people should be involved in every aspects of the decision-making process from the beginning to the end. This is only possible if the structure allow for participation in a democratic and transparent way. ... Following on, we also strongly suggest implementing and developing in all Member States a youth proofing article, this avoids tokenism and ensures young people's voices are heard. (*The Declaration of Vienna and Bad Ischl*, 2006, pp 5–6)

At the same time, it needs to be stated that this quotation represents a minority of so-called 'organised' youth which in most cases is highly educated. This means that accepting the political forms and concepts of struggling about participation means excluding and/or alienating a majority of non-organised youth (cf. Matthews, 2001).

Jean-Claude Richez's assertion may enlighten our approach:

> There is a true paradox in the discourse that our society develops on young people's involvement. On the one hand, a discourse about young people who do not want to militate any more, who are no longer involved, who refuse to take responsibilities in associations, and on the other hand, large mobilisations of young people on numerous subjects and occasions. ... Today, young people are involved but in a new way. This new deal is quite difficult to understand, in particular because we are still largely

> prisoners of a conception of involvement that is reduced to political involvement and – in a minor way- to union and associative involvement, to the detriment of other forms of involvement. ... Formerly, the socialisation process led the individual to a predetermined place. ... Today, there is no more traditional transmission by legacy. This legacy does no longer go without saying; on the contrary it is debated, discussed and experimented. The acquisition of a capacity to deliberate, to assess, to choose, to negotiate becomes crucial. (Richez, 2005, pp 9–12)

The analysis of the relationships and tensions between participation within current societal institutions, and within new forms of participation, and relating this analysis to public co-citizens form the core objectives of this book.

Which forms and conditions of participation (both initiated by public actors and emerging from young people's own activities) are attractive for young people? Which forms and conditions contribute to their recognition and position as co-citizens and are likely to increase their influence on their own lives in the context of their communities?

The meaning of participation in different societal contexts

Young people's participation takes place on all levels; from the local to the global, from informal settings such as groups, networks and communities, to formal structures such as youth organisations, municipal youth councils, school councils and elections. Different forms of participation can be distinguished with respect to a multitude of dimensions:

- voluntary (e.g. youth organisations, demonstration) versus non-voluntary (e.g. unemployment scheme);
- bottom up, top down or in a cooperative form;
- active (e.g. charity work) versus passive (citizenship, passive membership in voluntary organisation);
- conscious or unconscious;
- socially or institutionally sanctioned, conforming (voting, charity work) versus non-sanctioned, challenging, radical participation (riots, resistance, political extremism);
- collective (institutionalised: e.g. activity in a trade union; non-institutionalised: e.g. local pressure group) versus individual (e.g.

talking to school teacher to 'sort out things by myself') as highlighted by Biggart et al: 'Participation is complementary to citizenship, as in democratic societies individuals' rights are connected with their citizenship status. Participation implies an at least partial correspondence between the individual and the collective, in other words the active negotiation between personal interest and the demands of society and therefore processes of identification' (Biggart et al, 2006, p 12).

In relation to young people Walther et al (2006) have also distinguished between participation as a *principle* of societal practice from participation as a learning *objective*, illustrating that young people first have to be prepared for participation in terms of acquiring participatory competencies (cf. European Commission, 2001, 2007).

Different meanings and forms of participation are related to different societal contexts and arenas which will be presented briefly in the following: political participation, social or associative participation, civic participation, user or consumer participation, participation in and through education, and participation in employment. This list – which is by no means complete, exhaustive or representative – reveals that the appeal of the word participation has lead to an inflation of use in both directions: on the one hand any involvement in socially institutionalised contexts such as being part of the workforce or being enrolled in education is referred to as 'participation in society' (European Commission, 2007, p 1); on the other hand, social change has lead to an increasing differentiation in forms of participation.

Political participation

Mainstream research on political participation, by comparison, tends to focus on citizens' engagement in institutionalised political processes within nation-states and the relationship between citizens and the political system.

Political participation can be inspected from at least two different approaches in democratic theory. The realist approach is based on notions of representativity and democratic elite rule which see democracy not as the rule of the people but as the rule of politicians with the consent of the people. Accordingly, voting is the crucial form of citizens' participation and serves to install a functioning government. Political participation is restricted to the legal activities of the citizens which 'are more or less directly aimed at influencing the selection of governmental personnel and/or the actions they take' (Verba and Nie,

1972, p 46). The role of the citizens is more like that of spectators and consumers of politics. The normative approach to democracy, by contrast, sees the aim of participation not so much in safeguarding the functioning of institutions but in keeping a check on the political elite and the prevention of a hiving-off of elected politicians. Active participation that involves public discussion, common decision making and political action (Barber, 1984) as well as direct forms of democracy are preferable since they ensure that the people's needs and interests remain the basis and focus of policy making. Beyond its immediate role within a democratic system, political participation is seen as a value in itself through increasing citizens' self-confidence, social and political skills, as well as their social and political integration. Indeed, active participation in a lively democracy is often seen as a counterweight to processes of social disintegration and fragmentation. With this approach goes the normative expectation that the more participation the better.

Social and civic participation

Since the 1960s participation has become a political tool to address the decreasing legitimacy of political institutions. A primary area in this regard has been urban planning. It is this strand of participation to which youth participation programmes (e.g. White Paper, European Commission, 2001, 2005; cf. Williamson, 2002; Council of Europe, 2003a, 2003b) have their greatest affinity. Recently, it has also become a major issue in the politics of international development (e.g. the World Bank; cf. Cooke and Kothari, 2001).

While political participation refers to the relationship between the individual and society in terms of citizen and state, social or civic participation refer to the relationship between the individual and a group or a community. The political term of participation has both individual and collective aspects; terms such as civil society and civic participation refer primarily to collective action: membership, especially active membership, in associations and organisations. It is in this regard especially that (new) social movements deserve mention (although overlapping with political participation). Referendums, initiatives and demonstrations related to political issues of political participation are other forms; some refer to issues from official policy agendas while others refer to issues which are (apparently) non-political. Youth councils and forums might also be listed here inasmuch as they are located somewhere between contributing to community life and the official political agenda (Barber, 1984; Matthews, 2001).

Terms such as social and civic participation reveal the limitations to an understanding of participation that coincides with democratic politics. Although membership of a sports club will only in exceptional cases be intended and perceived as a political act, it still represents a practice whereby individual needs and interests are connected and transformed into collective action in a more or less public way. It is not only the link to individual needs but also the public nature of belonging to something that makes membership an issue of social identity.

Due to the blurring of the boundaries of political participation the notion of civic participation has become attractive at European level. Here, participation is connected to democracy without being restricted to elections (partly also because of the limited scope of elections) and the need for legitimation and a sense of shared identity, without disposing of the clear-cut assets of organisational membership or national citizenship (Williamson, 2002; Siurala, 2005). At the same time, civic participation is connected to the concepts of civil society and social capital. While there are different interpretations, these discourses are often used for de-legitimising welfare in weakened nation states in the context of globalisation and neoliberalism (Cooke and Kothari, 2001; van Berkel and Hornemann-Møller, 2002).

User participation

Because of the reality wherein modern states not only organise membership in terms of rights and responsibilities but also provide services to their citizens it has become common to refer to citizenship in terms of user participation. Such a perspective has been developed especially in regard to social services and social work, although reference to participation is ambivalent as social work is always characterised by the simultaneity of help and control; including individuals in the 'normal' life course while at the same time accepting and depending on subjective aims, orientations and resources.

This has been reflected in social work theories through concepts such as everyday life or life- world orientation, by social work practice as client-oriented service, participation as user involvement or, more recently, empowerment (Thiersch, 1992; Askheim, 2003; Payne, 2005). On the one hand, social work acts upon a mandate of the welfare state (inclusion as normalisation); on the other it depends on the active co-production of the client (who has to actively 'normalise'). Therefore, concepts of and reference to participation are wide spread – but always questionable and contradictory. In the 1980s self-help was promoted as a balance against paternalistic welfare and social work undermining and disabling individuals' resources. The contradiction is especially visible in youth welfare, e.g. young people in public care. According to professional principles they should be assigned participation rights. At the same time, professionals (and parents) fear loss of their own authority (Hodgson, 1995; Pluto, 2007).

The overlap between user participation and civic participation in the case of community development had its high tide in the 1960s and 1970s in the context of social (urban) planning: citizen involvement whilst balancing individualisation with structure-related approaches against disadvantage are the most important issues in this regard (Powell and Geoghegan, 2004; Herrmann, 2004). In contrast, a community work perspective values and includes as a necessity of opening spaces for societal conflicts, rather than seizing on them or cooling them out. Especially under conditions of late modern individualisation the divergence of individuals' and groups' interests seems inevitable. If democracy is to be the primary means of societal integration arenas are required in which struggles and conflicts can be acted out – and negotiated (Stevens et al, 1999).

The control aspect inherent in user participation has been reinforced under conditions of the activation of welfare policies in which the citizenship are primarily conceptualised as consumers or users of public services; this activation transforms questions of adequacy and legitimacy from public political issues into a question of market competition (Clarke, 2006; Barnes et al, 2007).

Participation as activation for education and employment

In modern and late-modern societies paid (and unpaid) work and education are fundamental mechanisms of social integration and social reproduction; it is therefore worthwhile to briefly reflect on their relationship to participation. Modern capitalism conceives of the market as the primary societal area in which individuals build relationships by means of exchange. Most notably in the Fordist period, social democracy and trade unions achieved a qualification of this form of participation through work by endowing individuals with social rights (cf. Marshall, 1950) including participation at the work place. In the post-Fordist world however, this concept of participation is apparently being re-conceived. Not only has the increase of atypical work arrangements and globalisation contributed to the curtailing of workers' participation rights within companies; the introduction of group work type practices have increased the responsibilities of individual workers. Similarly, activation in labour market policies implies that individuals are expected to increase their job search activities – including the willingness to reduce aspirations – while benefit entitlements are more and more being made conditional upon active job search (van Berkel and Hornemann-Møller, 2002; López Blasco et al, 2003).

With regard to education, activation is reflected by the trend towards lifelong learning which implies individualised responsibility for the own learning biography but also the potential freedom to organise learning according to one's own needs and interests and to integrate it with other obligations (Field, 2000). The notion of participation is also included in the concept of non-formal learning which describes all learning that does not follow a clear curriculum and does not subsume learning processes to external measurement. It relies on the assumption that learning is an activity of individual subjects which however can be facilitated within specific contexts and arrangements. Nevertheless, in educational policy and administration participation it is largely restricted to mere attendance – at least as long as predefined qualifications are being achieved. However, comparative research has also shown that activation has different meanings in different welfare states (cf. van Berkel and Hornemann-Møller, 2002; Pohl and Walther, 2007).

In sum, this assessment of different areas, forms and meanings of participation entails the consideration of a wider interpretation. Participation cannot be reduced to formal decision making, it can also characterise the practice of everyday life: 'children initiated political acts are woven into everyday cultural frameworks of being and adding to the world that exist in their own child/youth realities, not to the world structured and organised by adults who offer a space for children to "participate" along with them' (Malone and Hartung, 2010, p 35).

The comparative perspective: participation across different welfare and youth transition regimes

More widely, Barry Percy-Smith and Nigel Thomas (2010) underline that young people's participation cannot be understood in isolation from its social, cultural and political contexts: 'Whereas interpretations of participation in "Western" countries have tended to emphasise the expression of views in public sector decision-making, in majority world countries expression participation often has a wider meaning of "active contribution" to the family and community' (Percy-Smith and Thomas, 2010, p 357).

The impact of different national contexts is also relevant for the analysis of participation in a European perspective, as is intended by this book. One may locate the international comparison of youth policy and youth participation within the wider context of comparative welfare research. Here, the most influential contribution has been made by Esping-Andersen (1990) with his distinction of three 'welfare regimes', which focuses on the degree to which individuals' labour is being de-commodified from the labour market (i.e. to what extent individuals are secured by the state against the loss of income from paid work). Esping-Andersen distinguished three regime types: a social-democratic or universalistic in the Nordic countries, where access is regulated through the citizenship status and a high level of compensation; a liberal or residual in the Celtic and Anglo-Saxon countries where access is again regulated according to citizenship while the level of compensation is much lower and the focus lies on individual provision; and a conservative or corporatist model gathering the Continental countries where access to social security depends on occupational and family status. While being still a key reference, this model has been widely discussed and criticised for being 'blind' with regard to gender and ethnicity or for neglecting huge differences between Western and Southern Europe (cf. Sainsbury, 1999, 2006; Gallie and Paugam, 2000).

It also does not differentiate with regard to young people. The development of a comparative model with regard to the way in which modern societies regulate young people's transitions into work and adulthood differently was therefore a key task for theorists of youth and young people's lives. The notion of youth transition regimes refers both to the existing institutional settings and also to the values and interpretations which they constantly reproduce (Walther, 2006; Walther et al, 2006; see also Chapter 2).

Applying a typology of welfare regimes to the comparison of youth transition contexts requires an extended perspective. Whereas the social security arrangements that compensate for a lack of income through unemployment (benefit) remains important, the structures of education and training also need to be considered – especially according to dimensions of stratification and standardisation (Allmendinger, 1989) – likewise their relation to concepts of work and employment (Shavit and Müller, 1998). Employment and welfare, along with education and training, include mechanisms of doing gender through which the relations between men and women are shaped in particular ways (e.g. Sainsbury, 1999). The combination of these structures results in the particular design of programmes for unemployed young people. A comparison of such policies at the same time provides evidence of dominant interpretations of youth unemployment and 'disadvantaged youth' – in terms of ascribing disadvantage to either individual deficits or structures of segmentation. Policies also depend on and reproduce context-specific notions of youth, reflecting the main societal expectations towards young people (Walther et al, 2002).

Outline of the book

This book invokes a wide approach to youth participation based on both a comparison between national experiences and on a deep examination of the various domains of participation in Northern and Southern European countries. Starting from the existing international (mainly Anglo-American) literature on youth participation, this book intends to delve further into the gaps and the contradictions between policy makers' intentions and the reality of youth participation and culture in formal and informal contexts.

It is partly based on the research project UP2Youth, Youth as Actor of Social Change funded by the European Commission under the 6th Framework Programme of Research (Loncle and Muniglia, 2008; Walther et al, 2009; see www.up2youth.org). Half of the chapters of the book present the main results of this comparative research with regard to the countries Austria, Ireland, Italy, France and Slovakia. Nevertheless, in order to deepen our analysis, other contributors will present research and propose a focus on different fields of participation (information and communications technology or school participation) and on single countries (Finland, France, Italy, Ireland and Spain).

This volume is split into five parts. Part One explores the different meanings of participation regarding, on the one hand, young people's attitudes and, on the other hand, the structural aspects of policy making across Europe. In Chapter 2, Patricia Loncle, Pat Leahy, Virginie Muniglia and Andreas Walther describe the various weaknesses of youth policies looking at the difficulties at stake when defining youth policies and the various weaknesses of youth policies at every stage of the decision-making process. In Chapter 3, Reingard Spannring suggests that, contrary to the commonly held vision which considers that young people have become increasingly egocentric and are therefore uninterested in political involvement, some young people have actually moved beyond this individualistic stage and represent a world view that is community oriented – not in the old authority-oriented 'elite-directed' form we already know, but in a more egalitarian, 'democratic' form; it is the politicians who appear ego-centred. In Chapter 4, Filip Coussée and Tony Jeffs explore the history of youth work in Flanders and point out common items between Flanders and other European countries, as well as analogies between, on the one hand, the discussion on the past and contemporary policy and, on the other hand, the discussion on youth work. They show youth work as a central part of an educational-civilisation strategy that paradoxically empowers the powerful and has served (often unconsciously) an agenda of enforcing social control on vulnerable youth to maintain order in capitalistic societies.

Part Two brings together different national experiences of participation. In Chapter 5, Lasse Siurala and Heini Turkia analyse the way we talk about youth participation, how it is constructing participation models – with the hegemony of municipal youth councils – and how this keeps us from seeing other ways to deal with this issue. They discuss an alternative model of local youth participation in Finland as effort to break out of the hegemony of conventional youth council formats. In Chapter 6, Morena Cuconato, Nicola De Luigi and Alessandro Martelli analyse the ambiguous relationship among youth, participation and politics by proposing a critical excursus of the Italian local youth policies and their attempt to promote individual participation. Doing so, they highlight the large hiatus still existing between the rhetoric of the institutional principles and the real praxis of Italian youth policies, which very often continue to be limited to cultural practices, neglecting the need of a redistributive approach. In Chapter 7, Paul Burgess and Pat Leahy examine Irish experiences of youth participation in the context of severe social change in the wake of a major economic recession. They review the notion of change in relation to the status of young people in Irish society and the role of the youth work as the 'engine' driving young people's participation, before concluding on the current configuration represented by the connection between participation, youth and social change. In Chapter 8, Lourdes Gaitán examines the situation of youth participation in Spain trough three main structures: the educational system, juvenile associations and local programmes.

Part Three explores the new spaces taken up by young people to participate. In Chapter 9, Morena Cuconato and Natalia Waechter analyse the role of youth culture in participation examining the connection between Web 2.0, politics and participation, discussing to what extent youth culture may be considered participative and analysing the elements of online participation and youth cultural participation throughout the Arab 'youth quake'. In doing so, they question a possible new meaning of young people's participation in the second decade of the new millennium. In Chapter 10, Shakuntala Banaji and David Buckingham, reporting back on the triangulated, cross-cutting findings from surveys and textual case studies of youth civic websites in seven European countries, examine whether and how young people are involved in civic action on- and offline, looking for their general and specific motivations, concerns and constraints on participation. In Chapter 11, Camilla Granholm gives an insight in how participation through information and communication technologies (ICT) and particularly the Internet can be and is used for maintaining and promoting mental wellbeing by young people in Finland by providing an overview of recent research and literature describing the current situation in Finland.

Part Four examines the links between participation, education and learning. In Chapter 12, Andreas Walther questions the assumption that the relationship between participation and learning is normally constructed in a way that suggests that young people need to acquire participation competencies and, with reference to educational theory and research, he argues that the learning of participation also depends on participatory learning, that is on subjective experiences of participation. In Chapter 13, Valérie Becquet analyses the gradual construction of participation in French secondary schools, examines the rationale of pupils' participation methods and the approaches to citizenship that they are based on, and considers the concrete implementation of participation in schools.

In the Conclusion, Andreas Walther provides a comparative overview over different constellations of youth participation suggesting three main lines of analysis: an ideology-critical perspective analysing the meaning and function of current participation discourses; a comparative perspective on national configuration of participation related to existing comparative models of youth policy and youth transitions which proposes a critical view of a universal trend towards participation; and a biographical cultural perspective which refers participation to all action of young people in or directed to the public as potentially participatory. In doing so, he tries to transgress institutional dichotomies between 'real and false' or 'more and less' participation.

References

Allmendinger, J. (1989) 'Educational systems and labour market outcomes', *European Sociological Review*, vol 5, no 3, pp 231–50.

Arnstein, S. R. (1969) 'A ladder of citizen participation', *JAIP*, vol 35, no 4, pp 216–24.

Askheim, O. P. (2003) 'Empowerment as guidance for professional social work: an act of balancing on a slack rope', *European Journal of Social Work*, vol 6, no 3, pp 229–40.

Barber, B. (1984) *Strong Democracy: Participatory Politics for a New Age*, Berkeley: University of California Press.

Barnes, M., Newman, J. and Sullivan, H. (2007) *Power, Participation and Political Renewal: Case Studies in Public Participation*, Bristol: The Policy Press.

Biggart, A., du Bois-Reymond, M. and. Watlher, A. (2006) 'Introduction', in Walther, A. and du Bois-Reymond, M. (eds) *Participation and Transition, Motivation of Young Adults in Europe for Learning and Working*, Frankfurt: Peter Lang, pp 11–20.

Clarke, J. (2006) 'Consumers, clients or citizens? Politics, policy and practice in the reform of social care', *European Societies*, vol 8, no 3, pp 423–42.

Cooke, B. and Kothari, U. (eds) (2001) *Participation, The New Tyranny?*, London: Zed Books.

Council of Europe (2003a) *European Charter on the Participation of Young People in Local and Regional Life*, Strasbourg: Council of Europe.

Council of Europe (2003b) *Experts on Youth Policy Indicators. Final Report*, Strasbourg: Council of Europe.

Declaration of Vienna/Bad Ischl (2006) online: www.jugendvertretung.at.

Esping-Andersen, G. (1990) *The Three Words of Welfare Capitalism*, Cambridge MA: Cambridge University Press.

European Commission (2001) *White Paper. A New Impetus for European Youth*, Brussels, 21.11, 681 final.

European Commission (2005) *Addressing the concerns of young people in Europe – implementing the European Youth Pact and promoting active citizenship*, Communication from the Commission to the Council. Available at http://europa.eu.int/comm/youth/whitepaper/post-launch/com_206_en.pdf

European Commission (2007) *Promoting young people's full participation in education, employment and society*, Communication from the Commission to the European Parliament, the Council, the European Economic and Social Committee and the Committee of the Regions. COM (2007) 498 final. Download: http://eur-lex.europa.eu/LexUriServ/site/en/com/2007/com2007_0498en01.pdf

Field, J. (2000) *Lifelong Learning and the New Educational Order*, Stoke on Trent: Trentham Books.

Gallie, D. and Paugam, S. (eds) (2000) *Welfare Regimes and the Experience of Unemployment in Europe*, Oxford: Oxford University Press.

Giddens, A. (1994) *Beyond Left and Right. The Future of Radical Politics*, Cambridge: Polity Press.

Hart, R. (1992) 'Children's participation: From tokenism to citizenship', *Innocenti Essays*, no 4, Florence: UNICEF.

Herrmann, P. (ed) (2004) *Citizenship Revisited. Threats or Opportunities of Shifting Boundaries*, New York: Nova.

Hodgson, D. (1995) *Participation of Children and Young People in Social Work*, New York: UNICEF.

Loncle, P. and Muniglia, V. (eds) (2008) *Youth Participation, Agency and Social Change. Thematic Report*, Deliverable in 21 of the project 'Youth – Actor of Social Change' (UP2YOUTH).

López Blasco, A., MacNeish, W. and Walther, A. (eds) (2003) *Young People and Contradictions of Inclusion: Towards Integrated Transition Policies in Europe*, Bristol: The Policy Press.

Malone, K. and Hartung, C. (2010) 'Challenges of participatory practice with children', in Percy-Smith, B., Thomas, N. (eds) *A Handbook of Children and Young People's Participation – Perspectives from Theory and Practice*, London, New York: Rutledge, pp 24–38.

Marshall, T. H. (1950) *Class, Citizenship and Social Development*, Chicago: University of Chicago Press.

Matthews, H. (2001) 'Citizenship, youth councils and young people's participation', *Journal of Youth Studies*, vol 4, no 3, pp 299–319.

Payne, M. (2005) *Modern Social Work Theory* (3rd edn), Chicago: Lyceum Books.

Percy-Smith, B. and Thomas, N. (eds) (2010) *A Handbook of Children and Young People's Participation – Perspectives from Theory and Practice*, London, New York: Routledge.

Pluto, L. (2007) *Partizipation in erzieherischen Hilfen. München* (Participation in youth welfare services. An empirical study), Weinheim: DJI-Verlag.

Pohl, A. and Walther, A. (2007) 'Activating the disadvantaged', *International Journal of Lifelong Education*, no 5, pp 533–53.

Powell, F. and Geoghegan, M. (2004) *The Politics of Community Development*, Dublin: A&A Farmar.

Richez, J.-C. (2005) 'Avant-propos' (Foreword), in V. Becquet and C. De Linarès C. (eds) *Quand les jeunes s'engagent, entre experimentations et construction identitaire* (When Young People Commit Themselves, between Experiments and Identity Building), Paris: L'Harmattan, pp 9–12.

Sainsbury, D. (1999) *Gender and Welfare State Regimes*, Oxford: Oxford University Press.

Sainsbury, D. (2006) '"Immigrants" social rights in comparative perspective: welfare regimes, forms of immigration and immigration policy regimes', *Journal of European Social Policy*, vol 16, no 3, pp 229–44.

Shavit, Y. and Müller, W. (eds) (1998) *From School to Work: A Comparative Study of Educational Qualifications and Occupational Outcomes*, Oxford: Oxford University Press.

Siurala, L. (2005) *A European Framework for Youth Policy*, Strasbourg: Council of Europe.

Stevens, A., Bur, A.M. and Young, L. (1999) *Partial, Unequal and Conflictual: Problems in Using Participation for Social Inclusion in Europe*, Canterbury: University of Kent.

Thiersch, H. (1992) *Lebensweltorientierte Soziale Arbeit* (life world oriented social work). *Weinheim*, München: Juventa.

Van Berkel, R. and Hornemann-Møller, I. (eds) (2002) *Active Social Policies in the EU: Inclusion Through Participation?*, Bristol: The Policy Press.

Verba, S. and Nie, N. (1972) *Participation in America; Political Democracy and Social Equality*, New York: Harper & Row Publishers.

Walther, A. (2006) 'Regimes of youth transitions. Choice, flexibility and security in young people's experiences across different European contexts', *Young*, vol 14, no 2, pp 119–39.

Walther, A., Stauber, B., Biggart, A., du Bois-Reymond, M., Furlong, A., López Blasco, A., Mørch, S. and Pais, J. M. (2002) (eds) *Misleading Trajectories – Integration Policies for Young Adults in Europe?*, Opladen: Leske & Budrich.

Walther, A., Du Bois-Reymond, M. and Biggart, A. (eds) (2006) *Participation in Transition. Motivation of Young People in Europe for Learning and Working*. Frankfurt am Main: Lang.

Walther, A., Stauber, B. and Pohl, A. (2009) *UP2YOUTH – Youth – Actor of Social Change, Final Report*, Tübingen: IRIS.

Williamson, H. (2002) *Supporting Young People in Europe. Principles, Policy and Practice*, Strasbourg: Council of Europe.

Part One

Same word, same meaning?
Participating in a changing world

TWO

Youth participation: strong discourses, weak policies – a general perspective

Patricia Loncle, Pat Leahy, Virginie Muniglia and Andreas Walther

Introduction

> On November 27th 2009 the Council of Ministers responsible for Youth in the 27 Member States of the European Union adopted a resolution endorsing a new EU Strategy for Youth. This strategy, which is based on a proposal by the European Commission made in April of the same year, will guide both the EU institutions and the Member States in pursuing policies to improve the lives of all young people in the coming decade. (Odile Quintin, 2009)

This statement from the general director of the direction of education and culture of the European Commission appears to belatedly recognise the progressive institutionalisation of a sector of youth policies at European level.[1]

Nevertheless, despite the many efforts of the European institutions to orientate in favour of youth policies, despite their attempts to designate priorities and to organise decisions in a comprehensive way, youth policies, at least in national arenas, seem to remain weak, fragmented and poorly funded. Our hypothesis is that a deep hiatus exists between the multiplicities of political discourses on youth on the one hand and the weakness of youth policies on the other hand. One might say that the emphasis on youth participation actually reflects the weakness of youth policies and the lack of strong political will and strategy regarding youth; participation takes the place of political aims and strategies. The discourse on youth participation implies that policy contents are actually being replaced by policy procedures.

One explanation for this discrepancy is that youth policies belong at least partly to the category of symbolic public policy (Edelman, 1960).

Youth research has repeatedly pointed to the fact that addressing youth issues serves for reassuring societal actors with regard to concerns of societal reproduction (Kelly, 2001). The notion of youth is itself blurred enough to develop ideological and collective postulates for two main reasons: youth is considered as a problem and/or as a resource for society and it is seen as a way of legitimisation for decision makers. Images of youth as a resource and as a problem have a long history: they appear all across Europe in the context of nation state building at the end of the 19th century; youth was then envisaged as a soldier (or a mother of future soldiers) eager to defend their homelands. Many historians refer to the simultaneity of the creation of public education and compulsory conscription as indicator for the growing importance of youth for nation states, as it appears in this quotation from an Italian congressman in 1890:

> The soldier citizen has not to be trained in the barracks but in school; because the soldier citizen can only be the one who, in school and in his family, has learned what is the fire of freedom and the holy love of the homeland, and that he has, for it, on the battle field, to win or to die. (Bonetta, 1990, p 84, quoted by Loriga, 1996, p 28)

This image of youth as a resource has been transformed during the 20th century and in particular after the Second World War but it still exists: in peace time, youth is considered as the future of the territory it belongs to and this is true at local and national level as well as at European level. Rather than soldiers, the contemporary meaning of youth is now human capital; with the aim of securing the success of the European knowledge society in global economic competition. Pierre Mairesse, the director of the youth directorate in the European Commission, referred to youth's responsibility in creating the future Europe:

> Each new generation has its own dynamism, its own vision of utopia and its own sense of commitment. That is true for the young people in Europe today, just as it was true for their predecessors. It is our task to give them the opportunities they need to create the Europe and the world of tomorrow and up to them to seize their chance. (2007, p 48)

Connected to the image of youth as a resource is the image of youth as a problem, the EU White Paper explicitly claims that the 'youth as a resource' approach will replace the 'youth as a problem' approach (European Commission, 2001). However, reference to youth as a resource implies instrumentalisation by society; youth also tends to be perceived as a problem where its resourcefulness is questioned as parallel to the promotion of youth participation, early school leavers are increasingly being blamed for actually wasting their human capital and for producing societal costs while more and more punitive measures are advocated against deviant behaviour among young people. While this shows that youth as a resource always implies the notion of youth as problem, it shows also that youth as resource does not necessarily imply emancipatory potential: indeed youth is primarily referred to as a resource for societal and economic purposes rather than as subjects of their own lives (IARD, 2001; Walther et al, 2006).

The second reason for the symbolic use of youth lies in its capacity of the legitimisation of decision makers. According to Le Bart and Lefebvre (2005, p 13), youth produces 'interplays of naturalised equivalences whose symbolic effect is powerful': youth = resource = adaptability = legitimacy. These interplays of equivalences represent considerable advantages if one considers them from the perspective of political legitimisation mechanisms. For decision makers, these equivalences develop and produce public interventions addressed to young people. Legitimacy allows the obtainment of population adhesion to specific decisions through the recourse of broadly accepted social norms. This could explain why policy makers are so eager to talk about youth.

Having focused on the symbolic use of youth, how can we describe the various weaknesses of youth policies? To develop our argument, we first concentrate on the difficulties inherent in defining youth policies and then examine the various fragilities of youth policies at all stages of the decision-making process. For this purpose, we refer to the cases of the five countries studied in the framework of the UP2YOUTH project and on the existing literature from youth policy.

The difficult definitions of youth policies as a characteristic of weakness

Defining youth is an extremely difficult task, not least as a sociological issue. So how can youth policy be defined? According to Williamson (2007, p.100), 'All countries have a youth policy – by intent, default or neglect. In other words, young people continue to have to live their lives, whatever the policy context.' In contrast to this minimalist approach of defining youth policy as all policies affecting youth, Siurala suggests a broader prospective definition of youth policy:

> A public youth policy should reflect the challenges and
> obstacles young people face in their transition from
> childhood to adulthood and it should be based on the
> political objectives and guidelines adopted by a local
> city council, national government or intergovernmental
> organisation. (Siurala, 2004, p 7)

At European level, this has been reflected by the distinction between
a broad concept of youth policy as cross-sectoral, referring to youth-
related issues in different policy fields, and a narrower concept of
specialised youth policies. While the broad concept is ambitious in
terms of 'mainstreaming youth' it is also too vague for concrete action.
In contrast, the narrow concept risks reducing youth policy to youth
work with the adverse effect of becoming marginal (Siurala, 2004).

Whereas the European level concept appears to have progressively
arrived at a transversal and subtle definition of youth policies, it is much
more difficult to define youth policies from their real implementation
in national and local territories.

As shown by Walther (2006), concepts of youth as well as youth
policies are strongly linked to the types of welfare regimes the
countries belong to: focusing on transition policies, he highlights
how socioeconomic structures, institutional arrangements and
cultural patterns interact in shaping their transitions between youth
and adulthood. The typology of transition regimes clusters countries
according to structures of education and training, access to welfare and
labour market while it also reveals that the way in which activation is
being interpreted and implemented in these countries shows effects of
path-dependency. The model of transition regimes can also be relevant
for a comparative analysis of participation as it includes the different
concepts and representations of youth and disadvantaged youth. Up
to now four transition regimes can be distinguished.

Transition regimes have both a significant influence on and are the
expression of different representations of youth and disadvantaged
youth. These regimes can therefore be seen as the relevant contexts
of youth participation. Up to now four transition regimes have been
firmly distinguished.

The *liberal* transition regime in the Celtic and Anglo-Saxon countries
is best characterised by the notion of individual responsibility. Young
people without work face major pressure (workfare) to enter the
workforce; the underlying principle being that that young people
should lead into economic independence as soon as possible. The labour
market is structured by a high degree of flexibility. While this provides

multiple entry options, especially also for young women, it also implies a high level of insecurity. In the context of highly individualising policies young people face considerable risks of social exclusion.

The *universalistic* transition regime of the Nordic countries is based on inclusive education systems and individual access to welfare. Rather than primarily pointing to direct labour market relevance the education system reflects the individualisation of life courses. While youth is first of all associated with individual personal development, young people's status is that of 'citizens in education'. This is reflected by an education allowance for all who are over 18 and still in education which contributes to a partial independence from their families. Throughout education and labour market oriented activation policies, individual choice is rather broad to secure individual motivation. Gendered career opportunities are highly balanced due to the broad relevance of the public employment sector and the availability of child care.

The *employment-centred* regime of countries such as Austria, France and Germany, in which a differentiated (and partly even highly selective) school system leads into a rigidly standardised and gendered system of vocational training. The dominant task of youth is to socialise for a set occupational and social position – through education and training. This is reflected through the provision of a two-tiered division of social security, favouring those who have already been in regular training or employment, while others are entitled to stigmatised social assistance. Those who fail to enter regular vocational training are referred to as 'disadvantaged' from a deficit-oriented perspective. Pre-vocational measures are governed by the objective 'first of all, they need to learn to know what work means', in other terms: adaptation, reduction of aspirations, holding out.

In the Mediterranean countries transition regimes are under-institutionalised (see Chapters 5 and 7). Although the school system is organised in a largely comprehensive way, transitions often imply a waiting phase until the mid-thirties with unequal outcomes. Structural deficits regarding access to welfare and the lack of reliable training as well as youth policies affect young men and women as they are not entitled to any kinds of social benefits. They depend, to a large extent, on their families who are referred to as 'social amortisator' for the socio-political vacuum. Long family dependency stands for the fact that youth does not have a formal status and place in society – but recent research suggests that there are big differences also among Mediterranean countries, from the positive pole of 'big freedom' for young people living with their parents (as in Northern Italy) to the quite pessimistic pole of 'forced harmony' (as in Southern Italy). Young women have fewer career opportunities and anticipate responsibility for later family obligations.

In the post-socialist countries one cannot speak of a single transition regime. On the one hand, the past held reliable but choice-less trajectories. This still influences what is perceived as normal so that the existing regime types do not apply. On the other hand, differences existing prior to 1990 have increased since the post-socialist governments – under pressure of World Bank and EU – adopted liberal (e.g. Poland) or employment-centred (e.g. Slovakia) structures. Thus, complex mixtures have emerged which are still in dynamic processes of transformation. So far it seems wise to analyse the developments according to the dimensions applied in the regime typologies without subsuming the countries under existing typologies (Walther and Pohl, 2005).

This model of youth transition regimes helps to explain differences in young people's life course structures. The question of participation and the extent to which it is considered finds its place in this context.

It is important to note that regime models are not descriptive but heuristic. They are too broad to explain structural differences in detail which also occur between national transition systems clustered in the same regime type. They refer to the different logic underlying transition structures.

An attempt to compare youth policies

To what extent is it possible to ground a comparative analysis of participation on comparative research on national youth policies? The IARD study (2001) in 18 European countries on the 'state of youth and youth policies' attempted to cluster countries according to distinct youth policy models by applying a set of dimensions; four of which are briefly introduced here.

The dimension of governance at national level asks whether or not youth policy is regulated in a *comprehensive* way by a specific youth ministry (or a ministry with a special responsibility for youth matters, a specialised department or secretariat-general on youth matters within one ministry plus specific youth legislation); whether youth matters and youth provisions are *fragmented* among several ministries, authorities and agencies and youth related measures are regulated by more general legislation; or where there is *no clear system* of responsibility or where there is no regulation at all.[2] The study found that:

In practice, there are no countries in which all youth matters are united in one youth sector, and – on the other hand – there are also tendencies towards amalgamating youth matters in countries without a youth sector. Hence, the Western countries cannot be classified in two distinct groups: with and without a youth sector. It would be more correct to say that the European countries can be placed on a continuum from countries with a well-developed youth sector to countries with only a few elements of a self-contained youth sector. (IARD, 2001, p 60)

The construction of youth as a public action category significantly affects the target of youth policies: the dimension of target groups (vulnerable youth, youth in difficulties, excluded youth…) or – more generally – of defining youth starting either with early childhood or around the age of 14 or 15, ending somewhere between the mid-20s and the mid-30s.

The dimension of issues and activities which range from an infrastructure of leisure activities for all young people to the focus of integration measures for disadvantaged or at-risk youth or even to the sector of public care. This element is not neutral: a narrow definition of youth policies implies an old-fashioned attitude of decision makers and the non-recognition of the transversal problems that young people have to face in contemporary societies.

The dimension of addressing youth as a resource (as promoted by the 2001 EU White Paper) or as a problem which may include both the problems that youth creates for society and the vulnerability issues that young people themselves face. Here again, the phenomenon is not neutral: when disposals are analysed they may imply distrust toward young people and a range of exigencies or, on the contrary propose a large access or permit a succession of attempts and errors.

These various aspects also feature strongly in the historical legacy of each country. Italy represents a good example:

Until 1995 there was no systematic national policy for the youth, but only laws on particular aspects that aimed to protect young people in various fields, with responsibilities shared among different ministerial cabinets. Moreover, there used to be no ministry or other equivalent institutional body to coordinate youth policies. Historical reasons for such a lack go back to the early post-war period, when the political forces of the newly established Republic wished to refrain

> from following the same policies for youth and families
> adopted under the fascist regime. Rather, they committed
> both education and transition to adult and professional life
> to the traditional education structures (family, school, and
> church) and to the political organisations close to the party
> system. (Montanari, 1996, pp 182–3)

This weakness appears all the more evident when one considers local youth policies: here the degree of fragmentation is perhaps even higher as the interest and activity of public actors (administrative personnel as well as elected representatives) appears to vary dramatically from one territory to another; over the past thirty years in Italy the northern part of the country has been very active in comparison to the southern regions.

In relation to institutional organisation at central level each national system has its own specificities concerning at least four aspects: the legal framework of youth policy; the fields of public intervention; the concerned administrative bodies and the types of relationships among and between these bodies.

In the following these dimensions shall be applied to youth policy structures in five countries that were analysed in the context of the EU-funded project Youth – Actor of Social Change (UP2YOUTH).[3]

Whereas youth policy appears to imply a large number of fields of intervention in France, Italy and Slovakia, it concerns a narrow number of sectors in Austria and Ireland. Here again this plain typology hides a deeply complex situation.

Inasmuch as Austria has given the role of coordinating the (large) field of child welfare and youth work to the Ministry for Health, Family, and Youth (BMGFJ, Ireland used to determine youth policy through the department of Education which constructs its interventions in terms of youth work (although structures in Ireland are changing at this point in time, see Chapter 7). In the first case, the relationships between the Ministry and its work committees are clearly defined, in the second case, the relationships with other administrative segments seem to be rather loose. Actually, these differences are both due to the disparities in the definition of youth policies and to the great variety of institutional combinations.

In Italy, youth policy has a large remit and was been placed under the responsibility of a Ministry for Youth five years ago. This new entity is endorsed with the responsibility for coordinating the different administrative bodies; at present it is still too early to assess the real impact of this development.

In France, youth policy holds significant responsibilities; however leadership and the relationship between ministries remain unclear. In Slovakia, youth policy is again supposed to be substantial and the responsibility of the Ministry of Education. This ministry is supposedly endowed with the competency to coordinate the totality of administrative actors. Nevertheless, until now youth policy is confined primarily to the educational sector and the leadership of the Ministry of Education does not appear to be fully consolidated.

These differentiations in content are very important when one considers the consequence of the structure of youth policies for the access to rights (in particular to social rights for young people). Gill Jones underlined the following questions, which could be raised to identify the inequalities of treatment that are coming along the diversity of contents:

> Do young people under the age of 18 have individual rights, or do they derive rights through their families? Are entitlements age-structured and, if so, is this consistent? What arrangements are there for cases where young people's families are not willing or able to support them? When does adulthood, in terms of social citizenship, occur? (Jones, 2005, p 50)

Apparently, the individualisation of society in general and youth in particular as well as changing structures and processes of governance in the context of reflexive modernisation contribute to blurring boundaries of active citizenship, especially inasmuch as youth and young adults are concerned (Beck, 1992). This diversity of definitions and contents becomes even more obvious if the different steps of the policy process in the field of youth are considered.

Weaknesses at all steps and focus on the implementation process

Weaknesses are present during every step of youth policy creation: in the formulation of public problems, within the agenda setting process, in the implementation and finally in the evaluation of policy.

The formulation of public problems of youth over the last decades witnessed the growth of moral panics as an important factor concerning young people and, consequently, of youth as a problem:

> Adult paranoia about young people ranges from concerns
> that they will upset the boat by challenging the consensus
> to blaming them for the current widespread fear of crime.
> Moral panics, based on worries that normative values and
> practices are under threat, develop too easily into a culture
> of blame, centred on young people, while the responsibility
> of older age groups for moral decline or criminal activity
> is barely acknowledged. (Jones, 2010, p 31)

As public policies reflect the evolution of society this trend is sensitive
in the many fields of public action that tend to be more and more
stigmatising and severe towards young people: health (Peretti-Wattel,
2010), delinquency (Bailleau and Cartuyvel, 2007; Le Goaziou and
Mucchielli, 2009) and welfare (in particular integration to work)
(MacDonald, 1997) are particularly influenced by this process.

This growth of severity is based more on European changes in terms
of ageing and increasing needs of security than on any great change
in young people's behaviour, and it reflects a fundamental weakness: as
severity-influenced policies affirm a strong will in channelling young
people in predefined directions, they also tend to reject the young
people concerned and thereby to jeopardise the social integration
process.

As for agenda setting; many of today's youth policies exist at multiple
levels of the decision-making process but these policies are rarely
formulated properly. They lack the framework of a transversal project,
with a cross-sectoral approach and a reflection on the link between
the different levels of decision. On the contrary, they appear largely
fragmented and difficult to identify (Loncle, 2010). In 2002, Williamson,
reporting on international reviews of national youth policies asserted
that:

> The international reports, in different ways, expose the fact
> that most, if not all, of the national youth policies reviewed
> fell substantially short of this "holistic" approach to the
> framing and shaping of youth policy. Priorities and focus for
> youth policy were often much more narrowly conceived,
> and derived from a much more narrow field of information
> and consultation. (2002, p 36)

Even if projects exist and frameworks are elaborated, the implementation
remains the central problem of youth policies. We can illustrate this
through an example: the White Paper of the European Commission

A New Impetus for European Youth (2001) is exceptionally ambitious in the formulation of policy goals:
Investing in youth is an investment in the richness of our societies, today and tomorrow. It is therefore one of the keys to achieving the political objective laid down by the Lisbon European Council: making Europe 'the most competitive and dynamic knowledge-based economy in the world.' (European Commission, 2001, p 6)

On the one hand, the White Paper refrains from explicitly stating what investing in youth actually means in terms of young people's rights, welfare entitlements and/or a work infrastructure. On the other hand, the means of implementation – participation, the open method of coordination and the mainstreaming of youth issues – are rather soft and rely on the goodwill of national and local decision makers. Clearly, the White Paper, despite the underlying consultation process and its ambitious objectives, is above all a tool meant to stimulating policy discourse.

If we take into consideration that procedures like the White Paper process reflect general trends while at the same time general trends are interpreted and implemented differently in different welfare, transition or life course regimes (see above), to what extent do we find repercussions of the shift from contents to procedures also in the exemplary countries analysed in the UP2YOUTH project?

In all cases the structure and nature of youth policy formation and delivery tends to mirror the ideological foundations of the relevant national/regional welfare regime. The five countries under analysis have a mixture of welfare economy insofar as young people's needs are fulfilled to various degrees by the state, voluntary or NGO actors, family and local community and market forces (particularly in the area of commercial leisure). One should not forget that alongside the other groups in any population young people are users of generic services such as education, transport, healthcare, utilities and housing. There is also a commonality with regard to age related protections that seek to protect children and young people from hazards of one sort or another; and a commonality in regard to age-related rights such as consumption of alcohol and access to motor vehicles.

Within this framework, the local level appears highly significant, with local authorities fulfilling various roles. An overall picture of youth policies structured by the principle of subsidiarity emerges; national governments legislating for the provision of certain services and opportunities with the levels next to target population (regional, provincial, departmental or municipal) being responsible for policy delivery.

France, in the past decades, has experienced a notable process of decentralisation in which the municipalities have become the core actor, working hand in hand with the voluntary sector. In contrast, the central role of municipalities in Italy is not a result of decentralisation but of a structural deficit at national level while the declining influence of the Catholic Church has been balanced by a dynamic Third Sector. The Irish case can be interpreted through the concept of devolution. Here, the local Vocational Education Committees have the task of implementing the National Youth Work Development Plan. This is to some extent similar in Austria where youth policy is partly regulated at national and at federal level while delivered by the municipalities in cooperation with voluntary actors. In Slovakia, finally, the youth strategy of the national government is administered at regional level with varying links to the municipalities.

Nevertheless, the influence of the local level is also an important problem when regarding the subsequent inequalities it frequently implies, particularly if the challenge is to answer the specific difficulties of young people in one specific territory. Such inequalities appear to be multiple: they arise from disparities in funding, from differences in public policy objectives, in the definition of public problems, and in the legal frameworks that determine access to rights (Loncle et al, 2008). Moreover, the distribution of power between different levels leads to a growing number of concerned public actors. Consequently, youth policies possess faint visibility and expenditure is difficult to analyse as it is close to impossible to know exactly what expenditure is attributed to which policy.

In this regard the development of youth policies at local, regional, national and European levels reflect a general trend towards multi-level and multi-actor governance which especially challenges the nation state level. Municipalities claim more and more influence together with the necessary resources, conversely, transnational actors such as the EU initiate discourses and implement benchmarking procedures (European Commission, 2001). This is particularly relevant in countries where youth policies have been traditionally underdeveloped insofar as the process is neither assessed according to developed standards nor moderated by powerful stakeholders (Williamson, 2007).

It is further noticeable that the voluntary/NGO sector plays a significant role in providing direct services for young people even within states that have heavily invested historically in public sector provision. The field of youth is deeply invested by voluntary organisations of every religious, ideological and political shade; from the international actors such as the YMCA to local micro-agencies that serve the needs of a neighbourhood. This field and its associated actors are very diverse from one country to another; in addition the structural arrangements depend on the historical legacy of each country (Vershelden et al, 2009). Nevertheless, it is by no means certain that these associative organisations are always able to play the role of counterweight or 'mediators' between young people and public actors and are influential enough to avoid the emergence of moral panics centred on young people.

Conclusion: participation reflecting weakness of youth policies?

In the main, youth policies tend to focus on the soft sector issues that affect young people in society as they generally aim to improve access to leisure and recreational opportunities such as national and international exchanges, non-formal and informal educational systems, and active citizenship programmes. Thereby policy and practice constantly and strongly encourage participatory principles.

The promotion of young people's participation in decision making has become a key driver of policy in the youth field in recent years. On the European level, the White Paper outlines participation as a cross-cutting imperative to the core objectives of cooperation (particularly in relation to integrating young people), promoting initiative, enterprise and creativity, voluntary activities and citizenship.

Could one assert then that this focus on participation is a means to overcome the weaknesses of youth policies and to give legitimacy to a sector that seems fragmented, difficult to identify and a creator of social and territorial inequalities? This leads to the question of the relationship between weak youth policies and other (stronger) policy sectors such as activating labour market policies which profit from both the structural weakness of youth policies and a powerful discourse on youth participation (van Berkel and Hornemann-Møller, 2002; Walther et al, 2006).

However, the picture outlined so far is fragmented and tentative due to a lack of systematic comparative research not only on youth policy structures but also on the relationship between national structures and policies at local level.

Both youth research and public policy research need to invest more in order to contribute to a valid distinction between youth policies and youth policy discourses on the one hand and between national youth policy rationales and local constellations of delivery on the other. This includes an analysis of different actors involved in youth policies and their diverging interest in and interpretation of youth participation. Apart from this, research needs to contribute to distinguishing to what extent participation is an integral element of youth policies or an objective of participation programmes aimed at forming young people as active citizens. Finally, more knowledge is needed on the extent to which young people's participation is secured by individual and collective rights as well as by welfare entitlements contributing to an autonomy of young people in relation to institutional and other societal actors.

Notes

[1] The notion of sector can be considered as the combination of three elements: a group of actors who express specific interests (youth organisations, youth workers, locally elected persons with responsibility for youth, for instance); an institutional dimension that corresponds to the creation of dedicated administrative bodies (youth ministries and youth services); and a cognitive dimension that permits one to express the vision of a given problem (Muller, 2004).

[2] This study applies the categories of the major youth sector (for comprehensive), minor (for fragmented) or no youth sector. We have replaced these categories as they can be misleading in terms of indicating a size rather a form of governance. For example, in terms of size the British youth sector is 'major' although for a long time there has not been a central responsibility at national level; while at the same time the fact that in Italy there has been created a ministry for the first time does not imply the formation of a well-developed youth sector (especially as this ministry does not have a relevant budget but is a ministry '*senza portafoglio*', i.e. without a budget).

[3] The UP2YOUTH project was concerned with the relationship between social change and young people's agency – to what extent social change affects young people's agency and to what extent young people's agency influences social change. This question was analysed comparatively in three working groups: on transitions to adulthood, transitions of migrant youth to the labour market, and youth participation (Loncle and Muniglia 2008: Walther et al. 2009; see www.up2youth.org).

References

Bailleau, F. and Cartuyvels, Y. (2007) *La justice pénale des mineurs en Europe: Entre modèle Welfare et inflexions néo-libérales*, (Children and criminal justice in Europe: between welfare model and neoliberal inflections), Paris: L'Harmattan.

Beck, U. (1992) *Risk society: Towards a new mordernity*, London: Sage.

Bonetta, G. (1990) *Corpo e Nazione. L'educazione ginnastica, igienica e sessuale nell'Italia liberale* (Body and nation: athletic, hygienic and sexual education in liberal Italy), Milan: Franco Angeli.

Bourgeois, E. and Nizet, J. (1995) *Pression et légitimation* (Pression and legitimation), Paris: PUF.

Burgess, P. (2001) *Ireland. National Report for the Yoyo Project*, Cork: University College of Cork.

Edelman, M. (1964) *The symbolic uses of politics*, Illinois Books Edition: University of Illinois Press.

European Commission (2001) *White Paper. A New Impetus for European Youth*, Brussels, 21.11, 681 final.

IARD (2001) *Study on the state of young people and youth policy in Europe*, Final reports.

Jones G. (2005) 'Social protection policy for young people', in H. Bradley and J. van Hoof (eds) *Young people in Europe, labour markets and citizenship*, Bristol: The Policy Press, pp 41–62.

Jones, G. (2010) *Youth*, Cambridge: Polity Press.

Kelly, P. (2001) 'Youth at risk: processes of individualisation and responsibilisation in the risk society', *Discourse: Cultural Studies in the Politics of Education*, vol 22, no 1, pp 23–33.

Le Bart, C. and Lefevre, C. (eds) (2005) *La proximité en politique, usages, rhétoriques, pratiques* (Proximity in politics, uses, rhetoric and practices), Rennes: Presses universitaires de Rennes.

Le Goaziou, V. and Mucchielli, L. (2009), *La violence des jeunes en question* (Youth violence in question), Nîmes: Champ social éditions.

Loncle, P. (2010) *Politiques de jeunesses: les défis majeurs de l'intégration* (Youth policies: main challenges of integration), Rennes: Presses universitaires de Rennes.

Loncle P. and Muniglia V. (2008) *Youth participation, agency and social change, thematic report, deliverable no 21 of the project Youth – Actor of Social Change (Up2youth)*, contract no 028317.

Loncle P., Muniglia V., Rivard T. and Rothé C. (2008), 'Les inégalités territoriales dans la décentralisation du fonds d'aide aux jeunes' ('Territorial inequalities in the decentralisation of the youth help fund'), *Revue française des affaires sociales*, no 1, pp 229–49.

Loriga, S. (1996) 'L'épreuve militaire' (The military event), in G. Levi and J.-C. Schmidt (eds) *Histoire des jeunes en occident, l'époque contemporaine,* (The story of youth in West, the contemporary period), Tome 2, Paris: Seuil, pp 19–50.

MacDonald, R. (ed) (1997) *Youth, the 'underclass' and social exclusion,* London: Routledge.

Mairesse, P. (2007) 'The impact of the White Paper on youth policies', Forum 21, *European Journal on Child and Youth Policy,* no 9, pp 42–8.

Montanari, F. (1996) 'I servizi per i giovani in Italia e i centri informazione, ('The services for young people in Italy and the information centres') in L. Guerra, F. Hamburger and L. Robertson (eds) *Educazione comunitaria in Europa. Dimensioni interculturali del lavoro con i giovani* (Community Education in Europe. The intercultural dimensions of youth work), Bergamo: Junior, pp 182–92.

Muller, P. (2004) 'Secteur' (Sector), in L. Boussaguet, S. Jacquot, P. and Ravinet (eds) *Dictionnaire des politiques publiques* (Dictionary of public policies), Paris: Presses de Sciences Po, pp 405–13.

Peretti-Wattel, P. (2010) 'Morale, stigmate et prévention' (Moral, stigma and prevention), *Agora débats/jeunesses,* no 56, pp 73–86.

Quintin, O. (2009) 'The new EU strategy for youth', Forum 21, *European Journal on Child and Youth Policy,* no 14, pp 20–5.

Siurala, L. (2004), 'A European framework for youth policy', *Directorate of Youth and Sport,* Strasbourg: Council of Europe Publishing.

Tétard, F. (1986) 'Sauver notre jeunesse ou la prévention dans ses rapports avec les politiques de jeunesse de 1945 à 1965' ('Save our youth or the prevention and its relationship with youth policies from 1945 to 1965'), *Les Annales de Vaucresson,* no 24, pp 163–78.

van Berkel, R. and Hornemann-Møller, I. (2002) *Active social policies in the UE: Inclusion through participation?,* Bristol: The Policy Press.

Vershelden, G., Coussée, F., van de Walle, T., Williamson, H. (2009) *The history of youth work in Europe, relevance for today's youth work policy,* Strasbourg: Council of Europe Publishing.

Walther, A. (2006) 'Regimes of youth transitions. Choice, flexibility and security in young people's experiences across different European contexts', *Young,* vol 14, no 2, pp 119–39.

Walther, A. and Pohl, A. (2005) *Thematic study on policies concerning disadvantaged youth. Final Report to the European Commission.* Download from: http://ec.europa.eu/employment_social/social_inclusion/studies_en.htm.

Walther, A., du Bois-Reymond, M. and Biggart, A. (eds) (2006) *Participation in transition. Motivation of young people in Europe for learning and working,* Frankfurt a.M.: Lang.

Williamson, H. (2002) *Supporting young people in Europe: Principles, policy and practice*, Strasbourg: Council of Europe Publishing.

Williamson, H. (2007) 'European youth policy', in *Children and young people in disadvantaged neighbourhoods, new cohesion strategies*, Documentation of EU Congress in Leipzig 26–28 June 2007, Munich: Deutsches Jugendinstitut, pp 99–104.

THREE

Participation and individualisation: the emergence of a new (political) consciousness?

Reingard Spannring

Introduction

Over the past decades, the development of political participation in Western democracies has often been characterised by a decrease in traditional forms of mass participation and voter turnout which has given rise to widespread concern for the future of democracy. Putnam (2000), for example, observed that civic engagement among Americans was high and stable at the turn of the century and through the 1920s but began to dwindle with the generation born between the two world wars. This development picked up speed with the post-war generation, the 'baby-boomers'. Generation X, born between 1965 and 1980, continued the course of the boomers (Putnam, 2000, p 250).

Other academics have interpreted the changes not as a decline but as a *transformation*, a shift in the repertoire of political engagement. The decline in traditional forms of participation seems to be partly counteracted by the expansion of new and 'modern' forms of political and social engagement, rejecting the old 'duty-based citizenship' (voting, paying taxes, obeying the law) in favour of an 'engaged citizenship', based on independent, assertive behaviour and concern for others (Dalton, 2007, p 4). Similarly, youth studies have highlighted young people's involvement in unconventional, elite-challenging participation, sub-politics and social action, single issues such as animal protection (Wilkinson, 1996), spontaneous direct actions and voluntary work (Hackett, 1997; Eden and Roker, 2002) as well as participatory projects on the local level (Riepl and Wintersberger, 1999). Young people are also actively involved in innovative forms of political protest such as 'street-party-protest' interweaving politics and culture (Brünzel, 2000).

The changes in political participation must be understood in the context of the shift from modernity to post-modernity, materialism to post-materialism and from collectivism to individualism. It involves transformations on the level of the economy and social institutions (e.g. Beck and Beck-Gernsheim, 2004; Giddens, 1990), epistemologies (Lyotard,1986) and value systems (e.g. Inglehart, 1977) that have reinforced processes of individualisation and pluralisation. Moreover, political institutions and their relationships to the economy and society have also changed (e.g. Habermas, 1975; Crouch, 2004), impinging on citizens' ability and willingness to get and be active.

These transformations do not concern all citizens in a uniform way. They differ according to their geographical and social positions, economic and socio-cultural resources as well as their epistemological frames. These epistemological frames influence which political issues are relevant, how different citizens perceive political processes, and what kinds of participatory settings they prefer. On the other hand, epistemologies also exist on the societal level where they develop the political structures and culture that fit into their world views. However, as epistemological frames change in (particular groups of) the citizenry, they can be at odds with the predominant epistemologies of the political structures or processes and therefore give rise to political dissatisfaction, criticism and reform.

Indeed the changes in participation towards elite-challenging and individualised forms of participation have beenpartly explained by the contradiction between formal political structures that are based on collectivist experiences and endeavours on the one hand, and on the other hand by life chances and life styles characterised by individualisation. This individualisation thesis is an important aspect for understanding the relationship between young people and politics. However, in the public debate these arguments are often misunderstood as implying that young people have become increasingly ego-centric and are therefore disinterested in political involvement. Against this simplifying equation, this chapter suggests that some young people have in fact moved beyond this individualistic stage and represent a world view that is community-oriented – not in the old authority-oriented 'elite-directed' (Inglehart, 1977) form we already know, but in a more egalitarian, 'democratic' form; it is the politicians who appear ego-centred.

This chapter therefore explores young people's criticism of politics and participation in the light of their own epistemologies. At first, a brief overview of young people's attitudes to politics and political participation shall be given based on the qualitative data of the EUYOUPART research project that was carried out between 2003 and 2005 in eight member states of the European Union[1]. These young people's statements will then be interpreted from the perspective of a developmental model (Beck and Cowan, 2006) in order to reveal their underlying epistemologies and to convert their negative assessments into a picture of what might be a positive, attractive form of politics and participation according to the respective epistemologies. In the conclusion, the implications and challenges of such a fragmentation with respect to democracy and political integration shall be considered.

Young people's relationships with politics

The research project EUYOUPART set out to develop a valid comparative measurement instrument for youth participation in Europe. In youth research, the concept of participation is a very broad one ranging from young people's engagement in the shaping of their own lives (Walther et al, 2006), the co-shaping of their direct environments such as schools and local communities, to young people's attempts to influence decision making and to challenge power relationships. The EUYOUPART study, by comparison, took a more narrow approach by focusing on political participation. In line with mainstream research on political participation it looked primarily at citizens' engagement in institutionalised political processes within nation-states and at the relationship between young citizens and the political system.

One major preliminary step of the EUYOUPART project was a qualitative study with in-depth interviews and focus group discussions with young Europeans in order to investigate how politics and political participation is understood and experienced. A total of 266 young people shared their views with the researchers. Those respondents who were or had been politically active especially offered very nuanced and critical comments that helped the researchers grasp the young people's understanding of and frustration with politics.

The results of the qualitative study fed into the design of the questionnaire which was then tested for reliability, validity and comparability and revised. The final version of the questionnaire was applied in representative surveys among 15- to 25-year-olds in eight countries with a total sample size of 8030. The questionnaire included traditional, institutionalised forms of participation such as voting and membership in political organisations as well as participation in social movements, political communication, protest and political consumerism in order to capture more individualised forms of participation. The survey data revealed that participation within the representative system (political party, trade union) tended to be lower than the rates for participation in NGOs and social movements and still lower than the rates for legal protest (demonstrations and strikes) and political consumerism (boycotts and buycotts) (Spannring, Ogris and Gaiser, 2008). This finding is in line with the individualisation thesis that draws attention to the de-standardisation and de-institutionalisation of life courses, the fragmentation of the structures of social reproduction, the increasing discontinuities and risk in respect to young people's labour market entry and social and economic integration (Spannring, Loncle and Walther, 2008). Individualisation implies more opportunities for self-actualisation, choice and autonomy, but also more pressure to actively negotiate transitions, to cope with risk individually, and to reflexively construct identities and biographies. Thus, short-term commitment and spontaneous political action seems more congruent with young people's individualised lives, and complete lack of participation may be the result of social and economic marginalisation. The feeling of being let down by the politicians as a fundamental experience colouring the relationship with politics was expressed by a number of respondents, one of whom said: 'We don't get help. ... I cannot get a bank loan because they do not want any people with fixed term jobs' (Spannring, Ogris and Gaiser, 2008, p 55).

The findings are also congruent with the post-materialism thesis which maintains that as post-war generations increasingly experience political and economic stability and security they replace old materialist values with values such as human rights, gender equality, environmental protection, pluralism and tolerance as well as individual autonomy and self-expression (Inglehart, 1977; Inglehart and Welzel, 2005). This does not contradict the individualisation thesis, since individualism does not necessarily imply ego-centrism, but can also lead to engagement in unconventional forms of participation (Welzel, 2007). However, the EUYOUPART data also show a certain tendency that all forms of participation correlate (Spannring, Ogris and Gaiser, 2008): those who are active in one form of political participation are likely to be active in other forms as well. This finding puts the individualisation theory in perspective because some young people who grow up under the conditions of individualisation are still prepared to commit themselves to collective political endeavours. It seems that a piece of the jigsaw puzzle is still missing in order to fully understand youth participation. Maybe this missing piece concerns meaning; as one young respondent ventured: 'The question is not whether we take part in elections, but what meaning we attach to them' (Spannring, Ogris and Gaiser, 2008, p 65).

Different forms of participation as well as non-participation cannot be fully understood without considering the changes that affect the political sphere itself such as globalisation, economisation and de-traditionalisation. Globalisation and economic rationalisation processes limit the sovereignty of nation-states. They are placed in a dilemma between their industrial location policy and fiscal crises, which impinges on states' ability to shape and integrate society. The resulting steering and legitimisation crisis (Habermas, 1975) also contributes to a de-politicisation (Felgitsch, 2006). This frustration was articulated by many respondents: 'Business and industry are incredibly powerful and, well … their influence is really really unbelievable. The individual citizen, after all, does not really have such a strong lobby' (Spannring, Orgris and Gaiser, 2008, p 43).

The process of globalisation has also led to a radically increased complexity of social and political problems that cannot be adequately tackled on the level of the nation-state, nor can they be accommodated within the traditional left-right framework (Biorcio/Mannheimer, 1995). The process of de-traditionalisation and weakening of class-based ideologies is another visible issue in the EUYOUPART interviews:

> For me the distinction between left and right makes so little … is so little telling. If I have an issue and, ehm, I take a side, then it does not matter to me, whether it's the left or the right, but one with which I can identify. (Spannring, Orgris and Gaiser, 2008, p 51)

How, indeed, would politics have to function under these conditions? How is the meaning that young people attach to politics and participation influenced by this crisis?

Thus, various structures exist that alienate young people from politics: precarious socioeconomic conditions, disempowered nation-states and ineffective party politics based on the traditional class-related cleavage. In addition to these structures there are cultural factors relating to how politicians work together and how they relate to young people. In this respect, young people are strongly dissatisfied with the regime's effectiveness in solving problems, that is, its performance and political outcomes (Montero et al, 1997). On the one hand, they criticise the lack of representativity and responsiveness. Politicians are not interested in young people's living conditions and needs; they are driven by their own self-interests and patronages, and they yield to the power of the economy. On the other hand, young people reject the political culture for its poor efficiency, exaggerated competitiveness, unconstructive quarrelling and power games. Furthermore, young people miss ideals, political visions (as opposed to ideologies) and ethics in politics or see them sacrificed to power. Their longing for idealism, authenticity and faithfulness is repeatedly disappointed by real politics, in particular after elections when it becomes evident that promises are not kept (Spannring, Ogris and Gaiser, 2008).

In addition to this political dissatisfaction young people also experience powerlessness and confusion with politics. This is not only a matter of lacking political knowledge and competence but also a sign of distrust in media information and politicians' proclamations. The latter are considered competition strategies rather than representations of truth or truthful exposures of political aims and strategies. This distrust reflects awareness of epistemological indeterminacy: that knowledge is fuzzy, multi-layered and socially constructed. It produces a critical distance toward ideologies, political organisations and participation. It expresses itself in young people's refusal to categorise people and ideas as simply 'good' or 'bad' or to see the world in black and white. Political arguments and ideas are always open to question, inviting counter-arguments and counter-views. Blindly following an ideology or a group is criticised as extremist. Even if the counter-argument is not known by the individual concerned there is an expectation that there is a 'yes, but ...' answer. The complexity of political issues and the pluralisation of policy dimensions and political perspectives weaken class-based ideologies and their capacity to generate consensus, identification, solidarity and mobilisation. In fact, ideologies and political truths are discredited and suspected to legitimise oppression, intolerance and violence.

Thus, there is a paralysing negative relativism that keeps many young people from taking sides or getting politically active (Spannring, Ogris and Gaiser, 2008). The possibility of a positive reconstruction of a politics not intended as universal truth but as participation of individuals in shared processes of social and political construction is cognitively not available for many young people (Felgitsch, 2006). Indeed, the productive means of dealing with epistemological uncertainty are missing in our societies and political forums (Murray, 2006).

Interest in politics is expressed by two groups of young people. One group, mainly older adolescents, has already experienced politics as impinging on their lives in the form of tuition fees, taxes, access to social welfare and interaction with public healthcare. Here, politics interferes with their personal interests. Another group of young people is driven by a longing for fairness, solidarity and equality. They express strong feelings about broader issues such as anti-racism, peace, animal rights and environmental protection. In general however, neither the public debate nor the culture of 'management politics', (i.e. politics that manages rather than shaping society), provide a bridge to young people's immediate material and social needs, or to their ethical beliefs. Political structures and processes therefore provide poor opportunities for young people to connect with the political sphere, leaving them alienated or frustrated (Spannring, Ogris and Gaiser, 2008).

Young people's attitudes toward all political activities are characterised by the principle of freedom of committing and disengaging at any time and the principle of participating on equal terms. They are only prepared to give their vote in a case of full approval with the party profile and candidates, which is hardly ever possible. Similarly, young people want to be able to withdraw support for an organisation whenever deemed necessary in order to remain flexible and autonomous. Even those young people who feel close to a political organisation or movement maintain a critical distance. This has to do with their denial of the existence of one objective truth, but also with their refusal to comply with a party discipline or to take responsibility for the group's actions and decisions that are not under their control. It is more important to live up and remain loyal to one's own truth and moral standard. Many young people fear that they would not be integrated in the political group on equal terms with adults and that their voices would be lost in group processes; that membership of an organisation forecloses open communication with non-members or members of other organisations (Spannring, Ogris and Gaiser, 2008). It is obvious that these attitudes are not congruent with party structures that expect members to be either party soldiers, who willingly carry out basic party work as the party leadership ordains (Inglehart, 1977), or cannot give them a meaningful role (Hooghe, 2003).

However, even with spontaneous acts of political participation scepticism remains a stable feature; demonstrations contain the danger that young people's principles are violated, good causes can be abused by certain groups with false motivations, or young people's motivations can be misinterpreted (Spannring, Ogris and Gaiser, 2008; Such et al, 2005). The desire for self-expression, self-determination and loyalty to one's moral convictions that comes to bear in these political activities is also expressed in life politics. The latter relates to the defence of life styles rather than life chances (Giddens, 1994). Life politics can encompass universal values – such as equality, fairness and sustainability – that form part of a young person's political identity. Strikingly, young people do not attach any missionary zeal to their life politics. From the viewpoint of structural constraints for politically effective action it seems that living up to one's own political and moral expectations is the minimal possibility in changing the world (Spannring, Ogris and

Gaiser, 2008). However, life politics also expresses a positive decision to take on responsibility for one's own ethics and actions without an external authority:

> What is personal is political and thus really ... any choice is political ... the travel you decide to undertake, the philosophy you follow, so it is something in which you find yourself immersed, that you practice both explicitly and implicitly, always. (Spannring, Ogris and Gaiser, 2008, p 79)

Variations in perceptions: epistemological frames

While young people's critical remarks fit quite well with academic analyses of the democratic systems (e.g. Crouch, 2004), it is clear that perceptions are always structured by epistemologies; meaning-making frames of mind that are made up of tacit assumptions and expectations relevant for interpreting the world. Consequently, the same political structure and culture is seen in a different light through different epistemologies. It is argued in this section that several epistemologies exist among (young) citizens and that political culture is also characterised by a particular dominant epistemology. The dynamic but rarely synchronous development of these epistemologies gives rise to criticism of the political sphere. Two important epistemologies have already been partly captured by the individualisation thesis and the postmodernity thesis. The following theoretical model is understood not as a contradiction but as a refinement of these epistemologies that allows for the development of a fuller account of the manner in which young people make meaning of politics, find access to political discourses, criticise politics and find motivation to become politically active.

The *developmental model* by Don Beck and Christopher Cowan (2006) sees – as do many other comparable models – the evolution of the human psyche in a series of unfolding stages or waves. Every human being starts from the lowest level and reaches progressively higher stages of development. Each new level includes and transcends the structures of all previous levels. Stage models do not suggest that development is linear, and 'higher' does not mean 'better'. Development is rather seen as something fluid, like a wave or spiral that includes potential for progress and regression and displays an indefinite number of combinations of manifestations across the various lines of development (e.g. cognition, morality, self-identity). Progress from one stage to the next presupposes successful integration of the former. Development is directional only insofar as the individual leaves a limited, self-centred perspective to incorporate increasingly more encompassing identities, for example from ego-centred, group-centred to socio-centred and world-centred.

Don Beck and Christopher Cowan's cultural anthropological model of human development (2006) proposes eight 'value-memes'[2]. Each ᵛMEME has its own linguistic reality, world view, and serves as a lens for the interpretation of the world. In the Spiral Dynamics model each ᵛMEME is represented by a colour. The Spiral starts with BEIGE, where life is all about subsistence, and PURPLE, which is characterised by an emphasis of social relations and a strong need for integration into a family-like group. The next ᵛMEME is RED, in which individuals develop independence and attempt to enforce power over the self and others, as can be observed in rebellious youth. The basic theme of BLUE is finding meaning and direction in life with a strong belief in one right way and obedience to authority. ORANGE is characterised by self-interest and individuality, while the emphasis of GREEN is on community concerns and tolerance for plurality. With YELLOW and TURQUOISE, Beck and Cowan suggest epistemological frames that go beyond the present paradigms but shall not be pursued here.

> MEMEs develop a particular dynamic in individual-psychological development as well as in socio-historic development (Beck and Cowan, 2006, p 30)[3].

Every society has a certain centre of gravity ... around which the culture's ethics, norms, rules and basic institutions are organised and this centre of gravity acts like a magnet on individual development. If you are below that level, it tends to pull you up. If you try to go above it, it tends to pull you down. (Wilber, 2001a, p 208)

Thus, the individual mental structure is not directly determined by the techno-economic base, but by the centre of gravity of a society at a given point in time together with the collective, dominant world view. Every ᵛMEME along the spiral develops 'its own political and organisational forms which fit its world view, perform the functions it deems necessary and meet its specific bottom lines' (Beck and Cowan, 2006, p 126). Changes in individual mental structures, behaviour and collective world views can lead to changes in the legitimacy of political systems and institutions (Wilber, 2001b, p 243).

The eight ᵛMEMEs evolve in the form of a pendulum-like shift between a focus on 'me' and concerns with 'us'. BLUE and GREEN, for example, are closer to the community pole, while ORANGE is near the individualistic pole. This position on the arc of the pendulum marks not only individual development but also 'sets the tone for generations ("Yuppie Baby Boomers" versus "Depression Era" and so on)' (Beck and Cowan, 2006, p 58).

Three of the eight ᵛMEMEs (BLUE, ORANGE and GREEN) that are most relevant in terms of distribution in contemporary Western culture and in terms of their expression through the statements of young people in the EUYOUPART project shall be explored further in the following – not as types of people but as types of thinking nested in people (Beck and Cowan, 2006, p 63). The interpretation of the qualitative data of the EUYOUPART study through the model of Spiral Dynamics is intended as a theoretical experiment that invites future empirical work.

BLUE finds it necessary to bring order to the chaos and establish a tight structure. BLUE is certain about 'good' and 'bad', imposes justice and hierarchical order, and appears rigid and dogmatic. BLUE expects higher authority to rule and is ready to fulfil his/her duties toward the Church, the employer, the state and the political party. BLUE was strongly present in elite-directed mass political participation, where party members were ready to follow and actively support the leadership that represented the correct ideology. One statement could be interpreted as a BLUE longing for clarity and order: 'Before, only the king decided. Today they don't all agree and they are not all together' (Spannring, Ogris and Gaiser, 2008, p 45).

Once a reliable order exists, however, the 'me' can grow in importance: with the development out of the BLUE ᵛMEME, authority starts to be questioned as independent thinking and autonomy become more important. An indication of exiting BLUE may be the depreciative comments on politics that were made by a number of young people, such as: 'Politics? Bigwigs, running things. Government. Lining their pockets' (Spannring, Ogris and Gaiser, 2008, p 41). Exiting BLUE 'becomes openly disdainful of any authority which does not act like good authority should' (Beck and Cowan, 2006, p 242).

Conversely, a reaction against the BLUE idea of authority-led or mass political participation is expressed by the following statement, obviously by a young respondent who has moved beyond BLUE: 'What is strange is that people follow somebody' (Spannring, Ogris and Gaiser, 2008, p 72).

There are, however, not many hints of BLUE in the qualitative interviews with young respondents of the EUYOUPART project. This may be the result of the sample structure. Possibly, those young people with elements of BLUE were less likely to agree to an interview exactly because they are politically disinterested, alienated or even hostile to politics being no longer experienced as providing the security of reasonable values and leadership. In fact, on a societal level, BLUE has been very active during the past two decades in many European countries, playing up virtue and morality as political issues, debating immigration rules and national identities.

Contrastingly, in ORANGE, freedom from constraints in the form of people or dogmas is central. Faith is replaced by experimental data and scientific method, equipping the individual for material and social success. ORANGE is oriented toward independence and control, and appears materialistic and acquisitive. Contrary to BLUE, ORANGE is loyal to a group or organisation if it proves useful to the individual, but this loyalty does not stem from any sense of obligation. This sentiment was expressed in a statement from a young interview respondent who maintained that unless 'the government decided to build a motorway through my house' he would not get politically active (Spannring, Ogris and Gaiser, 2008, p 35). In the social and economic sciences, this utilitarian approach is also to be found in rational choice models that grapple with the lack of incentives for individuals to bear the costs of collective engagement (Downs, 1957; Olson, 1965).

For ORANGE, pragmatism is more important than principles, short-range victories more attractive than long-term guarantees, prosperity more compelling than ethics. ORANGE personalities are calculating, have a sense of superior competences, and take on responsibility. If they are involved in group processes they want to be credited for the progress. These characteristics are found in some of young people's statements that stress their demand for self-authorship, responsibility and control in political processes.

> I met up with an excellent, very dynamic team and fitted in at once. I was given responsibilities. I must say there is no better way of motivating people than giving them responsibilities. My opinion counted, I wasn't just a little first year student. (Spannring, Ogris and Gaiser, 2008, p 73)

Governments in Europe have a lot of pragmatic, economic and power-oriented ORANGE in their leadership that is harshly criticised by those young respondents who are not predominantly ORANGE themselves. They point to the politicians' will to power and domination, and their political manoeuvres that include espionage, liaisons, allies, intimidations and cover stories. '… there is no will to solve our country's problems. The chair is a continual fight, not working together to solve problems, but a continual fight' (Spannring, Ogris and Gaiser, 2008, p 44). And again: '... but for them it was more important to remain in power than to defend their own ideals. There I think, what kind of people are they?' (Spannring, Ogris and Gaiser, 2008, p 45).

(Neo) liberal economic theory is rooted in ORANGE; each is responsible for him or herself. The best will succeed and prosper. ORANGE attracts individuals who oppose social programmes supporting people who do nothing to earn what they get. Work-fare replaces entitlements to social security. ORANGE can be unscrupulous, justifying harms done to others as necessities that 'had to be done' or rationalising them as 'actually for his/her own good' (Beck and Cowan, 2006, p 250).

ORANGE is the manifestation of modernity with its liberation of individuals, technologies and the willingness to explore ideas. However, it has also produced problematic life conditions. Eventually, it becomes evident that despite all the success there is still no equality among people. Mechanistic science and technology as well as economic competitiveness have led to the exploitation of humans and the depletion of the Earth. For many, these problems have lead to doubts about the effectiveness of government and politics and to concerns about the possibility of billions of humans coexisting with a reasonable quality of life, and about the viability of the planet under current and future levels of consumption. As the influence of ORANGE gets weaker and GREEN emerges on the scene, there is a shift from 'me' to 'we'; from individualism to collectivism.

The GREEN ᵛMEME responds to these ORANGE excesses by emphasising legislation in favour of community good, support for the marginalised and protection for the endangered. There is acute awareness of the interconnection among humans, animals, plants and landscapes. It finds its political expression in campaigns for women's, gay and lesbian, children's and animal rights as well as humanitarian and environmental engagement.

> A sort of ethical spur, ethical motivation – it comes from the fact, I think, that the world you have in front of yourself does not stick to the way things should go. To change a reality essentially unfair and wrong ... not equal. (Spannring, Ogris and Gaiser, 2008, p 60)

GREEN prefers flat hierarchies and team orientation with discussion, the sharing of feelings and the sharing of ideas. It stresses understanding, cooperation, appreciation and tolerance. Every member of the community should have a say and be included in decision-making.

Sharing and participation are seen to lead to better results than competition. Open-mindedness and acceptance of pluralism are of utmost importance:

> I left certain groups because I realised that in the microcosm of students' collectives, associations, social centres, there was a trend to recreate a structure actually belonging to another tradition, say that of the Stalinist party, in a vertical sense … while in fact the intention was to create a horizontal situation of collective participation. (Spannring, Ogris and Gaiser, 2008, p 75)

However, as mentioned above, pluralism and relativism can impede decision making and action; 'It's difficult anyhow, because there are topics where one can argue in this or that way' (Spannring, Ogris and Gaiser, 2008, p 51). Under GREEN, decision making can take a long time and political activities can lack a BLUE policy foundation or ORANGE strategy (Beck and Cowan, 2006, p 266). Tolerance for the diversity of lifestyles, values and norms further leads to a homogenisation nurturing the false hope that 'everything and everybody is beautiful'. This approach obscures the fact that not everything is healthy or beneficent for the individual or community and that behind the beauty of diversity there are still oppressive structures in place (Eagleton, 1996). This tolerance may also be a reason for the lack of missionary zeal and the retreat to lifestyle politics as a private affair, for how can one persuade somebody else if all opinions and behaviours are equal? On the other hand, excessive GREEN can also develop strong group pressure to support collective decisions and actions, and it can be very rigid with respect to its demands for pluralism and egalitarianism and get rather militant about its values of liberation and human rights. It can be haughty and intolerant towards other ^vMEMEs. In the German language, the notion of *Gutmensch* (good person or 'do-gooder' in English) has developed to denounce GREEN's feeling of superiority.

The majority of the young people's accounts of politics in the EUYOUPART qualitative study can be related to the GREEN ^vMEME. Seen from a generational perspective, Generation X places more emphasis on collectivism and pluralism than their predecessors, the baby boomers, who now hold political positions and who have more ORANGE qualities. However, this is not exclusively a generational problem, since human growth is not limited to children and young people. Adults develop equally to subsequent stages, especially when the overall distribution of the ^vMEMEs changes.

Conclusion: politics for all perceptions?

This contribution started with the observation of a change in forms of political participation and some theories on the reasons for this change. These were explicated with the young people's own accounts of politics and participation. Interestingly, the qualitative interviews from the EUYOUPART project revealed very critical attitudes irrespective of whether the young people were politically active or not. The alleged decline in political participation has often been interpreted as threat to democracy. In many countries as well as at European level programmes were initiated to boost participation among the younger generations. However, it is not clear as to whether this effort has led to more efficient participation or to more satisfaction with the democratic system. The fact that criticism of politics is not limited to those who do not participate suggest that the key issue is not to increase participation rates but to improve the way in which politics and citizenry relate to each other and the way in which politically active people work together.

This contribution has further argued that perceptions of the political are influenced by different epistemologies that produce different expectations toward political leadership, towards motivations to get engaged and towards demands on participatory settings. While BLUE is associated with elite-directed participation and engagement based on duty, ORANGE prefers settings and processes that are under their control, that make use of their competences and yield benefits to the individual. GREEN opposes authoritarian BLUE as well as strategic, individualistic ORANGE and opts for pluralism, team-orientation and consensus. It is obvious that people are never completely characterised by one epistemology but rather 'host several ways of thinking which may mix-and-match to the subject areas' (Beck and Cowan, 2006, p 63) and that the relative strength of these epistemologies changes throughout people's lifetimes. However, knowledge of meaning-making frames with respect to politics provides a broader basis for understanding alienation and frustration and for developing more appealing participatory offers for young people.

What are the implications of the simultaneousness of different ᵛMEMEs for political leadership and participatory settings? Dissonance and conflict between different vMEMEs challenge political players to develop new strategies – impossible in conventional partisan politics – which should recognise the whole spiral and its dynamics, not as a jumbleof independent perspectives but as a complex whole. The aim is not only to resolve conflict between two sides but to develop and transform the community (Atlee, 2010). Political processes that start from this premise should place particular emphasis on communication and dialogue, as highlighted by many scientists (e.g. Habermas, 1985; Bohm, 1996). However, this strategy seems to have found no application in real politics yet. Empowering settings call for a participatory, emergent world view that is provided by a servant leadership.

Participation would not be reduced to being part of a decision-making process in order to 'buy-in' to the results. It would mean being involved in various ways, not necessarily in the form of mass participation or citizenship, but in ways that the result of the political process makes sense within the different epistemologies (Atlee, 2010).

Notes

[1] "EUYOUPART. The Political Participation of Young People in Europe – Development of Indicators for Comparative Research in the European Union" (2003–05), funded by the European Commission. The research consortium included partners from Austria, Estonia, Finland, France, Germany, Italy, Slovakia and the UK. The qualitative study, on which this article is based, included a total of 224 young people in focus groups and 41 individual in-depth interviews. The final survey with young people aged 15 to 25 had a sample size of 8,030.

[2] Value-memes ("vMemes") denote cultural bits of information such as epistemologies, ideas, symbols, rituals, ideologies (Beck and Cowan, 2006, p 30).

[3] Similarly: Taylor, 1999; Habermas, 1979; Gebser, 1973; for a discussion of theories of social evolution see: Niedenzu et al, 2008.

References

Atlee, T. (2010) 'Integral politics as process', *Integral Review*, vol 6, no 1, pp 274–85.

Beck, D. and Cowan, C. (2006) *Spiral Dynamics. Mastering Values, Leadership, and Change,* Malden, MA: Blackwell Publishing.

Beck, U. and Beck-Gernsheim, E. (2001) *Individualization: Institutionalized Individualism and Its Social and Political Consequences*, London: Sage.

Biorcio, R. and Mannheimer, R. (1995) Relationships between Citizens and Political Parties, in H-D Klingemann and D. Fuchs (eds) *Citizens and the State. Vol. 1: Beliefs in Government*, Oxford: Oxford University Press, pp 206-226.

Bohm, D. (1996) *On Dialogue*, London: Routledge.

Brünzel, S. (2000) 'Reclaim the Streets. Karneval und Konfrontation' ('Reclaim the Streets. Carnival and Confrontation'), *derive – Zeitschrift für Stadtforschung*, no 2, pp 41–6.

Crouch, C. (2004) *Post-Democracy*, Cambridge: Polity Press.

Dalton, R. (2004) *Democratic Challenges, Democratic Choices*, Oxford: Oxford University Press.

Downs, A. (1957) *An Economic Theory of Democracy*, New York: Harper.

Eagleton, T. (1996) *The Illusions of Postmodernism*, Malden, MA: Blackwell.

Eden, K. and Roker, D. (2002) ' … *doing something': Young People as Social Actors*, Leicester: The National Youth Agency.

Felgitsch, S. (2006) 'Die Rekonstruktion des Politischen' (*The reconstruction of politics*), in Ch. Flatz and S. Felgitsch (eds) *Dimensionen einer neuen Kultur des Politischen* (*Dimensions of a new culture of politics*), Wiesbaden: VS Verlag, pp 10–40.

Gebser, J. (1973) *Ursprung und Gegenwart. Die Fundamente der aperspektivischen Welt*, München: dtv (English translation: Ever Present Origin: Foundations of the aperspectival world, Ohio: Ohio University Press, 1986).

Giddens, A. (1990) *The Consequences of Modernity*, Oxford: Polity Press.

Giddens, A. (1994) *Beyond Left and Right. The Future of Radical Politics*, Cambridge: Polity Press.

Habermas, J. (1975) *Legitimation Crisis*, Boston: Beacon Press.

Habermas, J. (1979) *Communication and the Evolution of Society*, Boston: Beacon Press.

Habermas, J. (1985) *The Theory of Communicative Action*, Boston: Beacon Press.

Hackett, S. C. (1997) 'Young people and political participation', in J. Roche and S. Tucker, (eds) *Youth in Society: Contemporary Theory, Policy and Practice*, London: Open University Press, pp 73–95.

Hooghe, M. (2003) 'Youth Organisations within Political Parties. Political Recruitment and the Transformation of Party Systems', paper presented at the research seminar 'What about Youth Political Participation?' organised by the Council of Europe and the European Commission, November 2003, Strasbourg.

Inglehart, R. (1977) *The Silent Revolution: Changing Values and Political Styles Among Western Publics*, Princeton: Princeton University Press.

Inglehart, R. and Welzel, C. (2005) *Modernization, Cultural Change and Democracy*, Cambridge: Cambridge University Press.

Lyotard, J.-F. (1984) *Postmodern Condition: A Report on Knowledge*, Minneapolis: University of Minnesota Press.

Montero, J. R., Gunther, R. and Torcal, M. (1997) 'Democracy in Spain: Legitimacy, discontent, and disaffection', *Studies in Comparative International Development*, vol 32, no 3, pp 124–60.

Murray, T. (2006) 'Collaborative knowledge building and integral theory: on perspectives, uncertainty and mutual regard', *Integral Review*, no 2, pp 211–68.

Niedenzu H.-J., Meleghy, T. et al (eds) (2008) *The New Evolutionary Social Science: Human Nature, Social Behavior, and Social Change*, Boulder, CO: Paradigm Publishers.

Olson, M. (1965) *The Logic of Collective Action. Public Goods and the Theory of Groups*, Cambridge, MA: Harvard University Press.

Putnam, R. (2000) *Bowling Alone. The Collapse and Revival of American Community*, New York: Simon and Schuster.

Riepl, B. and Wintersberger, H. (1999) *Political Participation of Youth Below Voting Age. Examples of European Practices*, Vienna: European Centre for Social Welfare Policy and Research.

Spannring, R., Loncle, P. and Walther, A. (2008) 'Youth participation under conditions of individualisation', in P. Loncle and V. Muniglia (eds) *Youth Participation, Agency and Social Change. Thematic Report of the UP2YOUTH research project.*(www.up2youth.org/downloads/task,doc_download/gid,73/).

Spannring, R., Ogris, G. and Gaiser, W. (eds) (2008) *Youth and Political Participation in Europe. Results of the Comparative Study EUYOUPART*, Opladen: Barbara Budrich

Such, E., Walker, O. and Walker, R. (2005) 'Anti-war children. Representations of youth protests against the second Iraq War in the British national press', *Childhood*, no 12, pp 301–25.

Taylor, A. (1999) 'Time-space-technics: The evolution of societal systems and world views', *World Futures: The Journal for General Evolution*, no 54, pp 21–102.

Walther, A., Du Bois-Reymond, M. and Biggart, A. (eds) (2006) *Participation in Transition. Motivation of Young People in Europe for Learning and Working,* Frankfurt am Main: Lang.

Welzel, Ch. (2007) *Wertewandel oder Werteverfall: Zersetzen Individualismus und Individualisierung die Grundlagen unserer Zivilisation?* (Value change or decay? Do individualism and individualisation corrode the basis of our civilisation?), (www.grassmedienarchiv.de/imperia/md/content/groups/schools/shss/cwelzel/papers)

Wilber, K. (2001a) *A Brief History of Everything*, Boston: Shambala.

Wilber, K. (2001b) *Sex, Ecology, Spirituality – The Spirit of Evolution*, Boston: Shambala.

Wilkinson, H. (1996) 'But will they vote? The political attitudes of young people', *Children and Society*, vol 10, no 3, pp 242–4.

Wilkinson, H. and Mulgan, G. (1995) *Freedom's Children. Work, Relationships and Politics for 18 to 34 Year Olds in Britain Today*, London: Demos.

Wilpert, G. (2009) 'Integrale Politik. Ein spiritueller dritter Weg' (Integral Politics. A Spiritual Third Way), in: www.integralworld.net/de/wilpert_de.html.

FOUR

Informal education in an historical perspective: between an instrument of social education and a socioeducational practice

Filip Coussée and Tony Jeffs

Introduction

Youth work and other forms of *informal education* have consistently played a role within broader social and educational strategies. However the focus of youth work and other forms of informal education has not been a fixed entity. In the case of youth work, for example, the equilibrium has constantly shifted: now upon 'the social question', how to preserve social cohesion in a society; and then upon 'the youth question', how to support young people's positive development. *Participation* is in both approaches a key concept. The social question refers to the necessary (re)distribution of resources in order to be able to participate in society. The youth question refers to the necessary skills to access those resources. Neither foci are ever fully eclipsed but the tension between them never fades. Rather we find the alternating attention given to each by governments, practitioners and others ensures an enduring 'field of tension' and 'war of position' between the two 'questions'. The former has historically focused on the social role of youth work whilst the latter on the pedagogical function. This illustrates how the inherent tensioned concept of social pedagogy is at the heart of youth work: transforming social problems into pedagogical questions and relating pedagogical questions to social contexts. As other social pedagogical professionals youth workers face a permanent challenge not to prioritise the pedagogical function above the social and the other way round (Coussée and Williamson, 2011). In youth work these two primary functions were glued together via the recreational function that for both served to make youth work appealing to young people. Gradually this recreational function, once the appetiser or bait, became the meal itself. This has led to an impoverishment of the youth work discussion and in the end makes youth work extremely vulnerable to instrumentalisation from external aims or objectives.

Informal education in an activating welfare state

Especially following the establishment of the welfare state and spread of universal schooling, recreation and activities increasingly constituted the prime focus of youth work. The social and pedagogical functions so crucial prior to the creation of universal schooling and universal welfare services were now to be the responsibility of others and youth work appeared to be left with the residual role of universal leisure provider. Subsequently during the past two decades in particular the ongoing move towards an enabling state has raised again pedagogical questions relating to youth work practice. Youth workers are now being asked to offer young people an activating role for example to motivate them to remain in education, take whatever job are offered however demeaning or short-term, or embark in training however narrow or irrelevant; to raise their aspirations, without in most instances providing the means to realistically achieve them. Currently against a backcloth of rapidly escalating levels of youth unemployment, youth workers like other social pedagogues and informal educators find their tasks are being rapidly re-pedagogised, especially with regards to vulnerable young people, who historically have been the prime target group. This means youth workers are 'retaking' one of their historical functions. However now it no longer relates to providing social services aimed at the redistribution of life chances or a 'liberal education' that augments their social capital and may better enable them to engage in, and comprehend, the discourses of the powerful and privileged. Now it is recalibrated so that youth workers provide 'training' not 'education' in order that individuals might better grab the very restricted opportunities being offered them. History shows, we believe, that this (re)pedagogisation of youth work practice will be counter-productive unless it is also re-socialised.

Informal education: stabilising societies in transformation

Young people do not start from some mythical zero-point without family, culture, class or religious stance. As with all social and pedagogical practices, youth work intervenes in settings that possess their own history and therefore is seeking to 'act upon' individuals and groups who likewise have a history. As a consequence the focus and practice of youth work is in a state of constant flux ceaselessly tacking in order to adjust to fresh winds created by the social, economic and technological changes that relentlessly reshape the life courses of young people and simultaneously realign the structures sustaining the youth work agencies themselves. However certain continuities exist and some of these can be identified.

First is the persistent longing for generational continuity within communities. The tenacity of which allows us to trace the threads of youth work practice back to before the rise of mass schooling and compulsory education. This persistence relates to the historic value placed upon the importance of enabling young people to learn what Robert Owen called the 'arts of humanity' outside of the home, classroom or workplace by way of relationships with wise and virtuous adults via dialogue, conversation and observation (Jeffs, 2001).

Second is a longstanding belief, well founded, that not everything a young person needs to know in order to become a mature, well-rounded individual can be taught during childhood but needs to be learnt later in life; hence the long history of adult education, circulating libraries, travelling scholars and clubs attached to both religious institutions and their secular counterparts. Modern youth work has inherited much that resided within each of these, oft forgotten, attempts to foster education beyond the schoolroom. Therefore a strong case can be made that, as with other forms of welfare, youth work pre-dated industrialisation for the simple reason that the educational and social needs it endeavoured to address existed prior to the appearance of mass industrialisation and the urbanisation that inevitably accompanies it (Quadagno, 1988).

The tap-root of youth work may run deep but in a form recognisable today it emerged into prominence during the early years of mass industrialisation that first occurred in Britain, then shortly afterwards in parts of Belgium and Germany. This is because the social problems created by rapid industrialisation and urbanisation were of such a magnitude they stirred a new generation of reformers and philanthropists into action. As levels of poverty and ignorance escalated in tandem with a growing disparity between urban and rural mortality rates so the prototypes emerged that eventually coalesced into contemporary welfare provision. Prototypes included the clubs, missions, Sunday schools, out-reach programmes, visiting schemes, adult education initiatives and school-based interventions from which youth work and social work eventually surfaced during the early to mid-eighteenth century (Jeffs and Smith, 2002). By the 1830s in Britain and shortly afterwards elsewhere in Europe, the state out of necessity began to act in a more interventionist manner within the social realm; notably regarding education, the control of disease and epidemics, management of crime and administration of basic provision for the destitute (Donzelot, 1984). Both new and emerging nation states were obliged to do so because a failure to address these manifest problems would corrode the political legitimacy of the ruling elite, sap economic competitiveness and the viability of nation-building projects by diminishing the flow of men fit enough for military service. Maintaining this fragile balance between the imperatives of accumulation, legitimisation and security remains something governments still, with scant expectation of lasting success, endeavour to achieve. Then and now it means that as the severity of one threat grows or falls so the configuration of governmental expenditure is re-aligned accordingly (O'Connor, 1973). With regards to state directed youth policy and government sponsored youth work the foci for intervention incessantly shifts creating a semi-permanent state of volatility. When accumulation is threatened the priority becomes skills and 'employability' and participation is restricted to inclusion in the labour market; when a crisis of legitimisation looms the focus switches to stimulating 'social participation' (either to dampen it down as in the 1900s and 1960s or heighten it as in the present day) and the promotion of social responsibility; when the menace is militaristic attention transfers to fitness, activities and the building of nationhood.

A youth work practice deeply rooted in welfare, culture and history

Because industrialisation within Europe was an uneven process, occurring at varying times and speeds, youth work, like social work and schooling for example acquired disparate structures across states and regions. For example the first international youth organisation, the Young Men's Christian Association (YMCA), was founded in London by George Williams in 1844 to cater for young men in white-collar trades and the semi-professions. The Young Women's Christian Association (YWCA) established eleven years later also sought to provide social, leisure and educational services for the growing number of young women entering office work, teaching, nursing and other emerging welfare professions. Both the YMCA and the YWCA grew rapidly in England, North America and much of northern Europe as the size of the social class they served proliferated. However there was a restraint upon that expansion for although both viewed themselves as non-denominational Christian organisations the founders were predominately Non-conformists or Anglicans of a particular persuasion, something which prevented them securing more than a tenuous foothold in places where Roman Catholic and Orthodox Churches held sway. Likewise neither gained a substantive presence in countries where Christianity had scant or no presence. This story has been replicated regarding most youth work organisations. Rarely do they secure a toehold outside a given region or what Esping-Andersen (1990) terms a welfare regime. Only the Scouts and Guides buck this trend, because the founder, Robert Baden-Powell, consciously endeavoured to craft a methodology and structure open to adaptation by discrete religious, national and political groups.

Proceeding from the previous discussion, although the pace of industrialisation and urbanisation shaped much of the development of youth work and youth policy, so did religion and other factors. For example the influence of the Roman Catholic Church ensured that the organisational configuration of for example Irish (Devlin, 2010) and Maltese (Teuma, 2009) youth work dramatically differed from that encountered in England even though during the formative years of development both were ruled from London. Religion, alongside other cultural and social factors, did not merely help to mould organisational structures. More significantly, each to varying degrees served to foster modes of practice and theoretical models that have remained at variance from each other. Consequently within different regions and states ideas and modes of intervention were appropriated from adjacent arenas of welfare, notably adult education, schooling and social casework which themselves frequently possessed discrete characteristics relating to a national or regional setting. Therefore it is possible to identify key ideas and modes of intervention that have had a profound impact in one locality but little or none elsewhere. For example *social pedagogy* has served as a core concept upon which much youth work is predicated in Germany and Scandinavia; whereas in England and Wales the concept of social pedagogy is barely acknowledged except as way of describing the training and preparation of individuals for a transition from residential care to living in the 'community'. Instead youth workers relate to the concepts of *social* and *informal education* in order to explain their practice to themselves and others. Likewise in Scotland youth workers usually describe themselves as *community educators*; whilst North Americans turn to the concept of *youth development* to account for their practice. Such variations are not a matter of semantics or the by-product of difficulties in translation. Rather they flow from entrenched differences in the way in which youth work is approached and practitioners understand their place in the world. Each reflects a reality that in different countries alternative structures emerged post-industrialisation which provided both a theoretical underpinning and a coherent way explaining youth work to others. Settlements were major providers of youth work in England, Wales, Germany and Austria, but were absent elsewhere. Foyers played a crucial role in France but barely developed elsewhere. Similarly the Folk High Schools although much admired elsewhere never acquired a serious presence outside of Scandinavia and the American mid-west. Likewise the study circle concept failed to establish itself as a form of intervention within youth work and adult education outside Scandinavia and New England. All this tells us that discrete histories relating to the development of youth work in specific locations are essential in order to foster meaningful dialogue across state and regional boundaries. Equally it suggests that overarching policies intended to standardise practice and the training of workers will have little meaningful impact, because youth work relates so closely to a given social context. The best that can be said is that whatever is called youth work will in most settings be based on voluntary affiliation on the part of the young person and will, as an educational relationship, be primarily based upon dialogical and experiential approaches. Therefore it is crucial to try to return to first principles in order to highlight communalities if some form of productive cross-border dialogue is to develop between workers.

The welfare state is one of the great commonalities of advanced industrialised societies, yet that must not be taken, as we have argued with regards youth work and informal education, as implying uniformity of structure. Irrespective of the format the common roots nevertheless create this universal tension regarding educational and social goals. The first, and dominant, issue relates to who defines the aim and purpose of the learning and the educational content. Whether we are discussing school-based or informal educational provision one must ask if the outcome sought is emancipation or domestication. Is the ambition of the providers to teach young people to adapt to the situation they occupy? Or is it to learn how to question their situation and translate their private problems into public issues (Mills, 1959)? For a relatively brief period post-1945 the creation of universal welfare states seemed to promise to make this persistent pedagogical dilemma a relic from a bygone age. For it was commonly held that social cohesion was being guaranteed by a benign welfare state that would guide and support people from the cradle to the grave whilst eradicating poverty through redistribution and economic development.

Seemingly, with the big issues solved, youth work became one of the social services in a welfare state or a 'licensed' activity delivered with state support by religious and charitable agencies. Security within the bosom of the welfare state encouraged youth work to lose sight of the broader social and pedagogical strategies which once were an essential ingredient. Debates during the period when the welfare state flourished became increasingly introspective – focusing on professionalisation of the sector, staff training, activities and the recruitment of 'numbers'. Therefore when the welfare state found itself under ideological attack from neo-conservatives, youth workers, like so many colleagues in other welfare sectors, frequently lacked the capacity to defend what existed and pose liberatory alternatives to the transformation of the welfare state into an enabling state. Youth work, like adult education, schooling and higher education found itself at every turn vulnerable to instrumentalisation, to being forced into becoming an agent for preparing young people to slot without complaint into the world of work or for the managing deviant behaviour within the public sphere (Gilbert and Gilbert, 1989). Alternatives to these roles have long existed but in part we must turn to history to rediscover them and likewise the radical traditions of which they were so often a part.

The three historic functions of youth work

Good works for youth, preventing social problems through individual education

Industrialisation raised what Castel (1995) termed 'the social question'; but the social problems this term encompassed were addressed in differing ways. Both in Flanders and England Ragged and Sunday schools were established to provide day care for those children too young to work who hung around the streets or were trapped in unhealthy housing. In Flanders, as the children patronised these centres they were called 'patronages'. The concept spread to other industrialising parts of Europe, but the name changed – in France they were *oeuvres de la jeunesse* and in Italy *oratorio*. One of the most famous *oratorios* was that of Father Giovanni Bosco, who transformed his confirmation classes into an alternative youth care practice. His premises offered a warm place where they could experience a sense of freedom and belonging whilst simultaneously receiving a basic education. Bosco introduced pedagogical and methodical elements which still remain an essential part of youth work's identity. By 1848 his Oratorio di San Francesco di Sales was visited by 400 to 600 boys (Coussée, 2006). Almost a century later De Hovre, a Flemish pedagogue honoured Don Bosco as a genius because he 'saw very early on that the social question was fundamentally a question of education' (De Hovre, 1935, p 548, our translation). Such pioneering interventions as those of Bosco and in

Britain Robert Raikes, Hannah More and Sarah Trimmer helped to transform the 'social question' partly into a 'youth question'.

Youth work in between the social and the pedagogical question

Much 19- and 20-century work with young people sought to provide a pedagogical answer to social problems, thereby creating a persistent tension at the heart of youth work. Although conservative and preservative 'patronages' were immensely popular in Belgium, young people attended not necessarily to pray or learn to behave, but frequently merely to play and meet friends. However, a minority of patronages were more concerned with the education and development of young workers rather than caritas, correction, compensation and surveillance. This 'social change' model became more influential, especially after Rerum Novarum, when some leaders of the Catholic pillar started searching for connections between patronages and trade union; gradually patronages of the moralising type became obsolete, although their preservation from secularisation and socialism remained important. Influential thinkers, like Father Joseph Cardijn, called for a more pro-active and self-governing approach to working with youth. Cardijn drew inspiration from British trade unions, the German Catholic Labour Association of Manual Workers and the French Sillon (Cohen, 1988) which each combined critical working–class education with social action aimed at achieving better working conditions and a fairer redistribution of wealth. During the inter-war years the social function eclipsed the pedagogical function in many patronages and youth work was increasingly reconstructed as 'education for social action'.

The recreational function moderates the tension between education and social action

There was a second reason why the patronages quickly lost their status of being the most popular place for working class young people 'to go'. They not only lost their appeal to the more progressive adult elite, but also to young people. Various laws and academic developments (for example compulsory schooling, prohibition of child labour and developmental psychology) created a different youth status. Leisure time became more accessible and important, both in quality and quantity. Methods that served to make patronages attractive to young people came to stand alone. Football, theatre, dance and film, for example, all became popular leisure activities disconnected from broader social and pedagogical strategies and accessible without having to attend a patronage. Both adherents of the (individual) pedagogical approach of working with youth and those who saw youth work as an instrument for securing social change found themselves obliged to accept more recreational approaches to youth work. Both the pedagogical and the social functions of youth work were linked to the tenet of 'learning by doing'. The scouting method imported from the UK from 1910 onwards gained ground in Belgium, but not without a struggle. Cardijn was conscious that the patronages could not survive, but he wished to avoid adopting an apolitical scouting method. Eventually both church and trade union, respectively standing for the individual pedagogical and social justice approaches pushed Cardijn into the recreational youth work corner. The Catholic Church could not appreciate his revolutionary language and the trade unions rejected the idea of establishing a separate trade union for young people. By 1914 the idea of youth work as 'organised leisure time' with positive and guaranteed effects on individual citizenship and social cohesion was fast emerging as the dominant mode.

A triangular relationship under permanent tension

The 'social pedagogical tension' refers to the broader social pedagogical question of how to value diversity whilst preserving social cohesion within a society (Lorenz, 2009). It is this position that makes youth work in the first place social pedagogical work. The internal 'social pedagogical' struggle at the heart of youth work never disappeared although during the Fordist period the pedagogical and social functions of youth work were pushed into the background and it increasingly restricted itself mainly to leisure time provision, leaving its social and pedagogical functions to practices respectively to social work and the school. Throughout history we see this circumvention of fundamental social pedagogical questions being managed through the restriction of youth work to a method – like scouting or outdoor activities. This is exactly the reason why youth work today seems easily redefined or even dispensed with. Developing and optimising a certain method means making abstraction of context, fixing the eye on the desired 'incomes and outcomes' and in the end losing sight of the problem definitions upon which the method is deployed (Lewin, 1947). The Fascist Hitler Jugend, the Communist Pioneers or the Catholic Student Movement all adopted the scouting method but as this discussion between Cardijn and Chief-scout Baden-Powell illustrates, it was in order to achieve different ends. That was why Cardijn initially rejected the scouting method as the basis for youth work. This division is well captured in an exchange that occurred in London in 1911 between Baden-Powell and Cardijn. The former asked Cardijn to become Chief Scout for Belgium. According to Cardijn, Baden-Powell failed to grasp that there is a difference between 'youth in general' and 'working class youth'. He reports the exchanges:

> −'Cardijn: Do you know that there are young workers with their very own problems?
> −B-P: I do not know young workers. I only know citizens and I want to shape strong-willed men.
> −Cardijn: Do you realise how young workers have to survive in factories and how they are influenced by the workers' environment? How could we help them, not just to stay good, but even to have a positive influence in their social environment?
> −B-P: I do not know the workers' environment!'
> (Cardijn, 1948, p 137)

This fragment illustrates how the development of 'youth work' was from the outset interwoven with questions of diversity and equality as well as issues of exclusion and inclusion. Do we invest in youth work as a universalist service departing from the standard positive developmental model and thereby try to reach out to all young people (the youth question)? Or do we aim towards a differentiated youth work field that supports young people's aspirations and works with distinguished categories (the social question)? Which investment gives which young people the best chances for empowerment? And which investment supports developments towards a more socially just society?

Both movements and models – Scouting and the Catholic Workers Youth – conquered the world, but the tension between the two fundamental youth work questions has partially faded as youth work has become evermore a 'method'; a means of providing positive leisure activities.

Reconnecting to society?

Different welfare regimes fostered discrete evolutions, but broadly speaking there was one common denominator: methodisation, a focus upon the ways in which the work should be undertaken, as opposed to what the educational content should teach. The growing obsession with method, reflected not merely within practice but also in the content of the training of the youth workers and the public discourse relating to youth work, led to a demotion and even in some areas the disappearance, of the social and pedagogical functions of youth work. Generally these functions ceased to be explicitly discussed any more. This is illustrated in the Flemish history. In the interbellum period the youth work field showed a great diversity captured within the discussion between Baden-Powell, emphasising one single educational method, and Cardijn, taking distinguished social groups as his starting point. Following the ideas of Cardijn each social group had its own youth work organisation, one for boys and another for girls: the young farmers, the young merchants, students, working class youth. They all tried to make the combination between class-related study, social action and recreation. Only a few organisations aimed to recruit from the 'general' public. Those that did overwhelmingly followed the scouting model. Scouting was popular but that popularity faded as childhood merged into adolescence. Once their members reached the age of 14 they were generally referred to, or moved of their own volition, to the appropriate class-based organisation.

In the first decennia after the Second World War this picture got completely turned over. The different interest groups and ideological pillars lost their grip on society and governmental interference increased. Government wanted youth work to be a non-ideological, universal provision, which in fact meant a-pedagogical and a-social. Youth work was restricted to its methodical aspects: learning relatively simple things via doing and having fun. Scouting became the pre-eminent concept of youth work, a universal method reaching out to all young people in all their diversity. Suddenly accessibility became the main problem, for scouting up to then only reached out to middle-class youths. A differentiated youth work approach rooted in a social analysis and connecting to the life world of young people had been replaced by a methodical approach based on a single concept of youth (work) and by implication of what it meant to be a good citizen. In this agency-driven approach, non-middle-class young people became relabelled as 'hard-to-reach'. The same happened in other countries, even in the UK, despite the fact that the Youth Service acquired statutory recognition there. As Pearl Jephcott, later member of the Albermarle committee, concluded in her research report:

> The most convincing reply to the charge that the youth organization is a redundant institution was that given by the boys and girls who were themselves members. Those adolescents who belonged to a society were definitely easier

> to come to terms with than the non-members. They were not only willing but able to talk, and they generally had something worth saying. And were not those youngsters who were active members a shade more reliable, a shade more open-handed than the rest? (Pearl Jephcott, 1954, p 151)

For one decennium, the golden sixties, there was the firm belief that social class was outdated and poverty a phenomenon that would soon pass. Soon the economic crises of the 1970s raised awareness of social problems as inherent to the structure of our society. Policy makers in the field of youth work consequently urged that it should address social problems. Therefore a universal youth work provision aiming at 'learning by playing' was no longer sufficient or anything but a luxury. They reinvented the patronages – although sold through 'an appeal to newness' – and called it 'open youth work'. However, open youth work had not an existential right of its own, but was seen as the stepping stone to the 'mainstream' youth work. This meant a complete reversal of the pre-war model.

Reconnecting to a society that has disappeared

Every now and then there were impulses to re-pedagogise and re-socialise the youth field. This happened earlier in the UK than in Flanders, thanks to the more professionalised Youth Service and the successive policy committees and reviews (especially Albermarle in 1960 and Fairbairn-Milson in 1969; see Davies, 1999). Continental Europe followed, especially in the 1970s, when open youth work became increasingly professionalised and the theories of Paolo Freire and Oscar Negt gained currency within swathes of the youth field. Youth workers, who had excluded themselves from the social pedagogical debate, made frenetic attempts now to reconnect to society. It was not just their ambition to reconnect youth and youth work to society, but to do that in a critical way. The social and educational function in some areas began to push aside the recreational function and was seen as a means of achieving, for some, a redistribution of possibilities and resources. The economic crisis however halted this re-socialisation of youth work. The pedagogical focus remained, but turned rapidly into a narrow, outcome focused policy, targeting marginalised young people, who it was believed were in urgent need of education for good citizenship. Eggleston concludes his research on 'the Youth Service in

Britain' with the thesis that changing society is an adult desire, not really something that is widely articulated by young people. He notes:

> Our evidence suggests that the majority of members are well aware of the nature of contemporary society and are well disposed to accept it as it is. Most are content to find a meaningful place within it that is consistent with a satisfying self-image; to be able to make decisions in the present society rather than refashion it. (Eggleston, 1976, p 201)

From the late 1970s onwards youth work became less and less about social change and increasing obsessed with the prevention and management of social drop-out. The activating welfare state may put a humane face on this management of social exclusion (Scherr, 1999), but the ideological fault-lines are firmly fixed.

History and youth work's re-socialisation

In the redefining and reframing of youth work the role of workers themselves often remains underexposed. Youth workers (especially managers) seem to simply accept this redefinition of their work which raises the question Jordan (2004) asked social workers: 'Is this a matter of strategy, opportunistic trimming or powerlessness?' We hold that both youth workers and young people are not powerless and that youth work interventions are not only an answer to social problems, but can be closely connected to a radical defining of those problems. As a consequence social interventions themselves can either confirm or question the bounds of possibility (Roose et al, 2010). Within the current environment youth workers, we hold, need to be more explicit about their possible roles and practices. Furthermore, to achieve this confident and deliberate youth work practice help may come from constructive and supportive research, for social scientists not only describe realities but also help bring into being what they discover (Law and Urry, 2004). Unfortunately at the time of writing little in the way of contemporary, creative or constructive research relating to youth work is to hand. University-based researchers now predominately investigate those aspects of practice that others pay them to look at. Overwhelmingly, research is undertaken with the eyes down and the palms up thereby enabling those who control access to funding to mould the research agenda as they do the agenda of practice (Jeffs and Spence, 2008). This means that for the foreseeable future if practitioners wish to redefine the focus of their practice they will also have to seek to look to themselves rather than the compromised university sector to create a critical, radical and liberatory corpus of research.

It is interesting to see how this brief history of ideas relating to youth work shows 'the road not taken' (Reisch and Andrews, 2002) thereby highlighting how youth work must wrestle with the social pedagogical field of tension, while usually restricting itself to being a pedagogical instrument for social education. We suggest this encourages the easy option of retreating to the third function: youth work as leisure-time provision. It seems that a risk society has fostered risk-aversion policies. As a society we ask for confident, autonomous and strong young people, but from the 1980s on we have not stopped to cut down the supportive frameworks to make that possible (Giesecke, 1981). The focus in terms of policy across Europe has been towards the creation of an all-encompassing repertory of corrective interventions designed to keep young people 'on track'. Youth workers need to ask if they are content to tolerate this reframing of their work into corrective, conditional or coercive work. For those who reject this model then the worst case scenario means seeking to eliminate their own field. If youth workers cannot articulate the social and pedagogical dilemmas they encounter or if they fail to convince policymakers of the social pedagogical responsibilities of society, then they will be eliminated anyway. Or they won't be doing youth work anymore.

Conclusion

History shows us that only a social pedagogical approach of youth work has the potential to take us beyond the methodical discussions on the accessibility or the efficiency of youth work. It makes the shift from an agency-driven approach to a lifeworld-oriented one. In this respect youth work shows itself as social spatial work, as a support structure in the lifeworld of young people (Böhnisch and Münchmeier, 1990). The strength of youth work lies in its ability to create free spaces for young people characterised by safety, a sense of belonging, the art of conversation, challenge, friendship and convivial relationships; spaces different from schools as they are founded upon voluntary affiliation and free dialogue. Within such settings and relationships the focus is not upon certification of measurable skills, but life skills, biographical, institutional and political competencies; skills that are useful for young people given the life they lead and the aspirations they have or may acquire. Informal education starts from the assumption that young people do participate, here and now, not (only) from the aim to learn how to participate in society. The format and context in which youth work and informal education occurs will, as we argued earlier, not be uniform, being shaped by different social, economic, political and religious factors. Therefore there exists no single European model, but what we do hold is that a universal social pedagogical tension does exist within youth work and indeed within other forms of informal education. This is a tension that can not be resolved, but if neglected will challenge not only the survival of creative and liberatory practice but also of youth work itself.

References

Böhnisch, L. and Münchmeier, R. (1990) *Pädagogik des Jugendraums. Zur Begründung und Praxis einer sozialraumlichen Jugendpädagogik* (Pedagogy of youth space. On the establishment and praxis of a socio-spatial youth pedagogy), München: Juventa Verlag.

Cardijn, J. (1948) 'Arbeidersapostolaat in het leven. Tweemaal drie lessen gegeven op de nationale studieweken voor gewestleiders' (Apostolate in the life of the working class. Two times three courses given at the national study weeks for district leaders), in J. Cardijn (s.d.). *En nu vooruit!* (Let's start!), Merchtem: Kajottersbeweging, pp 96–9.

Castel, R. (1995) *Les métamorphoses de la question sociale. Une chronique du salariat* (The transformations of the social question. A chronicle of the salaried class), Paris: Fayard.

Cohen, P. (1988) 'Heroes and dilettantes: The action francaise, le Sillon and the generation of 1905–14', *French Historical Studies*, vol 15, no 4, pp 673–87.

Coussée, F. (2006) *De pedagogiek van het jeugdwerk* (The pedagogy of youth work), Gent: Academia Press.

Coussée, F. and Williamson (2011) 'Youth worker, probably the most difficult job in the world', *Children Australia*, vol 36, no 4, pp 203–7.

Davies, B. (1999) *From voluntarism to welfare state. A history of the youth service in England*, vol 1, 1939–1979, Leicester: Youth Work Press.

De Hovre, F. (1935) *Paedagogische denkers van onzen tijd* (Pedagogues of our times), Antwerpen: Standaard Boekhandel.

Devlin, M. (2010) 'Youth work in Ireland. Some historical reflections', in F. Coussée, G. Verschelden, et al (eds) *The history of youth work in Europe and its relevance for youth policy today*, vol 2, Strasbourg: Council of Europe Publishing, pp 93–104.

Donzelot, J. (1984) *L'invention du social. Essai sur le déclin des passions politiques* (The invention of the social. An essay on the decline of political passions), Paris: Faillard.

Eggleston, J. (1976) *Adolescence and community. The youth service in Britain*, London: Edward Arnold.

Esping-Andersen, G. (1990) *The three worlds of welfare capitalism*, Cambridge: Polity Press.

Giesecke, H. (1981) 'Wir wollen alles, und zwar subito. Ein Bericht über jugendliche Aussteiger' (We want everything, right now. A message on young drop-outs), *Deutsche Jugend*, vol 28, no 6, pp 251–66.

Gilbert, N. and Gilbert, B. (1989) *The enabling state: Modern welfare capitalism in America*, New York: Oxford University Press.

Jeffs, T. (2001) 'First lessons: historical perspectives on informal education', in L. D. Richardson and M. Wolfe, (eds) *Principles and practice of informal education*, Abingdon: Routledge.

Jeffs, T. and Smith, M. (2002) 'Individualization and youth work', *Youth and Policy*, vol 76, pp 39–65.

Jeffs, T. and Spence, J. (2008) 'Farewell to all that? The uncertain future of youth and community work education', *Youth and Policy* 1997/98, pp 135–66.

Jephcott, P. (1954) *Some young people*, London: Allen and Unwin.

Jordan, B. (2004) 'Emancipatory social work: opportunity or oxymoron?', *British Journal of Social Work*, vol 34, no 1, pp 5–19.

Law, J. and Urry, J. (2004) 'Enacting the social', *Economy and* Society, vol 33, no 3, pp 390–410.

Lewin, H. S. (1947) 'The way of the Boy Scouts', *Journal of Educational Sociology*, vol 21, no 3, pp 169–176.

Lorenz, W. (2009) 'The function of history in the debate on social work', in F. Coussée, G. Verschelden, et al (eds) *The history of youth work in Europe and its relevance for youth policy today*, Strasbourg: Council of Europe Publishing, pp 19–28.

Mills, C. (1959) *The sociological imagination*, New York: Oxford University Press.

O'Connor, J. (1973) *The fiscal crisis of the state*, New York: St Martin's Press.

Quadagno, J. (1988) *The transformation of old age security*, Chicago: University of Chicago Press.

Reisch, M. and Andrews, J. (2002) *The road not taken. A history of radical social work in the United States*, New York: Routledge.

Roose, R., Coussée, F. et al (2010) 'Going beyond the bounds of possibility: questioning the delimitation of the social in social Work', *Social Work & Society*, vol 8, no 1, http://nbn-resolving.de/urn:nbn:de:0009–11–26946.

Scherr, A. (1999) 'Transformations in social work: From help towards social inclusion to the management of exclusion', *European Journal of Social Work*, vol 2, no 1, pp 15–25.

Teuma, M. (2009) 'Youth work development in Malta – a chronicle', in F. Coussée, G. Verschelden, et al (eds), *The history of youth work in Europe and its relevance for youth policy today*, Strasbourg: Council of Europe Publishing, pp 87–94.

Part Two

National and local policies for youth participation

FIVE

Celebrating pluralism: beyond established forms of youth participation

Lasse Siurala and Heini Turkia

Reintegrating citizens

The emergence of populist parties in Europe may be a result of the inability of the established parties to articulate the interests of citizens. This reflects a broader lack of trust between government institutions and civil society, an increasing dissatisfaction of citizens in representative politics, politicians, established parties and elections, and 'the feeling of helplessness and impotence in relation to government' (Chomsky, 2009). Young people, in particular, exhibit low voting turnout, feel disaffected from representative politics and politicians, and are distancing themselves from political youth organisations. Youth participation has been promoted as an effort to link the interests of young people to those of decision makers. However, there is a discrepancy between rhetoric and reality. At the same time as current formats of youth participation seem to fail in articulating the interests and aspirations of young people, there has been an emergence of a myriad of unconventional ways that young people express their identities. There is an apparent misfit between the offered spaces for participation and the emerging forms of expression.

In Finland there are 200 youth councils, in France about 4,000 local or regional youth councils, and in the UK about 500 youth or student councils. In Finland youth councillors are typically elected through elections in the schools. These youth councils are placed within the municipal administration and youth councillors often have the right to attend meetings of the political bodies.

They provide opportunities for young people to discuss local youth policies and have a dialogue with decision makers. However, there is increasing criticism regarding the deficiencies of this type of youth participation.

The youth representation of these youth councils is often restricted to a limited group of 'insider' youth; disadvantaged and marginal young people tend to be underrepresented, participation stays at the level of consultation, there is little actual impact and the dialogue with decision makers is occasional and tokenistic (Matthews and Limb, 2003; McGinley and Grieve, 2010; Kallio and Häkli, 2011). Clearly, local youth participation needs redirection. McGinley and Grieve suggest that 'Part of the answer may be to move from a representative approach, symbolised by youth councils, to create a participatory culture… [and] a nurturing relationship which encourages active listening and moves into purposeful conversations and meaningful dialogue' (McGinley and Grieve, 2010, p 258). Or, as Malone and Hartung put it, '[we need to] think of new ways to interact with children outside the predefined ways in predefined structures' (Malone and Hartung, 2010, p 36).

Searching for a conceptual framework of participation

The democratic deficit, the feeling of citizens that their voices are not heard and that their efforts to influence government policy are ignored or inconsequential has led to debates on alternatives forms of democracy. 'Participatory democracy' includes forms of direct democracy (referendums, electronic direct democracy, participatory budgeting) and different forms of dialogue between the citizens and the government. 'Deliberative democracy' (Bessette, 1980; Cohen, 1989; Dryzek, 2000) is based on the idea of gathering a mini-sample of a population for 3–5 days to study and formulate a consensual opinion on a given subject (citizens' juries, consensus conferences and deliberative polls). 'Governance' refers to efforts to include a broader range of actors within the democratic processes. It aims at reconciling the interests between government and civil society. This is felt to be urgent, but at the same time challenging: '… radically new ways of thinking about democratic engagement are needed which can work with complexity, conflict and difference' (Cinefogo, 2011, p 3).

'Complexity' and 'difference' refer to ambiguities of civil society and its networks. These include the plurality of civil society actors with different rationales and goals, the tension between bottom-up and top-down processes and the asymmetrical distributions of resources (Bozzini and Enroljas, 2011). The ambiguities and diversities bring 'conflicts' which are difficult to manage and reconcile, but which are also a source of innovation and richness of views. Such conflicts are inevitable; or, as Chantal Mouffe (2000, p 13) has put it, 'ineradicable'.

—

Current modes of youth participation do not necessarily reflect the complexity of young people's social networks. Kay and Tisdall (2010, p 326) criticise student and youth councils for their isolation from other associated activities and their inability to use young people's own networks. Following the governance agenda, schools 'could be a central node in broader networks of community participation' (Kay and Tisdall, 2010, p 326). Another challenge presented by youth councils is their homogeneity; regardless of whether the councillors are invited, nominated (by teachers or school councils) or even elected, the 'achievers' tend to be overrepresented. This lack of diversity contributes to deficient representation and limits social tensions and conflicts, thereby neutralising the essential characteristics of a vivid civil society. To combat this, special efforts are sometimes taken to guarantee broader representation of youth groups. An empirical study in New Zealand quotes a youth worker struggling for a diverse youth council: 'We work very hard to get a diverse youth council, and we do. Incredibly diverse. That brings another set of problems because you end up with a group of young people sitting around a table who actually don't have a lot in common' (Nairn et al, 2006, p 259).

But, youth today is a 'mosaic' (Chisholm and Kovacheva, 2002) or 'atomized' (Salasuo, 2006). Salasuo summarises his ethnological study on youth cultures in the Helsinki Metropolitan area by stating that: 'The atomised generation forms a particle-like mosaic, constantly moving in the shivering field of cultural phenomena. It is characterised by the freedom and the demand of choice. It does not have a linear direction, in a way it has stopped in constant change' (Salasuo, 2006, p 20). A youth participation model has to find a way of dealing with the inevitable diversity of the youth scene.

The difficulties of youth and school councils becoming isolated from their social relations and networks, and the difficulties of managing discussions and consensual processes of decision-making with a 'too diverse' youth group, brings us to a key issue in current models of democracy.

Could it be that the procedures of representative and deliberative democracy are too restrictive within the complexity, variance and conflicts of civil society, and within the diversity of life worlds among young people? This is exactly what Chantal Mouffe (2000, 2005 and 2009) and others (Honig, 1993; Tully, 2008; Connolly, 2011) maintain when criticising representative and deliberative democracy. According to Mouffe (2000) Rawls and Habermas both overemphasised the capacity of rational procedures to arrive at consensual decisions. Politics becomes 'the exchange of rational arguments among reasonable persons guided by principles of impartiality' and procedural rules (Mouffe, 2000, p 4). Mouffe argues that Rawls and Habermas do not acknowledge 'the ineradicability of antagonism and the impossibility of achieving a fully inclusive rational consensus' (Mouffe, 2000, p 4). Or, their efforts to deal with the inevitable value pluralism, forces them to make compromises.

Rawls makes a distinction between public and private life, leaving the latter with its pluralism outside the public pursuit of consensual justice. Habermas does the same saying that there are certain competing ethical questions like that of the good life, which must be left outside moral and social issues where consensus is possible through rational and impartial procedures. These compromises are felt necessary to solve the issue of allegiance or legitimacy of democratic decisions.

Mouffe maintains that we should not circumvent the essentially pluralist nature of the society in our search for a just and legitimate democracy: 'This is not a matter of *rational justification* but of *availability* of democratic forms of individuality and subjectivity... [where]... the crucial role is played by passions and emotions in securing allegiance to democratic values. (Mouffe, 2000, p 10).

Mouffe becomes a proponent of 'agonistic pluralism' which argues that we should acknowledge the inevitability of pluralism in society and find ways to deal with this complexity and conflict. She makes a difference between 'antagonism' and 'agonism'. Antagonism is a struggle between enemies and agonism is a struggle between adversaries: 'the aim of democratic politics is to transform antagonism into agonism'. To achieve this we need 'the availability of those contending forms of citizenship identification' (Mouffe, 2000, p 10) tolerance and dialogical spaces.

Tokenism: why is the voice of the youth council not heard?

> ...simply mimicking adults is not always the most authentic, empowering and beneficial type of participation. (Malone and Hartung, 2010, p 26)

A youth council is typically a copy of municipal government. Thus it also shares the weaknesses of representative democracy. One of them is the disregard of alternative ways of expression and engagement. Perhaps the underlying concept of power is too simplified to allow for the myriad of ways that young people today express their citizenships. A broader concept is provided by Foucault (1978, p 93) who maintains that power is everywhere, because there are versatile ways of using power. It is not only those who govern that exert power, but also the governed utilise their own power through multifaceted forms of resistance and action. Young people use power through their organisations, networks and action groups, through media and the Internet, through cultural expression, forms of resistance and lifestyle choice, to name a few. Power becomes essentially diverse and difficult to pinpoint. Malone and Hartung note that 'Any "one size fits all" model will fail to account for the very contextualised and unique ingredients that make up any children's participatory project within a community' (Malone and Hartung, 2010, p 32).

Why do we then have only one model for youth participation – the youth council? Why are we assuming that the only power involved is that between the youth councillors and the decision makers of the city?

Foucault (1983, p 219) also says that 'power exists only when it is put into action'. Thus the power of a youth council should not be assessed through its placement in city organigram or through its official terms of reference and objectives (the public intentions), but through its actual impacts. The rhetoric in favour of youth councils is overwhelming; ranging from recommendations of international organisations (such as Council of Europe, 2003) to national policy documents and lobby groups. But how well does the practice meet the rhetoric?

Without doubt the strength of youth councils is in their educational effects on the councillors. These include a developing sense of self-estimation, the acquisition of new skills, increased confidence in presenting their ideas to others, a better personal understanding of local issues, and an increased interest in their environment. Youth councils work well as an apprenticeship for a small cohort of young people who wish to continue their involvement in politics (McGinley and Grieve, 2010, p 258).

A weakness of youth councils is the lack of their overall impact (Matthews, 2001; Matthews and Limb, 2003; McGinley and Grieve, 2010). Despite political efforts to promote children's and young people's involvement in the delivery of services:

> There is little evidence of children and young people making an impact at the central government level in England. Children and young people's views are invited at the consultation stage and examples of children's views are cited in government reports, but there are no significant examples of children initiating a policy change at the heart of government. (Cockburn, 2010, p 307)

At the local level there are many efforts to gap the 'democratic deficit' of young people, but 'even when young people acknowledge that there are opportunities to participate they sometimes abstain, assuming that their views will either be given little status or simply ignored' (Councillors Commission, 2007, cited in Cockburn, 2010, p 308). Many studies suggest that in most cases youth councils are limited to 'having a say' and consultation (Matthews, 2001; McGinley and Grieve, 2010). Mostly these hearings tend to concern 'safe' issues which do not significantly challenge the power or agenda of the adults. It has been argued that 'having a say' and 'consultation' takes on very passive connotation and has become an illusion of empowerment.

The City of Helsinki has organised four annual Regional Youth Forums for young people to discuss a theme, firstly among themselves and then with decision makers. The main proposals of young people from the 2009 Forums were officially forwarded to the respective administrative bodies of the City. The follow-up of the proposals showed that most city sectors did not even reply to them and those few who replied did not come up with any concrete action. Even the Youth Board itself forgot to follow up the proposals.

Dominance of the established forms of participation

Youth Councils in Finland represent the dominant discourse on youth participation; they also restrict experimentation with other forms of youth participation. When the Department of Youth at the City of Helsinki decided in 2010 to search for an alternative model for local youth participation the local and national lobby organisations started a large campaign against this action. Lobbyists met City Councillors, parties of the City Council and senior civil servants to argue for an elected youth council. Media were frequently used to attack the alternative plans of the Youth Department.

The Finnish experience has to be put into a cultural context. A comparative study of youth participation in Finland and Germany found marked differences in the two countries (Feldmann-Wojtachnia et al, 2010). In Germany youth participation was understood as civic activities and projects carried out by young people in NGOs, while in Finland participation was about activities in formal representative structures like youth councils and youth parliaments. The authors recommend that Finland should promote youth agency outside the predefined top-down frameworks of representative structures, enhance diversity in the forms and methods of participation, improve accessibility to youth participation and offer a variety of ways to act, exert influence and become involved (Feldmann-Wojtachnia et al, 2010, pp 65–75).

In other Nordic countries, which might not be dominated to the same extent as Finland by the representative youth participation ideal, we do find examples of experimentation with alternative approaches. The City of Lund (population 100,000) in Sweden has established a 'bottom-up' participation model. Young people and decision makers gather to negotiate issues raised by young people four times in a year. These meetings are open to all young people in Lund. Between the meetings young people work in topic-based committees. Apparently, the City of Lund has understood that participation is not just engagement with the city administration, but also with the personal power to act as a citizen. The experience has been positive and the model has been adapted to other Swedish cities as well. In the Danish City of Aarhus the youth council is made up of local youth organisations covering 120 member organisations which operate predominantly with young people between 18 and 28 years of age. The Youth Council actively takes part in the local youth political debate and promotes the work of the local voluntary children and youth organisations. These examples indicate that it is possible to break away from the traditional youth council format.

Promoting variety of expression and dialogic space

For years Helsinki has been the only big city in Finland without an elected youth council. Being aware of the limitations of the youth council format the Youth Department together with the Education Department decided to search for an alternative model. In spring 2010 two focus groups were set up, one for researchers, civil servants, politicians and a diversity of youth organisations, and another for young people1. The model developed in the focus group was adopted (June 2011) by the City Board (executive body of the City Council).

The key elements of the model were inspired by (1) agonistic pluralism (acknowledging the variety and complexity of the youth scene), (2) the changing nature of youth engagement and expression (need for low threshold participation and opportunity for a variety of expression) and (3) the need for collaborative intergenerational dialogue (structures for continuous, open and tolerant dialogue). Accordingly, the following criteria for a youth participation model were formulated:

• providing a maximum number and a broad variety of young people an access to express their citizenships (access)

- supporting easy to get in and out spaces for versatile agency (spaces)
- developing dialogue between the actors, like young people and the City's decision makers (dialogue).

Figure 5.1: Key elements of the Helsinki participation model: access, spaces, dialogue

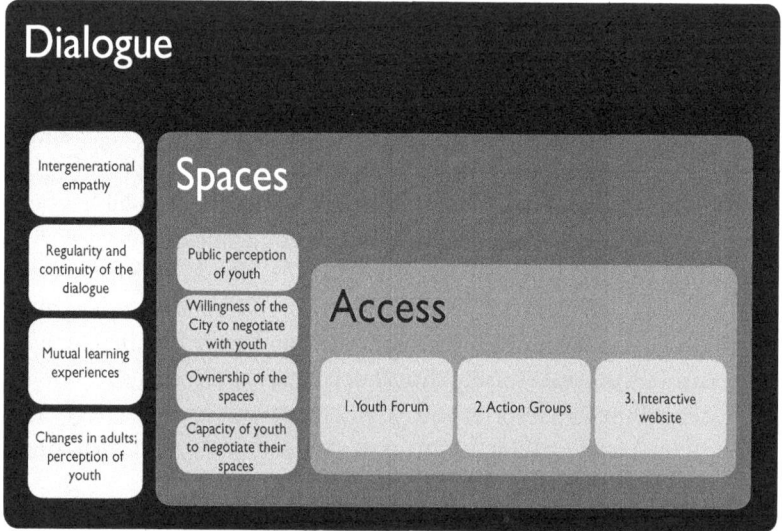

As described in figure 5.1, we need to develop open access to as many young people as possible to create spaces for young people to deliberate their own views and enter into dialogue with other actors.

The access

Normally, youth councils attract 'achievers', active and socially capable young people, leading sometimes to efforts to recruit the marginal and the hardest to reach youth groups. To promote diversity of youth participation in Helsinki, three main efforts are taken (figure 5.2). First, once a year Youth Expo will meet to display the variety of ways that young people express themselves and to discuss their concerns and aspirations. The Youth Expo is not profiled as a meeting, but as a youth event with a mixed programme of activities. The event is targeted at the about 130 youth organisations, school councils, students, the city's 50 youth centres and any young person. Second, young people are encouraged to join in open activity groups based on topics they have found pertinent. The activity groups are supported by youth workers and the young people decide on their own how to develop and put their ideas into action. The groups are based on ongoing recruitment. Ideally, there will be a large array of groups providing young people an opportunity to choose and no preconditions for long-term commitment. It is easy to step in and out. Third, there is an interactive web channel to facilitate young people's possibilities to contribute with an initiative. The overall aim is to maximise the number of young people involved.

The Youth Expo agrees on persons to be nominated to an executive board, which is in charge of the continuity of the discussions of the Youth Expo, which oversees the action groups, functions as link to other actors (such as the City), and which prepares the next Expo. It is not a body which pronounces itself as youth at Helsinki, but a body which facilitates the dialogue among young people and between other actors such as the City.

Figure 5.2: Main efforts to promote diversity in the Helsinki youth participation programme: action groups, Youth Expo and meeting with decision makers

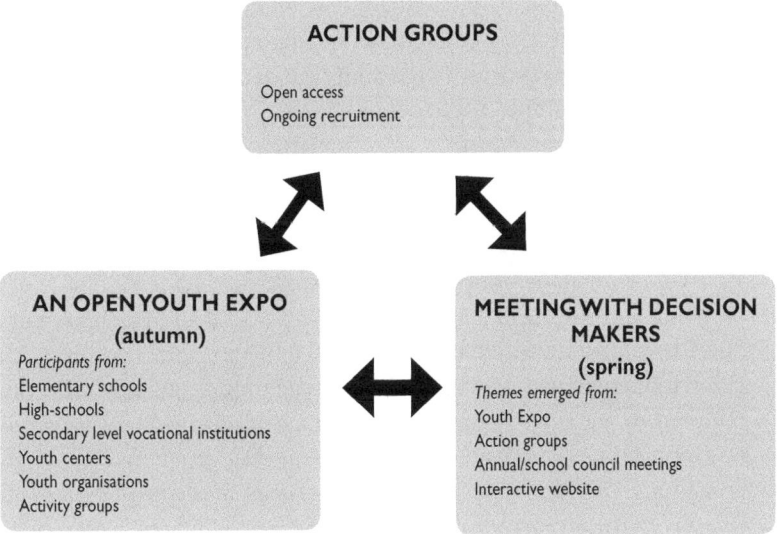

The spaces

We identify four factors to how the space for youth agency becomes shaped; (1) public perception of youth, (2) willingness of the decision makers to negotiate with youth, (3) the extent to which decision makers structure the space and (4) the capacity of young people to negotiate their own space.

- *Public perception of youth.* There is a societal level tendency to categorise youth. Youth is perceived either as a problem (needing support or intervention) or a promise (being a resource). The more pronounced is the perception of youth as a problem, the less space for autonomous youth agency. As for youth participation; it is important to work for a positive public image of youth and to counteract the stereotypic negative images. The City of Helsinki has always invested substantially in youth work. Recently the City Council has made children's and young peoples' welfare one of its key strategies. Of course, it is not always easy to say as to what extent the underlying motive is control and care instead of support to the autonomy and agency of young people. However, the decision of the City Council (June 2011) to provide young people a higher profile in its decision making can be seen as an indication of its trust in youth.

- *Willingness of the decision makers to negotiate with youth.* Cities are sectorised organisations which might not be willing to negotiate with young people, as potentially this entails sharing power. The willingness of the City of Helsinki to share power with youth was tested through the process of the adoption of the youth participation model. It was unanimously accepted by the Youth Board in February 2011. It was then (April 2011) circulated for comment to eight administrative sectors. All eight were in favour of the said model, even if the degree of interest to make use of it varied among the sectors. Some sectors, like City Planning, felt that they already had enough measures to engage young people in their field of activities. Most sectors, like Education, Park and Building, Social and Health Affairs and Environment, said that they wanted to be actively involved with the youth participation model. Finally the model was unanimously adopted by the City Board in June 2011. Such attitudinal climate is an important prerequisite for a successful dialogue between youth and adults. Of course, it is the implementation of the model that will provide us the answer to what extent the positive interest materialises itself in intergenerational dialogue.

- *The extent to which decision makers structure the space.* There are a number of spatial factors controlled by adults, which limit the expression of young people. When the Youth Council meets at City Hall, the mere location at the heart of adult power structures, the linkage to representative modes of democracy and the assumption that participation is about having a meeting with consensus protocols, already signifies the use of adult power. To avoid this, the Helsinki model organises the encounters of young people in their own territories; open to whatever form of expression. The physical context and ambiance are to send the message that young people are operating on their own turf and on their own conditions.

- *The capacity of young people to negotiate their own space.* Martina Löw (2008) uses the term 'duality of space' to clarify how spaces can both constrain and enable action. Spaces structure action but are also an outcome of action. Young people can act on spaces and negotiate for more freedom to express themselves. In the case of Helsinki the City Board decided that through the Youth Expo, action groups and dialogue with decision makers, young people are expected and legitimated to negotiate their views in the City of Helsinki. At the same time the City Board 'obliges the administration and the political bodies to utilise the youth participation model when preparing and taking decisions concerning young people' (City Board 13 June 3011, 615 §). Secondly, the dialogue is structured and continuous. Once a year the young people and the decision makers gather to share ideas on young peoples' initiatives and their action group projects. In six months both parties report their advancements to the Youth Expo. Thus young people and decision makers establish a regular dialogue through which they may expand the space for young peoples' own agency. Finally, the success of young people in negotiating more space is very much dependent on how the dialogical culture and the quality of dialogue develop in the City.

The dialogue

> It is easy to organize forums between young people and the decision makers, but very difficult to achieve a true dialogue. (Dr. Herbert Wiedermann, Director of Youth, City of Hamburg)

There is plenty of research on the very different ways that young people and adults interpret the same phenomena. For example in a study of school dropouts (Ahola and Galli, 2010) the respondents provide structural reasons for their situation saying that the entrance examinations are too difficult, the medium scores of entry too high and the number of student places too few. The special education professionals of these same young people tend to give individualistic reasons for their problems; learning difficulties, mental problems and unstable home conditions. Other examples of generational differences of interpretation include leisure, lifestyle, graffiti and the modes of expressing political identities. Sometimes the differences between young people and adults are not that pronounced. Marjatta Bardy (2010, p 172) suggests that the relationship between the generations is rather 'furtively adjacent': 'It is not about hostility, but somehow those present do not seem to sit around the same table'. Dialogue is needed to promote better mutual understanding.

Learning each others' cultural languages is a two-way traffic. Young people need to become acquainted and trained in the rational and oral discourse of the decision makers, but likewise the decision makers need to learn the variety of symbolic languages, cultures, sub-cultures, lifestyles and digital lives of young people. A municipal youth participation model based on agonistic pluralism requires an introduction, or training, of both young people and the adult decision makers (civil servants and politicians) to each others' ways of understanding democracy and citizenship. In this context youth worker's competence as a cultural interlocutor should be seen as an asset.

The Helsinki participation model provides spaces for dialogue. Once a year young people and decision makers gather in a face-to-face dialogue. The themes are set by young people. The City provides civil servants and decision makers responsible for those themes. The idea is to deliberate issues together as a dialogical negotiation rather than a monological consultation. In the following autumn young people and decision makers return to these issues and see how they are progressing. In addition, young people's action groups may hold continuous deliberations with municipal civil servants during the year. The dialogue is an ongoing process, not a set of isolated events.

Discussion

New thinking on youth participation is needed. Considering the problems of liberal democracy with its rational consensus procedures of the mandated few to meet the demands of the ever increasing 'complexity, diversity and conflictuality' of civil society, the idea of agonistic pluralism seems appropriate. Celebrating pluralism becomes appropriate when we remember the mosaic nature of youth scenes and the plurality of young people's identity expression. What young people need to know is how representative democracy works, and what they need to have is the space 'to sort out their thoughts' and to express them in ways that suit them.

We also need new concrete models for young people to act out their ideas within local government. New openings, like the Helsinki model, necessarily face uncertainty and constant modification. There are more questions than answers: How to profile Youth Expos as attractive youth events? How to turn youth council meetings into spaces for 'fun, elasticity, play and irony' as Paakkunainen (2003) characterises current modes of youth participation? How to guarantee a broad representation of youth? How to motivate young people to act through their own action groups? How to make the encounters of youth and decision makers a serious mutual challenge? These questions can only be answered through experimentation; youth work expertise and a commitment from decision makers to negotiate with youth.

Inspired by Benjamin Lee Whorf's (contested) idea that language shapes the way we think, and determines what we can think about, we should have another look at the term 'youth participation'.

'Youth participation' has become a youth policy tag word, almost an untouchable truism. Can anybody be against youth participation? Can one imagine an alternative to it?

As a policy tag word it is so vague that one is not promising anything concrete. 'Youth participation' as an expression is in this sense de-contextualised and perhaps meaningless.

Paradoxically, at the same time it has also become too concrete. Youth participation has come to denote formal participation structures within representative democracy: school councils, municipal youth councils, youth and parliaments, youth hearings and so forth. As youth participation comes with these concrete signifiers, it creates a dichotomy of what is and what is not participation. In municipalities youth participation is a youth council. UP2YOUTH, a European youth research project (2009), also raises this issue by pointing out that there is 'the obvious mismatch between institutional expectations of how young people should participate and young people's actual activities and priorities' (p 121). The study recommends:

> Accepting a diversity of conceptual and actual types of participation and overcoming the dominant dichotomies of what is and what is not participation ... because different types of participation hold the key to understanding the changing meaning of participation – including the changing meaning of politics, collectivism and public space – in late modernity. (Up2Youth, 2009, p 126)

Following this advice, the expression 'promoting youth participation' should perhaps be replaced by a new one to cover new and emerging forms of youth involvement and to stimulate our thinking on youth action. We propose the expression 'providing space for youth agency'. One could ask; why change a well-branded political tag word into a theoretical sociological term? One reason is that 'youth agency' is a contextualised and open term. It is linked to structural constraints, individual biographies, and the myriad of ways young people negotiate and act out their future through the present. It simultaneously opens our eyes to see new roles for youth work; celebrates the diversity of grassroots action, links with virtual and other social communities and provides opportunities for negotiating the future.

Note

[1] Despite efforts to guarantee diversity of young people in the focus group for youth, it was taken over by an active group of young people dedicated to the dominant youth council model. The two focus groups also held joint meetings which made transparent the differing views of the two groups. In the media the youth group did not hesitate to pronounce that they represented 'the voice of young people' at Helsinki.

References

Ahola, S. and Galli, L. (2010) 'Dimensions of exclusion discourse among young school drop-outs and their tutors' [in Finnish with abstract in English], in A.-H Anttila, K. Kuussaari and T. Puhakka (eds) *[Talking Past Each Other] Adolescence* [in Finnish], Helsinki: Finnish Youth Research Network.

Bardy, M. (2010) 'Generations Furtively Side by Side?' [in Finnish] in A.-H. Anttila, K. Kuussaari, and T. Puhakka (eds) *[Talking Past each Other] Adolescence* [in Finnish], Helsinki: Finnish Youth Research Network.

Bessette, J. (1980) 'Deliberative democracy: the majority principle in republican government', in *How Democratic is the Constitution?*, Washington DC: AEI Press, pp 102–16.

Bozzini, E. and Enjolras, B. (eds) (2011) *Governing Ambiguities. New Forms of Local Governance and Civil Society*, Baden-Baden: Nomos Verlagsgesellschaft.

Chisholm, L. and Kovacheva, S. (2002) *Exploring the European Youth Mosaic*, Strasbourg: Council of Europe Publishing.

Chomsky, N. (2009) *What is the Most Dysfunctional Thing about American Democracy?*, http://bigthink.com/ideas/16051

Cinefogo (2011) *Policy Briefing: WP 14 – Citizen Participation in Policy Making*, www.cinefogo.com City Board of Helsinki, 13 June 2011, 615 §.

Cockburn, T. (2010) 'Children and deliberative democracy in England', in B. Percy-Smith and N. Thomas (eds) *A Handbook of Children and Young People's Participation. Perspectives from Theory and Practice*, London: Routledge, pp 306–17.

Cohen, J. (1989) 'Deliberative democracy and democratic legitimacy', in A. Hamlin and P. Pettit (eds) *The Good Polity*, Oxford: Blackwell, pp 17–34.

Connolly, W. (2011) *A World of Becoming*, Durham, NC: Duke University Press.

Council of Europe (2003) *Revised European Charter on the Participation of Young People in Local and Regional Life*, Adopted by the Congress of Local and Regional Authorities of Europe, Strasbourg.

Dryzek, J. (2000) *Deliberative Democracy and Beyond: Liberals, Critics, Contestations*, Oxford: Oxford University Press.

Feldmann-Wojtachnia, E., Gretschel, A., Helmisaari, V., Kiilakoski, T., Matthies, A.-L., Meinhold-Henschel, S., Roth, R. and Tasanko, P. (2010) *Youth Participation in Finland and in Germany – Status Analysis and Data Based Recommendations*, Helsinki: The Finnish Youth Research Society.

Foucault, M. (1978) *The History of Sexuality*, vol 1, Harmondsworth: Penguin.

Foucault, M. (1983) 'Afterword: the subject and power', in H. Dreyfus and P. Rabinow (eds) *Michel Foucault: Beyond Structuralism and Hermeneutics*, Chicago: Chicago University Press.

Gallagher, M. (2008) 'Foucault, power and participation', *International Journal of Children's Rights*, no 16, pp 395–406.

Honig, B. (1993) *Political Theory and the Displacement of Politics*, New York: Cornell University Press.

Kallio, K. P. and Häkli, J. (2011) 'Tracing children's politics', *Political Geography*, vol 30, no 2, pp 99–109.

Kay, E. and Tisdall, M. (2010) 'Governance and participation', in B. Percy-Smith and N. Thomas (eds) *A Handbook of Children and Young People's Participation. Perspectives from Theory and Practice*, London: Routledge, pp 318–29.

Löw, M. (2008), 'The constitution of space: the structuration of spaces through the simultaneity of effects and perception', *European Journal of Social Theory*, vol 11, no 1, pp 25–49.

Malone, K. and Hartung, C. (2010) 'Challenges of participation practice with children', in B. Percy-Smith and N. Thomas (eds) *A Handbook of Children and Young People's Participation. Perspectives from Theory and Practice*, London: Routledge, pp 24–38.

Matthews, H. (2001) 'Citizenship, youth councils and young people's participation', *Journal of Youth Studies*, vol 4, no 3, pp 299–318.

Matthews, H. and Limb, M. (2003) 'Another white elephant? Youth councils as democratic structures', *Space and Polity*, vol 7, no 2, pp 173–92.

McGinley, B. and Grieve, A. (2010) 'Maintaining the status quo? Appraising the effectiveness of youth councils in Scotland', in B. Percy-Smith and N. Thomas (eds) *A Handbook of Children and Young People's Participation. Perspectives from Theory and Practice*, London: Routledge, pp 254–61.

Mouffe, C. (2000) 'Deliberative Democracy or Agonistic Pluralism', *Political Science Series*, no 72, Vienna: Institute for Advanced Studies.

Mouffe, C. (2005) *On the Political*, Abingdon: Routledge.

Mouffe, C. (2009) 'The Books Interview: Chantal Mouffe', Published 19 November 2009, www.newstatesman.com/books/2009/11/agonistic-democracy-bnp-post

Nairn, K., Sligo, J. and Freeman, C. (2006) 'Polarizing participation in local participation in local government: which young people are included and excluded?', *Children, Youth and Environments*, vol 16, no 2, pp 248–71.

Paakkunainen, K. (2003) 'Yes to politics, but...' [in Finnish], Finnish Youth Research Network.

Percy-Smith, B. (2010) 'Councils, consultations and community: rethinking the spaces for children and young people's participation', *Children's Geographies*, vol 8, no 2, pp 107–22.

Percy-Smith, B. and Thomas, N. (eds) (2010) *A Handbook of Children and Young People's Participation. Perspectives from Theory and Practice,* London: Routledge.

Salasuo, M. (2006) 'The atomised generation', *City of Helsinki Urban Facts, Research Series*, no 2006/6 (English summary).

Tully, J. (2008) *Public Philosophy in a New Key* (two volumes), Cambridge: Cambridge University Press.

UP2YOUTH final report 2009, www.up2youth.org

Youth participation in the framework of the reformulation of local youth policies in Italy

Morena Cuconato, Nicola De Luigi and Alessandro Martelli

Introduction

When focusing on concepts such as *youth, participation* and *local policies* in Italy, some key aspects need to be underlined in order to provide a common conceptual framework.

The *first* aspect relates to the problem of defining youth and the related expressions of 'youth policies' and 'youth participation'. Italian literature has recently adopted the term *young adult* to denote people between the ages of 30 and 34; nevertheless a young adult can be female, male, student, professional, unemployed, single, married, a parent, live with parents and so forth[1]. At policy level the intrinsic differentiation characterising 'planet youth' is still based on the traditional distinction among 'children', 'adolescents' and 'youth', that implies both different disciplines and different professional skills and policy fields.

The *second* aspect is related to the structure of the Italian welfare system, characterised since the very beginning of the republican period through two core interrelated features that influence the entire policy scenario: the *breadwinner model*, on the one side, and on the other side the *weak stateness* of the social protection regime, traditionally centred on the individual-family couple (Sgritta, 2005b). According to Saraceno and Keck (2010), *familism* relies on a permanent trust on the family, on its intergenerational solidarity and on its gender structure as provider of work and assistance. This model makes the social chances of mobility and autonomy of young people dependant on the labour market position of the breadwinner, the social status of enlarged family and the socioeconomic context of birth and life.

The *third* aspect refers to territorial dimension and consequential policy scaling. In Italy there is a high percentage of towns with less than 5,000 inhabitants, representing about 70% out of 8,000 urban areas and home to approximately 17% of the total population. It has to be stressed that in referring to this territorial dimension, young people's conditions concern mainly but not only cities (in Italy about 45% of the population lives in highly urbanised towns). Beyond the traditional north–south educational, labour market and social participation divide, ongoing factors of differentiation affecting urban/rural, industrial/ agricultural, mountain/coast dimensions confirm the importance of socioeconomic context and 'local societies'.

Moving from this contextual framework, three main questions inform our reflections: 1) what forms of participation and intervention opportunities are offered to youth in a country characterised by a deeply focused *familistic* welfare regime; 2) to what extent do youth participation policies counteract the influence of this *familistic* structure? And, in particular 3), to what extent does the local dimension hold the capacity and resources to combat and reduce the inequalities inherent to this dimension?

In particular, in the first section we present the analysis of the ambiguous relationship existing in Italy between youth, participation and politics. In the second section we propose a critical excursus of Italian local youth policies, which are currently attempting to overcome the compensative approach of the 1970s and the 1980s in favour of proactive and participatory methods. The strengths and weaknesses of these policies will be reviewed based on some of the Italian case studies (Cuconato and Lenzi, 2004, 2008) undertaken during two European research projects carried out respectively between 2001 and 2004 (YOYO Project) and between 2006 and 2009 (UP2YOUTH Project)[2].

In the third section we analyse individual youth participation within the context of a *familistic* grounding of social policy. We conclude conclude the chapter by highlighting the large hiatus still existing between the rhetoric of the institutional principles and the real praxis of the Italian youth policies, which very often continue to be limited to cultural practices, neglecting the need for a redistributive approach.

Youth, participation and politics: an ambiguous relationship

Reflecting on participation implies first of all recognising its *multifaceted* nature, which is impossible to reduce to a single form or model; not only does it encompass individual and collective trajectories; it also embraces social, economic and welfare structures. Over the past decade, the European Union and the ministers responsible for youth in each country have underlined, often in a rhetorical manner, the desirability of active youth participation, a phenomenon considered to be an essential factor in the building of more democratic, inclusive and prosperous societies.

However, not all young people have got the same sociocultural resources and economic means, the aim of involving them in the decisions affecting their own lives requires different varieties of policy and support in order to democratise the meaning of participation (Cuconato, 2011). According to the notion of citizenship formulated by Marshall (1950), participation is connoted through an evident socioeconomic meaning as a sort of premise and empowerment for the cultural and civic engagement of young people, together with formal rights and duties. Under this perspective it includes dimensions such as education and vocational training, labour market, health and housing. These dimensions are essential for an independent and autonomous life as they create the conditions for the active participation of young people in the decisions concerning them and the life of their community (Fahmy, 2006; Tisdal et al, 2006; Walther et al, 2006).

As pointed out by Jill Jones, 'it is only through economic emancipation (particularly through labour market participation, but also through welfare system) that young people can enter a direct relationship with the state as a citizens' (Jones, 2005, p 55). From this perspective, the difficulties experienced by young Italians in entering the labour market and being supported by public policies show that in Italy youth citizenship remains largely a second-class citizenship, with entitlements derived from the family's status (Livi Bacci, 2005; Sgritta, 2005a; Boeri and Galasso, 2007; De Luigi, 2011)[3]. The persistence of this 'minority' condition is due to institutional delays in planning new categories of social protection to combat the widespread precariousness associated with the fixed-term and temporary contracts disproportionately offered to younger people (Barbieri and Scherer, 2009). This second-class employment situation has a potential to alienate the life and working relationships of young people as is evident in the words of the young people interviewed working in the FIAT factory in Turin:

> ... maybe these temping agencies are even worse, ... to me it's the worst thing that can happen to a guy because after all you even miss a good relationship with the other workers, because you are highly discriminated, because when you are in the production line of a factory, you are forced to produce more than a normal person, there is no Trade Union to defend your rights, you own nothing and you feel even like fighting with other workers because if

you don't produce as much as they want you to, then at the
end of the month you won't see your contract renewed,
nobody tells you so but it is common knowledge. (Cuconato
and Lenzi, 2004, p 27)

Furthermore, due to high youth unemployment rates (32.9% of 15- to
24-year-olds at the end of 2010), Italian young people are deprived of
social and citizenship rights regarding the basic level of material wellbeing
that is granted through state provision in other European countries
regardless of an individual's market capacities. Social expenditure in
Italy is unbalanced and features a disproportionally substantial provision
of resources towards pensions and a commensurate lesser allocation for
families, children and active labour market policies (ISTAT, 2010). This
policy and fiscal disparity hinders the implementation of policies aimed
at ensuring universal rights; if resources targeted to women and youth
are not increased this imbalance will continue to hamper progress for
the groups concerned.

Moreover, political actors and scientists are worried that the apathy
expressed towards politics and politicians by Italian young people
reflects an underlying indifference and mistrust that has the potential
to endanger the roots of democratic life (Sciolla, 2004). Italian young
people seem to exhibit scarce civic consciousness, low levels of
interpersonal trust, and a dangerous mistrust towards the traditional
languages, rites and forms of politics. The political engagement of
younger generations in traditional institutions (political parties and trade
unions) is very low, but the reality is even more faceted: Italian young
people seem to attribute great importance to universalistic values like
freedom, democracy, solidarity and social equality. The attention given
to these values is reflected in their engagement in youth associations: a
significant number of young people (between 15 and 29 years) appear
to play an active role in social work activities, youth associations and
voluntary organisations. Spontaneous and informal forms of association
attract a growing number of participants, who find themselves closer
to decision-making processes.

A recent and promising counteracting sign emerges from the
latest Italian referendums held in mid-June 2011. These referendums
maintain the participative trend that first appeared during the May
2011 municipal and regional elections, in which young people played
a major role.

In contrast to the paucity of information concerning the referendums
on the television and the government encourangement to abstain
from voting, young people themselves conducted an impressive 'yes'

campaign; predominantly through Internet platforms such as Facebook and Twitter (*informal participation*) in tandem with numerous committees and citizens' initiatives working outside officialdom and concentrating on the issues of the four plebiscitary questions. These single issues were (1) the ban on nuclear power plants; (2) the privatisation and (3) marketing of water; and (4) the so-called 'law of legitimate impediment', which would allow officials to ignore a summons, if they could not appear in court for 'important' reasons.

The Italian young people campaigned in an unconventional way, distancing themselves from the political parties' viewpoints of reality and oriented more towards a social engagement that offered greater opportunities for self-expression and the realisation of fundamental political opportunities right up to the limits and constrictions of political norms. Alongside these unconventional tactics the young people then had to vote (*formal participation*); and in so doing accepted the traditional method of participating. As this time they felt that the questions were meaningful for their lives and futures, the young people demonstrated that they are not disconnected from politics: it is politics that is disconnected with young people, politics that often fails to represent them.

Furthermore, it is worth mentioning that a conflictual field of youth participation and self-management, namely self-managed social centres, rich with experiences, also exists and is richly deserving of further investigation. Created in the late 1970s by young groups 'illegally' occupying unused buildings, these squats soon turned into centres for social aggregation as cultural and discussion centres, some of which have been recognised by the local authorities. They have thus become real alternative socioeconomic and cultural networks. Hand in hand with the demolition of the welfare state, we nowadays find migrants, unemployed or people with low income or drug-addiction problems beginning to seek out these self-managed centres as freely accessible places, wherein they can find a warm meal, the possibility of jobs and advice on how to obtain a residence permit. They are scattered throughout Italy and undoubtedly represent an important resource (though anti-institutional at times) in the process of youth participation and *empowerment* in large cities (Cuconato and Lenzi, 2008).

Local youth policies: the long way toward a participatory approach

Due to renewed attention towards youth and the desire to create youth policies similar to that of other European countries the (centre-left) government instituted a national Ministry for Youth and Sport in

2006, which apparently represented an 'unprecedented innovation' for Italy in the field of youth policy (Campagnoli, 2010). Prior to the establishment of this Ministry laws existed on only some particular aspects of youth issues. These laws aimed to protect young people in various domains, with responsibility shared between different ministries. This arrangement did not assist any form of central coordination; it was fragmented and heterogeneous in the different geographical areas and was oriented more towards governing emerging issues than to planning an integrated framework of intervention.

Therefore the new Ministry was assigned the task of coordinating the actions of several governmental actors responsible for specific aspects of youth issues, in order to optimise interventions aimed at fostering the social and economic autonomy of young people, promoting their right to get a job, financial credit, housing, and to form a family.

The creation of a Ministry for Youth and Sport seems to counteract the strong pressure towards decentralisation (vertical subsidiarity) in Italy over the past decade. Discourses and rhetoric around this kind of *double movement* hide some central facts: 1) youth policies were developed and promoted at local level a long time before this latest wave of federalism and local orientation; 2) the national structure of social protection (in both the financial and political-ideological spheres) has strongly conditioned local policy variants; and 3) up to now the (current) process of rescaling welfare policies has not granted local authorities the correspondent level of financial and normative autonomy required and suffers from the general delegitimisation of public social expenditure.

Moreover, the ambitious aims of this new-born Ministry as stated in the National Plan for the Youth will be difficult to achieve as the resources available under the National Fund for Youth Policies amounts to a meagre 130 million euro for the period 2007–09, which must fund both ministry activities and the activities of the regions and municipalities.

Despite the absence of a general national law on youth (a situation that persists to this day), some local authorities, in collaboration with not-for-profit associations, promoted a variety of experimental projects, interventions and actions in the field of youth policy, initiatives that were later supported at regional level and followed up through the 1980s and the early 1990s by other local administrations.

The original initiatives sprang up around the end of the 1970s and were predominantly located in the large cities and medium-size towns in Northern Italy such as Turin, Bologna, Milan, Modena and Reggio Emilia, where left-wing councils administrated municipalities. These first attempts charted their course through a process of institutional reform that in the 1970s led to a *devolution* of power to regions, provinces and municipalities in the field of social policies. They were also adopted to respond to youth protest movements and the social riots of the late 1960s and the early 1970s and to manage the grave crisis of political parties and associations at national level, aiming to regain the support of younger generations on at least the local level.

Among other experimental and participatory measures, the foundation of youth information centres known as *Informagiovani*[4], Youth Centres and Youth Councils marked a new era in the Italian approach to youth issues, intended to neither cure nor stigmatise, but rather to integrate different levels of intervention in the *Progetti Giovani* (Project for Youth).

The surplus value of this new approach is not only that young people began to be recognised as social subjects and a target of services and projects from local administrations, but that these projects made the first attempt to integrate several national measures at local level. These disparate national measures promoted by different ministerial cabinets contributed to the creation of new professional profiles and the establishment of the first education and youth work cooperatives, which have played an extremely active role in the decades since their foundation (Mesa, 2010). Moreover, several attempts have been made to encourage a deeper involvement of territorial resources, thus favouring the autonomy and participation of local youth associations[5].

At the beginning of the 1990s, D.p.r. (Decree of the president of the Italian Republic) 309/90 and Law 216/91 brought the national legislative focus on youth conditions. However, regarding the fields of drug use and juvenile delinquency, the approach was still grounded in the idea of youth as a problem and not as a 'proper' target of policies. Nevertheless, at local level funding has been used not only for compensatory measures, but also for implementing several pro-active interventions concerning school counselling, preventive healthcare, leisure time, youth work, youth association, volunteers and social communication.

In the meantime, some central and northern regions approved basic and organic laws for the promotion and coordination of youth policies, institutionalising the previous local authorities' experimentations. From an institutional point of view, all these laws were supposed to provide regional and local decision makers with the tools required to monitor youth conditions and to adopt integrated measures favouring the citizenship rights of adolescents and young people; in only a few cases were they promoted and developed into a territorial systemic coordination of youth policies (Dondona et al, 2004).

The weak point of these measures lies in the foundation services and projects offered by local administrations or youth associations; these structures have had difficulties in reaching young people who lack the social and cultural capital necessary to recognise the opportunities offered through a participative experience and their relevance for future life and social integration.

A young participant from the urban regeneration project *Youth and Suburbs* (Turin) informed us with disarming obviousness:

> You know, many people don't even know about the existence of Informagiovani, I worked for them in the international exchange programme, ... but who participates? The teacher's child or the architect's child, people who can afford to go abroad any time. Nobody here knows that there are international exchanges. None of us uses this opportunity. (Cuconato and Lenzi, 2004, p 18)

The second half of the 1990s marked a turning point in youth policies promoting the activation of the target group: in both Law 285/1997 (aimed at promoting children and adolescent participation in local community life) and in the National Plan for the Youth, expanded in 1998, *empowerment* and *participation* were championed as the main strategies for implementation. Law 285/1997 defined the concept of a *participation project*, which concerns both children and local agencies, whose aim is to promote children and adolescent participation in the local community's life. Baraldi (2001) analysed about 1,000 projects between 1998 and 2000 in relation to Law 285/97 so as to emphasise – beyond any rhetoric – the concepts of youth participation promoted. Analysis of these projects highlights the existence of two different cultural attitudes towards social interventions aimed at enhancing children and youth participation: the first (more prevalent) attitude is connected with the traditional models and concepts of education and adolescence, seeking more to prevent deviant behaviour than to enhance active participation. The second (emerging) attitude functions on the assumption that adolescents are 'complete' beings and social actors in order to promote their participation to collective life with equal rights and equal dignity. From this research it emerges that most of the projects financed under Law 285/97 are still inspired by the traditional approach, even if that law has been passed to enhance innovative form of active participation.

Under this law, a number of actions have been taken with the aim of setting up *Consigli dei ragazzi* (Local Youth Councils) for the community, but in some cases young people reacted with suspicion to this institutional participation offer. In Bologna, one of the liveliest towns for youth cultural and expressive ferment in Italy, the last attempt at building a Youth Council was made in 1998. Following election through districts consultations, the young people's council met four or five times and then disbanded as they were unsuccessful in generating interest among other young people.

In relation to the role of territories in promoting (or not) youth participation policies, a second process of institutional devolution of power occurred in 2001 through the reform of Title V – Art. 117 of the Italian Constitution; this process gave the Regions legislative and executive powers in all matters that were not expressly covered by state legislation (including youth policies), leaving the exclusive legislative powers regarding the determination of basic benefit levels in civil and social entitlements guaranteed throughout the national territory to the state.

However, one should not forget the qualitative and quantitative differences between geographical areas; these differences reveal that regional policies are not a coherent whole. While certain regions have undertaken unitary integrated projects, others retain a worrying lack of coordination between agencies (associations, local authority, family and schools).

Individual participation versus familism: a new trend in Italian youth policy?

How have the recent institutional innovations influenced Italian youth policy aimed at fostering the social and financial autonomy of young people and therefore their active participation? How do they interact with the supposed bottom-up benefits of a youth policy originally created through the autonomous experimentation of local government? Do they offer new perspectives for young people's participation in community life?

A new widespread governance programme in the field of youth policy is gaining a foothold, grounded in the devolution of resources from the Fund for Youth Policy and the implementation of the duties assigned to the Regions through the Framework Programme Agreements (FPA), within a broader process of devolution of power to Regions starting from 2001, with a specific reform of Italian Constitution. The FPA implements the principle of vertical and horizontal subsidiarity and specifies the national priorities in youth policy areas identified by the Ministry.

An analysis of 21 FPAs highlights a wide range of initiatives which promote youth participation in public life and aim to facilitate self-fulfilment as active and responsible citizens. However, the FPA confirms the patchy nature of Italian youth policy; the persisting lack of a strategic national plan and national law regarding youth affairs, and the different economic trends and priorities within the corresponding regional contexts of the nation, militate against a coherent approach. For example, the definition(s) of youth are so heterogeneous that in the 21 FPAs there are 14 age ranges delineating target groups.

Analysis of the current situation exposes two sets of consequences: firstly, this fragmentation could activate positive scenarios of normative and experimental planning and intervention; secondly, negative consequences emerge given that this arrangement exacerbates the chaotic patterns of activity across the country, thereby consolidating the territorial differences among the regions of Italy.

At local level, the most important and recent innovation consists of the Local Projects for Youth, established through cooperation between the Ministry for Youth, the National Association of Italian Municipalities and the national coordination of *Informagiovani*, which now faces the challenges inherent in the onset of new information and communication technologies. Through these projects, local administrations have been provided with the instruments required to develop specific social planning in the field of youth policy, designing a consultation path midway between public and private actors with the aim of harmonising the interests and objectives of youth policy and improving the life quality of the whole community, including previously disregarded intervention areas (e.g. access to housing, work and fiscal credit).

However, these projects are not always a total success. The above mentioned project Youth and Suburbs is sponsored by the Turin Municipality in cooperation with youthwork social cooperatives and youth centres. It aims to enhance the active participation of young people (from 15 to 25 years old) from four different suburban areas in a wider and more comprehensive project of urban development and reconstruction (Suburbs Special Project). The participatory approach foresaw on the one hand the creation of *tavoli di lavoro* (joint decision-making sites) comprised of young people, third sector organisations and the local authorities, and on the other hand pilot-projects based on 'youth protagonism': the involvement of young people in planning and implementing projects for themselves. The project involved young people in action research directed towards all those living in the area and, subsequently, in an action research project targeted at young people specifically. The initial aim of the participation action research was to carry out a *preliminary exploration of the youths' ideas on the planned interventions* concerning urban, social and economic transformation as upon decided by the local council. Subsequently, the aim(s) evolved into promoting concrete *action plans* for youth interventions around the planning and refurbishment of urban spaces. However, what did emerge from interviews (with the young people) was that the final decisions were always taken in a bureaucratic manner by the local administration. This state of affairs provoked both frustration and a progressive drop off from the young participants (Cuconato and Lenzi, 2004). This phenomenon of progressive disengagement due to official retention of decision-making power is an ever-present risk in the recent youth policies promoted by local administrations.

The initial raw analysis of the preliminary Local Projects highlights critical aspects beyond the encouraging innovations. First of all, it seems difficult to establish strong mixed partnership with local private social actors, in particular from the economic sector, when the role of the public sector is becoming more important, and the educational institutions (school, vocational training and university) are active partners. In order to enable young people to acquire the full autonomy available through work, housing and credit, the public-private actors' network must be improved. Crucially, it must seek local alliances with private enterprises and banking institutions to further the ambitious aim of influencing established socioeconomic and institutional mechanisms, which unfortunately have contributed to keeping young people locked into a sort of half or provisional citizenship relying still on *familism*.

Secondly, the aim of developing an organised system of youth policy does not seem to be high on the local administration's priority list, since local administration persists in maintaining a deep fragmentation of interventions and lacks coordination across municipal departments. The situation is even worse in those local contexts that demonstrate a poor institutional sensibility and a weak mobilisation of social and youth associations. In this framework, it is not unusual to find that decisions and agreements produced at local level through negotiated planning do not exert any great influence on local policy. Therefore the Local Projects for Youth risk being an arena of rhetorical principles, promoting good intentions that have no real power in regenerating the chain of representation, whose links today appear weaker and weaker.

Thirdly, the *syndrome of delayed youth* characterising Italian young people makes it necessary to focus on the *familistic* nature of the welfare regime and, more generally, on the need for new regulation in the area of inter-generational relationships and social expenditure. Italian young people have recently been slammed by an Italian Ministry as '*bamboccioni*' (big babies), who live as parasites in the comfort of home until marriage. The experience of 'T', a 24-year-old man living in Turin, who had to go back to live with his parents after a brief attempt at living on his own, offer a firm rebuttal to this ministerial assumption on young people's lives:

> If I only had the chance to spend the periods of unemployment [with more economic tranquillity] as a guy from the Netherlands or Denmark, I would have acted more rationally. Here instead, there are no certainties, continuously changing jobs, the rent and everything, it grows on you, and makes also study difficult. Indeed, there are not many people who have made my choice [to leave the parent's house], but there would be more of them if the Government understood that a young person needs to work and to be independent, and should be allowed to combine these things. It is not us being tied to our mothers' skirts, as some say, it's an objective difficulty, the situation is worse than in the rest of Europe. (Cuconato and Lenzi, 2004, p 37)

These questions are of a nature that cannot be solved at local level alone. If local strategies, the actors' power and the regulatory mechanisms remain self-sufficient and the analysis and action perspective remain within territorial borders, it will be near impossible to correctly understand the systemic integration (or disintegration) processes set up through dynamics which are often of supranational origin, thus risking an underestimation of the elements which cannot be seen, decoded and addressed from a local perspective.

The local contest, today more important than yesterday, cannot in any case withdraw into itself. Moreover Italy is a country which persists in a two-speed development process, especially regarding young people, with the south of the country reporting a significantly higher youth unemployment rate (42.4%) compared with the north (27.3%) and centre (31.3%) (ISTAT, 2010). For this and other reasons, the local governance of youth policy must also involve the upper institutional levels, upper levels which are 'more able to analyse the situation from a less local position' (Bobbio, 2006, p 73).

Conclusion

Notwithstanding the important innovations over the past few years, Italian youth policy still represents an unsettled system with restricted power, showing great variation across the country. The stated goal of introducing fiscal federalism in Italy could enhance the accountability and resources of local authorities to formulate policy in favour of young people, but it does not intervene on the culture orientation of youth policies; on the contrary, within generally unbalanced welfare-state social expenditure and arrangements, fiscal federalism could increase localised and fragmented positions.

Even if this development has been trying to overcome the traditional approach, which considers young people to be disadvantaged and dangerous subjects, who need both support and control, it seems to persist constructing young people as excluded from the socioeconomic context in which they live.

As in the past, recent innovations have to come to terms with the restrictions inherent in a *familistic* and to some extent *localistic* welfare regime, which make the full participation of young people almost completely dependent on their socioeconomic and cultural background. And more, youth policies suffer both of their still weak institutional legitimacy and of the difficult and somehow conflicting balancing between local and central power in the general redefinition of welfare policy. The result is a deep gap between on one side rhetoric and institutional principles, and on the other side effective interventions, which remain very often more concentrated on cultural practices than on redistributive approaches, thus substantially including young people with high levels of education, wide social relationships and clear life plans, and excluding those educationally and socially deprived from participating to formal institutional opportunities and, more generally, from a participatory citizenship (Martelli, 2011). The main risk is that the enhanced participative processes remain merely formal and fail in involving effectively the most vulnerable young people.

Notes

[1] More recently has been coined also the label of 'adult-young' for targeting those people between 35 and 39 years old (Cesareo, 2005), who despite their age still present a youth lifestyle and a weak economic autonomy.

[2] The YOYO project *Youth Policy and Participation* analysed the potentials of participation and informal learning for young people's transitions to the labour market. The qualitative study included a total of 365 biographical interviews to

young people and 27 case studies on participative youth projects. The Italian case studies took place in Campagnola, Palermo and Turin. The UP2YOUTH project *Youth – Actor of Social Change* analysed to what extent social change affects young people's agency and to what extent young people's agency influences social change. This question was examined comparatively in three working groups: on transitions to adulthood, transitions of migrant youth to the labour market, and youth participation. The Italian participation group carried out two case studies, in Bologna and in Palermo.

[3] In Italy the percentage of 25- to 29-year-old young adults still living at home with their parents has grown from 34.5% in 1983 to 59.2% in 2009 (with young men reaching 68.8%). Furthermore, in the same period the percentage of them aged 30 to 34 years old has increased threefold, with three out of ten adult young people now living with their parents.

[4] *Informagiovani* represents a sort of municipal help desk in the areas of socioeducational and prevention policies, a bridge between youth needs/interests (tourism, vocational guidance, spare time, culture, etc.) and (local) institutions and associations.

[5] The first form of direct participation of associations in projects of Forums and Councils (*Consulte*) saw the light in this context, with varying success.

References

Baraldi, C. (2001) *I diritti dei bambini e degli adolescenti. Una ricerca sui progetti legati alla legge 285 e le sue applicazioni* (The rights of children and adolescents. A research on the project based on Law 285 and its applications), Roma: Donzelli Editore.

Barbieri, P. and Scherer, S. (2009) 'Labour market flexibilisation and its consequences in Italy', *European Sociological Review*, vol 25, no 6, p 677–92.

Bobbio, L. (2006) 'Le politiche contrattualizzate' (Contractualised policies), in C. Donolo (ed), *Il futuro delle politiche pubbliche (The future of public policies)*, Milano: Bruno Mondadori, pp 59–79.

Boeri, T. and Galasso, V. (2007) *Contro i giovani. Come l'Italia sta tradendo le nuove generazioni (Against Youth. How Italy is betraying new generations)*, Milano: Mondadori.

Cesareo, V. (2005) *Ricomporre la vita. Gli adulti giovani in Italia (Reassembling life. The adult-young in Italy)*, Roma: Carocci.

Campagnoli, G. (2010) 'Vivere un "new deal" delle politiche giovanili' ('Living a "new deal" of youth policies'), in A. Bazzanella (ed) *Investire nelle nuove generazioni: modelli di politiche giovanili in Italia e in Europa. Uno studio comparativo (Investing in new generations: patterns of youth policies in Italy and Europe. A comparative study)*, Trento: Editore Provincia Autonoma di Trento – IPRASE del Trentino, pp 70–128.

Cuconato, M. (2004) 'Apprendimento e partecipazione: la sfida di un capitale sociale europeo' ('Learning and participation: the challenge for a European social capital'), in R. Prandini and S. Melli (eds) *I giovani: il capitale sociale della futura Europa. Politiche di promozione della gioventù in un welfare societario plurale (Young people: The social capital for the future of Europe. Youth promoting policies in a pluralist social welfare)*, Milano: Franco Angeli, pp 97–120.

Cuconato, M. (2011) *La mia vita è uno yo-yo. Diventare adulti in Europa tra opportunità e rischi (My life is a yo-yo. Becoming an adult in Europe between opportunities and risks)*, Roma: Carocci.

Cuconato, M. and Lenzi, G. (2004) *WP 2 – Analysis of explorative interviews in Italy*, Department of Education, University of Bologna.

Cuconato, M. and Lenzi G. (2008) 'Italian Case Study: Palermo and Bologna' in P. Loncle and V. Muniglia (eds), *Youth participation, agency and social change, thematic report, deliverable no 21 of the project Youth – actor of social change (Up2youth)*, contract no 028317, pp 188–99.

De Luigi, N. (2011) 'Les jeunes et le marché du travail en Italie: entre continuité et signaux de changement' ('Young people and labour market in Italy: changing and persisting dynamics'), in M. Vultur and D. Mercure (eds) *Perspectives internationales sur le travail des jeunes (International perspectives on youth and labour market)*, Québec: Presses de l'Université Laval, pp 33–51.

Dondona, C. A., Gallini, R. et al (2004) *L'osservatorio nazionale sulla condizione giovanile, le politiche per i giovani in Italia (The national observatory on youth condition, youth policies in Italy)*, Torino: IRES Piemonte.

Fahmy, E. (2006) *Young citizens: Young people's involvement in politics and decision making*, Aldershot: Ashgate.

ISTAT (2010) *Conti della protezione sociale 1990–2009 (Social protection expenditure 1990–2009)*, Roma: Istat.

Jones, G. (2005) 'Social protection policies for young people: a cross-national comparison', in H. Bradley and J. van Hoof (eds) *Young people in Europe: Labour markets and citizenship*, Bristol: The Policy Press, pp 41–62.

Livi Bacci, M. (2005) *Avanti giovani, alla riscossa. Come uscire dalla crisi giovanile in Italia (Forward young people, to the rescue. How to escape from youth crisis in Italy)*, Bologna: il Mulino.

Loncle P. and Muniglia V. (2008) *Youth participation, agency and social change, thematic report, deliverable no 21 of the project Youth – actor of social change (Up2youth)*, contract no 028317.

Marshall, T. H. (1950) 'Citizenship and social class', in T. H. Marshall and T. Bottomore (1992) *Citizenship and social class*, London: Pluto Press.

Martelli, A. (2012) 'The debate on young people and participatory citizenship: questions and research prospects', *International Review of Sociology*, forthcoming.

Mesa, D. (2010) 'Le politiche giovanili in Italia: attori, prospettive e modelli d'intervento' (Youth policies in Italy: stakeholders, perspectives and actions models), *Autonomie locali e servizi sociali*, no 2, pp 261–74.

Saraceno, C. and Keck, W. (2010) 'Can we identify intergenerational policy regimes in Europe?', *European Societies*, vol 12, no 5, pp 675–96.

Sciolla, L. (2004) *La sfida dei valori* (The values challenge), Bologna: il Mulino.

Sgritta, G. B. (2005a) 'L'Europa delle generazioni: l'ipoteca del passato' (Generation Europe: the legacy of the past), in Osservatorio Nazionale sulla Famiglia, *Famiglie e politiche di welfare in Italia: interventi e pratiche (Families and welfare policies in Italy: actions and practices)*, Bologna: il Mulino, vol. I, pp 13–51.

Sgritta, G. B (2005b) 'Famiglie di nazioni, nazioni di famiglie' ('Families of nations, nations of families'), *La rivista delle politiche sociali*, no 4, pp 9–23.

Sgritta, G. B., Laino, G., Leone, L. and Rossi-Doria, M. (2010) 'Persistenza della povertà e limiti dell'investimento sociale su infanzia e giovani nel Mezzogiorno' ('Lingering poverty and deficiencies of social investment on childhood and youth in Southern Italy'), *La rivista delle politiche sociali*, no 3, pp 231–56.

Tisdall, E. K. M., Davis, J. M., et al (eds) (2006) *Children, young people and social inclusion: Participation for what?*, Bristol: The Policy Press.

Walther, A., du Bois-Reymond, M. et al (eds) (2006) *Participation in transition: Motivation of young adults in Europe for learning and working*, Frankfurt am Main et al: Peter Lang, 2006.

SEVEN

Barriers to participation within a recessionary state: impediments confronting Irish youth

Pat Leahy and Paul Burgess

Introduction

This chapter explores the effects on young people's *participation* in an Ireland engulfed by a major economic recession. It reviews the notion of *change* in relation to young people in Irish society and the status of young people, with a particularly critical focus on the emerging trend of portraying young people as 'children' in a policy context.

Thereafter we explore the role the *Youth Work* as the 'engine' driving young people's participation, before offering the reader a concluding section focused on the current relationship represented by the participation/youth/social change nexus in contemporary Ireland.

The reader should bear in mind that in common with other jurisdictions, Ireland does not have a precise definition of participation; instead, the term is often bandied about due to its positive connotations. In reality, young people's experiences of participation run along a continuum, from the tokenistic 'attendance equals participation' version to what we might characterise as 'real and meaningful' participation. From this chapter's perspective, we have used the phenomenon of exercising power in the sense of having decision-making competences as our idealised opposite of tokenistic participation.

Background: a transitional society

Ireland has experienced vast changes in the past two decades: 'It would be difficult to find an example of such deep, intense and rapid transformation as has occurred in Ireland' (Peillon and Corcoran, 2002, p 1). Ireland during the 1980s saw recession, emigration and violent political activism. Unemployment and emigration had a heavy impact upon the young. The Irish state was conservative and secretive, and the Roman Catholic Church held an inordinate sway over politics, health and education policy and population control (Tovey and Share, 2003). From 1987 the government began using a *corporatist model* of governance to overcome economic difficulties. Through the 1990s improvements became noticeable (Allen, 2000). These encompassed a resolution of Ireland's historical meta-narratives (McCarthy, 2000) as represented by the peace process in Northern Ireland, globalisation, a free-market approach to business and the widening of participation in education. Ireland did experience a boom in the early years of the millennium. However, the government catastrophically mismanaged this boom resulting in a disastrous collapse of state finances.

O'Connor notes that alongside these sweeping changes Ireland witnessed: 'a series of scandals involving the abuse of authority in a number of male dominated institutions' (O'Connor, 2008, p 2). These scandals involved the sexual predilections of the Catholic Church and financial shenanigans in business and politics. These scandals have undermined young people's (and others') confidence in authority. The Catholic Church is losing adherents and authority: 'The institutional apparatus that had organised and managed Irish educational and social services, and by virtue its moral monopoly had governed Irish hearts and minds for at least one hundred year, is in deep crisis' (Kuhling and Keohane, 2004, p 1).

The individualisation of society over the 'Tiger' years weakened solidarity and collectivism; Tovey and Share referred to this as an 'obligation (on people) to construct their own do-it-yourself biography' (2003). This individualisation is visible in young people's transitions (Leahy, in Herrmann, 2008) and has had an impact upon young people's participation. Perhaps the most visible manifestation of shifting patterns of engagement lies within the political field.

The state, NGOs and the main political parties have all expressed unease at the decreasing levels of participation displayed by young people towards politics (O'Leary, 2001). Political parties are experiencing difficulty in recruiting young members (paradoxically, the youngest member of the Dail (Parliament) is the 24-year-old Simon Harris, with the youngest minister being the 32-year-old Leo Varadekar). Research amongst 18- to 25-year-olds by the National Youth Council of Ireland (NYCI) reinforces this picture of a decline in political participation by young people (National Youth Council of Ireland, 2009).

Ireland witnessed significant immigration; Powell et al point out that in relation to multi-cultural youth provision: 'Young people from different cultural and ethnic backgrounds are proportionally well represented overall in youth work interventions, however the experiences of youth work organisations on the ground seem to indicate that more could be done to support more multi-culturally integrated youth work groups' (Powell et al, 2010, p 6).

With these societal changes came the technological revolution. This revolution was embraced by young people through mobile phones and Internet usage; allied with a widespread subscription to satellite television these new forms of communication facilitated the dissemination amongst young people of new and alternative cultural ideas and ways of 'being young'. Osgerby suggests that 'perhaps the most dramatic impact of new technologies on young people's lives has been the way they establish, cultivate and maintain their social relationships. Here, the spectacular proliferation of mobile phones has been especially significant' (Osgerby, 2004, p 208).

Along with email, mobile phones allow for instantaneous communication outside adult control; the Internet has rendered any attempt at adult censorship futile. It is not unreasonable to expect increased access to innovative modes of communication to enhance the participatory process; the form that it may take is however an unknown quantity at this juncture.

With part-time employment available, young people's income rose and concern was expressed about teenagers missing school or being exploited by unscrupulous employers (Lalor and Baird, 2006). Young people's autonomy and mobility expanded; some school-going young people vied with teachers for parking spaces, and foreign holidays *sans* parents became a popular means of celebrating the completion of formal schooling.

These examples of change point to a youth population with increased income, technologically and socially interconnected in previously unheard of ways, and educated to a hitherto unimaginable degree. These factors influenced and reflected a fundamentally different country that championed a free-market model of economic development (Allen, 2000; O'Toole, 2003). The underlying assumption flowing from this ideology is that participation is primarily an economic activity, 'the role of the ordinary citizen is to be a member of a paid labour force and a consumer, in order to keep the economy going' (Ryan, in Coulter and Coleman, 2003, p 155).

Participation was in danger of being reduced to monetary exchanges with a correspondingly bleak outlook for marginalised groups in society. Before the economic downturn Kuhling and Keohane had warned that 'through pursuing a neoliberal economic policy, this economic modernisation has been accompanied by a variety of social inequalities and a strong decline in social cohesion' (2007, p 207).

Despite this rise in market-orientated capitalism and individualisation Ireland retained a strong voluntary sector that anchored civil society; this sector plays a pivotal role in facilitating participation in civil society among the population. This strength does not however entail a strong degree of participation in decision making. It can actually disguise a non-participative (in decision making) membership of spear-carrying followers beneath a thin veneer of equal participatory activity. In this regard, Honohan observes that: 'we should be wary of exhortations to be more active or civic spirited, or to join voluntary associations in order to strengthen social capital, unless ordinary citizens are given a larger voice in decision making' (Honohan, 2005, p 180).

Ireland developed a form of corporatism that in theory operates alongside the party-political system: allowing participation and policy input. Critics venture that the effect of this arrangement '...is that a small group of peak organisations have come to exert particular influence' (Tovey and Share, 2003, p 88).

Nevertheless, this partnership process is credited with being instrumental in opening limited avenues of participation for ordinary citizens in Irish society[1] (Meade, in Forde et al, 2009) without disguising a historical reluctance towards a fuller participatory democracy in Irish society. Powell has argued that in Ireland: 'Social citizenship rights have remained incomplete and chances for participation have continued, to the present day, to be more unequally distributed than the full status of citizenship in a modern democracy would permit' (2003, p 82).

During the economic boom years concerns were raised that the strength of the voluntary sector was exposed to grave risks. A 'Task Force on Active Citizenship' was launched in April 2006 to encourage and facilitate participation. This group reported that 'no firm evidence has emerged, so far, to support claims that social capital or volunteering has been declining' (Task Force on Active Citizenship, 2006) although anecdotal evidence of such a decline abounds.

Ireland's boom continued until 2007, led by an overheated property market (O'Toole, 2009). As the global economy foundered the bubble burst. This precipitated a severe contraction which saw the government resort to an extensive EU/IMF bailout.

The effect of this economic crisis on young people has been close to catastrophic: youth employment has collapsed with 24.2% of 15- to 24-year-olds being unemployed (MacAleer and Doorley, 2011) within an overall unemployment rate of 14.7% (Irish Examiner Statistics, 1 April 2011). Emigration by young people has reached levels not seen since the 1980s and youth suicide rates are a grave source of concern. Young people's entitlements were halved in May 2009 with the rate being reduced to €100 per week for claimants less than 20 years of age, while funding for various youth organisations was been cut by as much as 20% (Foróige, 2011).

The context of young people's lives in Ireland has therefore changed dramatically within a few short years. Rather than young people becoming an engine driving (positive) social change, social change is adversely affecting young people, as McLoughlin argues: 'the real cost of this crisis will fall on the shoulders of today's young people' (McLoughlin, 2010, p 2). The financial fallout from the economic collapse will be borne by today's young people through reduced opportunities, welfare rollback, and cutbacks in educational, recreational, cultural and social mobility programmes.

The status of young people in Ireland

An emerging trend in young people's status in the Republic of Ireland is the resurgence of the terms 'children' and 'child' in the official discourse around young people. The Government has indicated that it intends to hold a referendum on *children's rights* in the near future, there is an Ombudsman for children, and the definition of a child as a person under 18 years of age in the 2000 National Children's Strategy illustrates this trend.

Although a person is legally a child until the age of 18, the 2001 Youth Work Act defines a young person as between the ages of 10 and 21. The terms child and children betray a patronising attitude evident in the terminology used in the Children's Strategy and Dáil na nÓg (Parliament of the Young). For example, the term 'children' features in all of Dáil na nÓg's objectives (Office of the Minister for Children and Youth Affairs, 2010, p 28). There is a marked difference in what is appropriate participation for a child (generally under 12) as opposed to a young person. Martin points out that: 'Along that chronological spectrum, children as adolescents or as near adults must surely, as a matter of law and common sense, have nearly all the rights that adults possess' (Martin, 2000, p 5).

One area in which this lack of participation has serious ramifications is sexual relations. The current age of consent in Ireland is 17; young people who have underage intercourse are criminalised. A 19-year-old who had consensual intercourse with a 16-year-old girl in 2009 received an 11-month custodial sentence (Coulter, 2009). It is extremely doubtful that young people are either aware of or take much notice of laws prohibiting sexual behaviour. Mayock and Byrne found that sexual intercourse in some instances took place as early as 13 years of age and that: 'for the vast majority (practically all of the young men and 64% of the young women), first sexual intercourse was unplanned'(Mayock and Byrne, 2004, p 70).

Young people were consulted around the age of consent issue and participated in a discussion organised by the Joint Oireachtas[2] Committee on Child Protection in November 2006; this committee recommended 16 as the age of consent. This issue is sensitive however, with the protection of children, the declining – although influential – teaching of Catholic morality and traditional conservatism affecting the debate. In December 2006 it was reported that the then Taoiseach (Irish Prime Minister), the leader of the opposition and the Catholic bishops all disagreed with the committee recommendation. The bishops stated that: 'children needed to be protected not only from irresponsible adults but also from themselves, until they reached the age of maturity, currently considered to be 18' (RTE[3], 2006). It should be noted that the Catholic Church marries 'children' aged 17 and under. Ultimately, 17 was adopted as the age of consent[4], disregarding the recommendations of the joint committee, the various youth organisations and the input of the young people themselves. The tokenistic, patronising and condescending attitude shown towards young people is perhaps best explained as both moral and political expediency in an Ireland that still clings to authoritarianism, rather than naked cynicism.

This particular issue illustrates that designating young people as children legitimises adult control and validates McLaughlin's contention that although the state is strong on rhetorical rights for young people, '...their translation into reality is often weak' (McLaughlin, 2006, p 1). Treating young people as children equates with limiting and adult-dictated participatory structures; Christie notes that in Ireland: 'traditionally, children have not had the autonomy or the right to make decisions for themselves' (Christie, in Herrmann, 2004, p 127). Equally disempowering is the conceptualisation of childhood as a time of innocence and dependence, a concept that further justifies, through the nomenclature of childhood, the curtailment of young people's autonomy and rights over fundamental decision making concerning their own lives.

Young people's issues are in danger of being subsumed into children's rights with the consequential neglect of young people's rights. This development was exacerbated by the structural shift in which Youth Affairs was moved into the Office of the Minister for Children. It was identified at the time by Kearney as potentially damaging for the youth sector (Kearney, 2009, p 2) and as adding to the confusion around youth work's role and purposes.

The perception of youth

Ireland slots into the liberal 'Anglo-Saxon/Celtic' welfare regime with the consequential policy formulations that flow from this regime heavily influencing societal perceptions of youth and young people.

Across Europe, and (arguably) particularly in the liberal regime, the common perception is that young people are problematic and Ireland is no exception in this regard: '...the academic community, policy-makers and the popular media have tended to focus on the problematic aspects of young people and their lives: alcohol and drug use, early school leaving, early sexual behaviour, pregnancy, STDS (sexually transmitted diseases), delinquency' (Lalor et al, 2007, p 4). Moreover 'news stories tend in the vast majority of cases to portray young people either as being a problem or as having problems' (Devlin, 2006, p 47).

Youth organisations may inadvertently be complicit in this demonisation of young people through a 'following the funding' approach to service provision; government funding is overwhelmingly targeted towards 'at-risk' groups. By chasing this revenue agencies are constructing their activities as risk minimisation, strengthening the 'problem' perspective. Kiely notes that although youth services have a tradition of voluntary engagement, non-voluntary initiatives are becoming normalised: 'Included under the mantel of youth services in Ireland are projects that can be characterised as having more coercive kinds of participation and a greater orientation towards the surveillance and control of young people' (Kiely, in Forde et al, 2009, p 23).

This form of youth work provision has the further effect of downgrading, in the public and political eye, the efforts of 'mainstream' youth work to at best an amateurish attempt by well-meaning volunteers to keep the kids off the streets and to occupy them with harmless and uncontroversial activities while the professionals get on with the real business of tackling the hard case delinquents who threaten the fabric of society by wearing hoodies and hanging around on street corners.

A further problematisation is the attempt to link young people with reluctance to engage in low-paid work or training schemes. Announcing plans for a 'crackdown' on (especially young) unemployed people refusing such offers the Social Protection Minister, Joan Burton, stated that: 'we can't have a situation where somebody at very young age could almost drift into a life on welfare payments' (McEnroe, 2011). It is interesting that a societal failure to provide employment opportunities is ignored in the attempt to shift the blame on to the shoulders of the young people concerned.

We therefore arrive at a social construction which is broadly positive although patronising towards 'children', yet negative towards young people. This may seem a minor point but it is indicative of the state's manipulative and proscriptive practices and does have ramifications for perspectives on youth and the state's youth participation structures.

Youth participation in Ireland

Various studies strongly indicate dissatisfaction amongst Irish young people in regard to having their opinions taken into account: 'young people felt ignored and excluded by politicians, resident associations and community development committees' (Combat Poverty Agency, 2006). It would seem that at national, regional, municipal and most importantly, local levels, young people are frustrated and excluded.

This corresponds with Burgess and Leahy's findings from 2003; from Long's research amongst urban young people (2001) and with Burke's (2006) study of the setting up a youth café. Young people expressed of alienation from their own communities regardless of class background, with power and decision making controlled by adults.

Ireland has developed a set of initiatives under the 2000 National Children's Strategy (NCS) that aim to foster children and young people's participation; the equation of youth with childhood does suggest a more limited form of participation. The key initiatives are:

- Dáil na nÓg (Parliament of the Young) and Comhairle na nÓg (Municipal Youth Councils)
- Student Councils (National Children's Office, 2003 ; Keogh and Whyte, 2005).
- The Ombudsman for Children (Kilkelly, 2011).

The National Children's Strategy

In keeping with the 'child' designation mentioned above the Irish Government published the National Children's Strategy in 2000 (Government of Ireland, 2000) and established the National Children's Office (NCO), charged with implementing the strategy, (now the Department of Children and Youth Affairs) in 2001. In reviewing this strategy, the Children's Rights Alliance (which is comprised of over 90 non-governmental organisations) has commented on the impact of economic recession on this strategy:

The ten years covered by Our Children – Their Lives can be broken into two distinct halves – an initial active period marked by development of key infrastructure, and a latter period of reduced activity and investment, which, in some cases, risked undermining earlier achievements. The loss of momentum in the second part of the Strategy's ten year period corresponds with a more general tightening of Government expenditure, and, in recent years, cutbacks affecting services and supports for children. (Children's Rights Alliance, 2011, p 2)

Student councils

Student councils are a further tentative vehicle for participation; however, the Irish version again appears to be adult controlled: 'A student Council is a representative structure for students only, through which they can become involved in the affairs of the school, working in partnership with school management, staff and parents for the benefit of the school, and its student' (Keogh and Whyte, 2005, p 10).

Keogh and Whyte found that significant differences existed between rhetoric and reality, and between the students and the management as to the role of student councils. Management viewed these entities as a consultative forum whereas the students saw: '…their main role as one of action – they talked about representing students' views, changing school uniform, changing food in the canteen, fixing things, dealing with issues, solving problems, helping students, organising events, etc.' (Keogh and Whyte, 2005, p 10).

Amongst other findings, perhaps the most revealing was that although councils can make a positive contribution in enlightened schools, significant obstacles remain in many sites: 'Many students and student council members perceived that the attitudes of staff, and the Principal in particular, were obstacles to the council completing projects for a number of reasons, including the council having little status within the school and their role being undefined' (Keogh and Whyte, 2005).

Student councils have become a feature of school life in Ireland over the last decade; however, the degree of young people's control over decision making does not appear to equate with participatory decision making. Although there are doubtless excellent examples of fully participative student councils it would seem that the 'consultation' variety of participation holds sway in the majority of schools.

Dáil na nÓg

A further initiative is Dáil na nÓg (Parliament of the Young). Comhairle na nÓg (local structures) are operated under the aegis of municipal development boards that allow 8- to 18-year-olds a forum for discussion. These local groups select representatives for an annual Dail (Parliament) consisting of over 200 young people (aged 12–18). Relevant government bodies and NGOs also attend (the Government is usually represented by a Minister). The National Youth Council of Ireland is responsible for the operation of this forum.

Dáil na nÓg has come in for severe criticism: McMahon arguing that 'projects such as Dáil na nÓg can be criticised for the lack of any real say they offer young people in influencing public policy in relation to youth rights' (McMahon, in Forde et al, 2009, p 122). Murphy (2005) believes that improvements are required in at least three areas if Dáil na nÓg is to truly represent young people:

• The selection of young representatives at local level needs attention in order to develop relationships between the representative and the represented.
• Dáil na nÓg requires a statutory footing to underpin its' role and enhance its' position.
• The one-day format should be abandoned in favour of (at least) a two-day event so as to allow time for proper debate and discussion.

McLaughlin (2006) has argued that although Dáil na nÓg is a step forward and is worthy of support the real aim of organisations purporting to represent youth interests should be the lowering of the voting age to 16. Nevertheless, although tokenistic and possibly elitist (the delegates are not representative of all young people) this structure does represent a start in a heavily centralised polity, and Burke (2011, p 2) has listed the development of this structure as a priority for Youth Work organisations.

Alongside these core strands of participatory policy – some of which are progressive and some not so progressive – are located specific initiatives designed for selected groups; including input into residential arrangements (Health Information and Quality Authority, 2010) and the Irish Association of Young People in Care (Irish Association of Young People in Care, 2009).

The chief exponents of young people's rights and advocates for meaningful youth participation in Ireland are the youth organisations. Youth Work Ireland advocates for youth participation which: 'Not only seeks to involve young people in decision making within our organisations, but which works towards young people participating more fully in decisions in their own lives, the Irish Youth Work Sector, their communities and in Irish society' (Youth Work Ireland, 2010, p 10).

Similarly, Foróige takes participation as a central theme in its work: 'To ensure we take a leading role in the development of youth participation and advocacy, a Youth Advocacy Officer will be appointed to explore current practices and make recommendations to enhance youth participation at all levels of the organisation' (Foróige, 2010).

The National Youth Work Development Plan placed active participation at the core of good practice. The first goal under this plan, which forms the mechanism for implementing Irish youth policy, is: 'to facilitate young people and adults to participate more fully in, and to gain optimum benefit from, youth work programmes and services' (Department of Education and Science, 2003, p 18).

This plan has not been fully implemented, a matter of concern to the various youth organisations. The then chief executive officer of Youth Work Ireland stated that the integration of youth affairs into the Office of the Minister for Children and Youth Affairs is 'potentially signalling the end of the Youth Work Act 2001' (Kearney, 2008, p 2) and its offshoot, the Youth Work Development Plan. The NYCI's strategic aims include developing participation and of advocating for young people at the highest level (National Youth Council of Ireland, 2004).

Youth work has been attempting to overcome alienation and to offer meaningful participation opportunities. Two overlapping and complementary strategies are employed:

- Advocacy: lobbying for increased opportunities for meaningful participation and for resources to implement relevant programmes (National Youth Council of Ireland, 2005);
- Practice: searching for and implementing good practices in active participation (O'Donovan, 2006).

Notwithstanding the commitments of both state and voluntary sector to increasing the level of participation, the situation in practice requires a much fuller response.

The experiences of the young people researched in the case studies for 'Up2Youth' and 'Yoyo' (Walther et al, 2006; Loncle and Muniglia, 2008; Walther et al, 2009; Leahy and Burgess, 2011) suggest much remains undone in translating well-intentioned policy into practice. Gunning (2006) found a number of challenges inherent in raising participation. These ranged from the avoidance of tokenism to the provision of age-appropriate opportunities, and from the need to 'up skill' the young people to the need for adults to relinquish power.

The challenge from a participation perspective is to overcome the tendency for youth work participation in Ireland to revert to or remain stuck in offering 'opportunities for young people to practice participation for their future roles as adults' (McMahon, in Forde et al, 2009, p 122).

Conclusion

For the current generation of young people, this is an inauspicious time to be Irish. Pat Cox, the former Irish MEP and President of the European Parliament recently pointed out that: 'we have lost many of our friends in the most important place of all, the high temples of power in Europe' (RTE, 2011). The Secretary General to the European Commission, Catherine Day – the latest in a line of Irish officials who have risen to the highest ranks of the EU civil service – observed in an extraordinarily blunt comment on Ireland's engagement with the EU: 'the perception is that the more prosperous Ireland became, the more arrogant it became, and the less it engaged. The result was that the Irish were no longer seen as good Europeans' (RTE, 2011).

The situation regarding the potential for young peoples' participation in such a society – to meaningfully engage in social change – is now predicated on the interplay of a diverse set of dynamic and interrelated social and financial phenomenon. This 'nexus' is shaped by all manner of societal forces: some broadly progressive such as the youth work sector, some regressive, such as the creeping *infantilisation* through the 'child' misnomer.

Looming over all is the economic scenario: to participate within a liberal, free-market, capitalist polity, people require monetary and financial means. Lack of such means now defines the lived experience and the reality which faces many Irish young people. This scenario undoubtedly diminishes dramatically the potential to participate in such an overwhelmingly market-based society. Faced with such seemingly insurmountable odds, they may well choose the time-honoured Irish method of dealing with hard times by choosing emigration, thus rendering their potential input into progressive social change null and void.

The vital issue of young people's *own* social, political and civic perceptions will continue to go unheeded, as their self-worth – as potential actors of social change – is subjugated under the weight of poverty, lack of opportunity, political indifference and frustrated potential.

Notes

[1] The social partnership model has been severely criticised by left-wing authors as a free market by stealth and by the right-wing media as a sell-out to the unions.

[2] The Oireachtas is the Irish term for the national parliament.

[3] RTE; Raidió Teilifís Éireann, the Irish public service television and radio broadcaster.

[4] An exception to 17 as the age of consent exists if the persons concerned are married; the minimum age for marriage (heterosexual) is 16 (Bisset, 2006).

References

Allen, K. (2000) *The Celtic Tiger, the Myth of Social Partnership in Ireland*, Manchester: Manchester University Press.

Bisset, F. (2006) *Rights and Entitlements of Young People*, Dublin: Irish Youth Work Press.

Burgess, P. and Leahy, P. (2003) *Project Yoyo, Work Package 6, Final Report Ireland*, Unpublished.

Burke, I. (2006) 'Youth Participation', Dissertation, Applied Social Studies, Cork: University College.

Burke, P. (2011) *Irish Youth Work Scene*, Issue 67.

Children's Rights Alliance (2011) *Ten Years On: Did the National Children's Strategy Deliver on its Promises?*, Dublin: The Children's Rights Alliance.

Combat Poverty Agency (2006) Press Release, 22 November.

Coulter, C. (2009) 'Jail term for having sex with girl', *Irish Times*, 10 October.

Coulter, C. and Coleman, S. (2003) *The End of Irish History? Critical Reflections on the Celtic Tiger*, Manchester: Manchester University Press.

Department of Education and Science (2003) *National Youth Work Development Plan 2003–2007*, Dublin: Stationery Office.

Devlin, M. (2006) *Inequality and the Stereotyping of Young People*, Dublin: The Equality Authority.

Forde, C., Meade, R. and Kiely, L. (eds) (2009) *Youth and Community Work in Ireland, Critical Perspectives*, Dublin: Blackhall.

Foróige (2010) *Annual Review 2009–2010*, Dublin: Foróige.

Foróige (2011) *Annual Review 2010–2011*, Dublin: Foróige.

Government of Ireland (2000) *National Children's Strategy*, Dublin: Government Publications.

Gunning, A. (2006) *Report of a Consultation on Youth Participation in Youth Work Ireland and Recommendations for Developing a Strategy*, Dublin: Youth Work Ireland.

Health Information and Quality Authority (2010) *Draft Quality Standards for Residential and Foster Care Services for Children and Young People*, Dublin: Health Information and Quality Authority.

Herrmann, P. (ed) (2004) *Citizenship Revisited: Threats or Opportunities of Shifting Boundaries*, New York: Nova Science Publishers.

Herrmann, P. (ed) (2008) *Governance and Social Professions: How Much Openness is Needed and How Much is Possible?* New York: Nova.

Honohan, I. (2005) 'Active Citizenship in Contemporary Discourse', in C. Harris (ed) *The Report of the Democracy Commission: Engaging Citizens, the Case for Democratic Renewal in Ireland*, Dublin: TASC at New Island.

Irish Association of Young People in Care (2009) *Strategic Plan 2010–2012*, Dublin: Irish Association of Young People in Care.

Irish Examiner (2011) Business Section, General Financial Statistics, 1 April.

Kearney, D. (2008) 'A New Departure; Does It Bode Well for Youth Work?', *Irish Youth Work Scene*, Issue 56, June,

Kearney, D. (2009) 'Follow the Yellow Brick Road', *Irish Youth Work Scene*, Issue 61, September.

Keogh, A. F. and Whyte, J. (2005) *Second Level Student Councils in Ireland: A Study of Enablers, Barriers and Supports*, Dublin: National Children's Office.

Kilkelly, U. (2011) *A Children's Rights Analysis of Investigations*, Dublin: Ombudsman for Children.

Kuhling, C. and Keohane, K. (2004) *Collision Culture, Transformations in Everyday Life in Ireland*, Dublin: Liffey Press.

Kuhling, C., and Keohane, K. (2007) *Cosmopolitan Ireland: Globalisation and Quality of Life*, Dublin: Pluto Press.

Lalor, K. and Baird, K. (2006) 'Our Views, Anybody Listening?, Researching the views and needs of young people', in *Co. Kildare, Executive Summary*, Kildare: Kildare Youth Services.

Lalor, K., de Roiste, A. and Devlin, M. (2007) *Young People in Contemporary Ireland*, Dublin: Gill and Macmillan.

Leahy, P. and Burgess, P. (2011) *Youth Participation in the Republic of Ireland*, Cork: Youth Work Ireland Cork.

Loncle, P. and Muniglia, V. (eds) (2008) *Youth Participation, Agency and Social Change. Thematic Report*, Deliverable No. 21 of the project 'Youth – Actor of Social Change' (UP2YOUTH), www.up2youth. org/downloads/task,cat_view/gid,19/

Long, A. (2001) *Levels of Participation of Youths Aged 18–22 in the Glen Community*, Cork City: Glen Leadership and Equality Network.

MacAleer, M. C. and Doorley, J. (2011) *Creating A Future For Young Jobseekers*, Dublin: National Youth Council of Ireland.

Martin, F. (2000) *The Politics of Children's Rights*, Cork: Cork University Press.

Mayock, P. and Byrne, T. (2004) *A Study of Sexual Health Issues*, Dublin: Crisis Pregnancy Agency.

McCarthy, C. (ed) (2000) *Modernity, Crisis and Culture in Ireland, 1969 – 1992*, Dublin: Four Courts Press.

McEnroe, J. (2011) 'Crackdown on jobless refusing offers of work', *Irish Examiner*, 26 April.

McLaughlin, (2006) *'Asking Young People about the Age of Consent'*, Youth Work Ireland Press Release, 28 June 2006.

McLoughlin, M. (2010) 'Meeting the challenge', *Irish Youth Work Scene*, Issue 66, December.

Murphy, T. (2005) *Review of Comhairle and Dáil na nÓg*, Dublin: National Children's Office.

National Children's Office (2003) *Annual Report 2003*, Dublin: Stationery Office.

National Youth Council of Ireland (2004) *Strategic Plan 2004–2007*, Dublin: National Youth Council of Ireland.

National Youth Council of Ireland (2005) *Budget 2006: 'Youth Forgotten', Post-Budget Analysis*, Dublin: NYCI.

National Youth Council of Ireland (2009) *The Truth About Youth*, Dublin: National Youth Council of Ireland.

O'Connor, P. (2008) *Irish Children and Teenagers in a Changing World*, Manchester: Manchester University Press.

O'Donovan, D. (2006) 'The Participation of Non-Traditional Groups of Young People in Irish Civil Society', Dublin, Annual General Meeting Presentation, Youth Work Ireland 2006, unpublished.

Office of the Minister for Children and Youth Affairs (2010) Dáil na nÓg Delegates Report 2010, Dublin: Government Publications.

O'Leary, E. (2001) *Taking the Initiative: Promoting Young People's Involvement in Public Decision Making in Ireland*, Dublin: National Youth Council of Ireland/Carnegie Youth Initiative.

Osgerby, B. (2004) *Youth Media*, London: Routledge.

O'Toole, F. (2003) *After The Ball*, Dublin: TASC.

O'Toole, F. (2009) *Ship of Fools: How Stupidity and Corruption Sank the Celtic Tig*er, London: Faber and Faber.

Peillon, M. and Corcoran, M. (eds) (2002) *Ireland Unbound, a Turn of the Century Chronicle,* Dublin: Institute of Public Administration.

Powell, F. W. (2003) 'The Third Sector in Ireland', EuroSET, Rome: Centro Italiano di Solidarietà di Roma.

Powell, F., Geoghegan, M., Scanlon, M. and Swirak, K (2010) *Working with Young People; A National Study of Youth Work Provision and Policy in Contemporary Ireland*, Cork City: University College Cork.

RTE, Raidió Teilifís Éireann (2006) http://www.rte.ie/news/2006/1208/consent.html

RTE, Raidió Teilifís Éireann (2011) *Marian Finucane Programme*, 2 April.

Task Force on Active Citizenship (2006) *Together We're Better, Background Working Paper*, Dublin: Government Publications.

Tovey, H. and Share, P. (2003) *A Sociology of Ireland* (2nd edn), Dublin: Gill and Macmillan.

Walther, A., du Bois-Reymond, M. and Biggart, A. (eds) (2006) *Participation in Transition, Motivation of Young Adults in Europe for Learning and Working*, Frankfurt am Main: Peter Lang, GmbH.

Walther, A., Stauber, B. and Pohl, A. (2009) *UP2YOUTH. Youth – Actor of Social Change, Final Report*, Tübingen, IRIS www.up2youth.org/downloads/task,cat_view/gid,19/

Youth Work Ireland (2010) 'Youth Participation Policy', Youth Work Ireland, unpublished.

EIGHT

Youth participation and local social and youth policies in Spain

Lourdes Gaitán

Introduction

The form, range and depth of participation is related to the democratic pathway of each country, and also to the nature of social relations, culture, habits and social representations around childhood and youth that prevails in each country. The histories of various organisations that offer and deliver services and activities for children and youth lead us to the pre-democratic (1936–76) stage in Spain. The Franco dictatorship considered youth education a core element in which the values of 'national spirit' gained significance, and, as in other fascist regimes, this polity organised its own youth movement. This movement lost importance in the twilight of the regime; other types of organisation gained credence, some promoted by the Catholic Church, others depending on secular non-profit entities.

Participation constituted a key concept in the new democratic era, commencing from Franco's death and sealed thereafter in the Spanish Constitution of 1978. 'Youth' was viewed as a privileged arena; to be nurtured and to assure the future of this new democracy. Different institutions for young people were created linked with the three existing levels of public administration: national, regional and local. Some years later, the influence of international debates regarding children's rights led to the creation of childhood institutions at these three levels.

This structure, together with the existence of different agencies responsible for child and youth policies, entails some fragmentation within policies. While youth policies sometimes include boys and girls aged 15 or more years, childhood policies extend from birth to 17 years of age. Consequently, young people aged between 15 and 17 may be the focus of two types of institutions or agencies; however, they may also fall outside the scope of both. In this chapter, we intend to examine the situation of youth participation in three main structures: (1) the educational system, (2) juvenile associations and (3) local programmes.

In each of these structures the degree, range and form that participation takes occupies a central area. We have focused primarily on the younger (0- to 17-year-old) group; it serves as an important mobilisation mechanism between the local administration levels as well as between NGOs. This group are also the target of measures that aim to improve children's participation in public matters, originating from the United Nations Convention on the Rights of the Child in 1989.

Our study of the situation is based on recent and relevant research projects, official data provided by different public institutions, and youth organisation networks. Our aim is to uncover the expectations, experiences and valuations that these networks have regarding Spanish young people.

Participation in the education system

The 1995 Participation, Evaluation and Government of Educational Centers Act (LOPEG) regulates student participation in Spanish educational institutions. According to this Act, there are three mechanisms for student participation in school:

- The **School Council**, wherein student representatives are directly elected by their peers;
- The **Students' Delegates**, who are the elected representatives of each class group. All the Delegates of a centre alongside students who are member of the School Council constitute the **Delegates' Board**;
- The **Students' Associations,** which were created to increase the involvement of students in their own education, to learn to assume responsibilities, to practise decision-making processes and to develop democratic attitudes.

To summarise, young students in Spain (from 12 to 16 years old) have the following possibilities of participation in the education arena (see figure 8.1):

Furthermore, the 1995 Act also foresaw the existence of a National School Council. The competences of this Council are the general programme of education and all the basic norms and regulations in relation to education at a national level. The composition of this Council includes eight student representatives. There are also 12 parental representatives, 20 teacher representatives and some 40 other representatives from different constituencies.

Figure 8.1: Possibilities of participation in the education arena

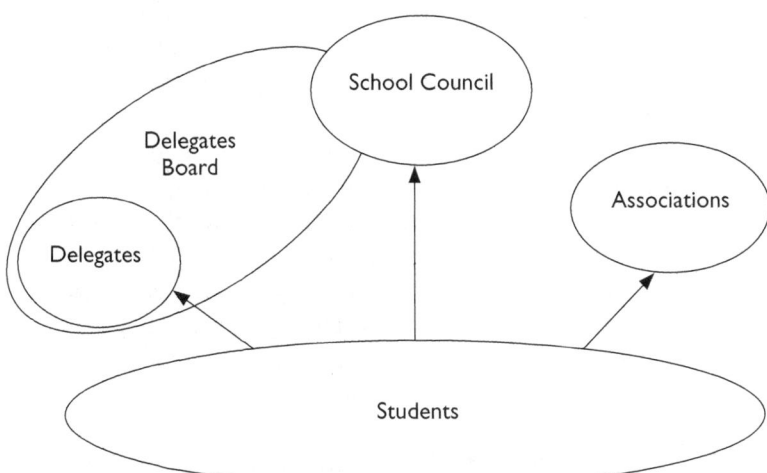

From the start of the contemporary democratic period, participatory methods were a condition of almost all reforms initiated as a means of dismissing the procedures of the dictatorship. This condition also applied to educational reform; therefore formal channels for children's participation were established early in the democratic period. However, the current question is: do children have real participation in school or is their participation rhetorical and tokenistic?

No specific studies inform of the level of young people's meaningful participation in the school. The available data refer to school programmes from 2000/01 to 2003/04 (Consejo Escolar del Estado, 2006). According to these data, student participation in the elections to School Councils on Secondary and Training Education runs at approximately 50%, with the highest point being in the academic year 2001/02 (57%); this relates to public education. Private schools (supported with public funds) report a higher level of participation: 70% above the average of the three years considered. Participation data from elementary school students was found to be higher, both in public and in private schools where the average percentage of participation of public education is 57% and private 77%. It should be noted that the student participation is much lower than that of teachers (more than 80% in public schools and 70% in private ones) but significantly higher than that of parents, which is less than 10%.

From the perspective of one student association represented in the National Council (CANAE, 2008) the causes for this low degree of participation can be explained thus:

- There is a clear deficiency in democratic practices, as the students do not exert a real influence in decision-making.
- The electoral process is flawed as it is not possible to hold assemblies to debate programs and proposals; additionally, there are few candidates for election.
- The School Council has become a place where people certify (some) previously adopted decisions. Students are not consulted; neither are their views they taken into account. Their position is weak as there is no parity with adult members. Students in general identify the Council with conflict and disciplinary matters. They only intervene when they are asked to, and feel that they are treated in a patronising manner.
- This is related to the absence of participation in the classroom. There are no interactive lessons conventional lessons only are provided, and all decisions are within the teachers' exclusive remit.
- The Students' Associations believe that the short period (one or two years) within which students can be active (due to the mobility of students or changes in level) makes continuity difficult if they have no support from the institution or from the relevant teachers. (CANAE, 2008)

These assessments reflect the powerlessness of children in general and the barriers they encounter when trying to participate on an equal basis and attempt to make use of their rights in Spanish society.

Juvenile associations

Spanish legislation considers 'juvenile associations' as those formed by people aged between 14 and 29 years old. In 1988 a Royal Decree regulated the registry of these associations. The statement of reasons from this legislation recognised that the previous (1977) regulations governing the registry of associations retained restrictive criteria of a tutelary nature. This was superseded by article 22 of the Spanish Constitution, which obliges associations to register for publicity and transparency purposes only. On the other hand, associations formed by people under the legal age (18 years) of adulthood could become part of the Spanish Youth Council (created in 1988). The Royal Decree emphasised that this opportunity should be seen from the most favourable point of view. Consequently it has been established that associations whose members were over 14 and under 30 years of age, who were not subject to a specific legal framework, must be registered as juvenile associations in the corresponding registry for the sole purpose of publicity. Likewise, those members of the association who belong to its governing body and are below the legal age may act within public administration to exercise the rights conferred to these associations by the legal and administrative order.

The scope of action of a juvenile association may be national or local. This circumstance conditions its registry in a national or autonomous (regional) registry. As each of the regional governments has competences to establish its registry of associations, as well as their own census and directories of juvenile associations established in the area, the available information is diverse and dispersed, making it difficult to establish an overall view of the number and composition of the juvenile associations in Spain[1]. This difficulty is compounded in attempting to ascertain the proportion of people under 18 in these associations. To further complicate this task the census includes institutions that provide services for youth, that is, institutions that work with children and young people without necessarily categorising their participation, the matter of interest to us.

The most common form of union or of joint work between juvenile associations in the same region is the creation of a Youth Council, either on a local, county, provincial, regional or national level. The Spanish Youth Council (Consejo de la Juventud de España (CJE)) is a platform of juvenile organisations legally established in 1983 and comprised of the Juvenile Youth Councils and other national youth organisations. The purpose of this Council is to promote juvenile participation in the political, social and cultural development of Spanish youth. Currently there are approximately 80 youth organisations involved in this joint project.

In 1997 this platform started to develop actions aimed at promoting children's participation. These actions were prompted by Spain's approval of the United Nations Convention on the Rights of the Child and the influence that this approval exerts over different Spanish public and private institutions. The constitution of a permanent working group, the instruction of trainers for the promotion and development of children's participation by means of the associations, and the publishing of guides or educational material (Consejo de la Juventud de España, 1999; Miguel and Bretones, 2008) were some of the actions carried out. At the same time the CJE took on board some of the aspirations of the youth population. Currently, for example, CJE has a document demanding a youth policy, featuring 10 key demands, amongst which is 'establishing the right to vote at the age of 16'. The notion of extending the voting age in this manner is virtually unknown amongst the general population in Spain.

Participation at a local level

In Spain policies for cultural, public entertainment and recreational activities fall under the remit of the Autonomous Communities. Apart from the National Act (Spanish Protection of Children Act, 1/1996) reference is made in the autonomous legislation on children's right to rest and have free time, to play and perform recreational activities, and to participate freely in the cultural life and the arts (Casas and Gaitán, 2008).

That sort of activity mentioned in the regulations, as well as the participation principles contained within the UN Convention on the Rights of the Child, appears to be the inspiration behind public policies implemented throughout the country by regional or local authorities. Plans for Childhood, Children's Councils, Youth Parliaments and so forth are widespread in many municipalities. A 2004 report explored the impact of these activities on the national level (UNICEF/UAM, 2004), finding that 1,605 among 8,108 Spanish municipalities had children's councils. In the municipalities with up to 20,000 inhabitants, the report found that 4–5% had a Plan and 21% had constituted Children's Councils.

In a report investigating children's social participation experiences Casas et al (2008) highlight the significant quantity of child participation programmes they managed to locate; this is interpreted as a sign of both awareness and interest on behalf of the authorities in this matter. The most significant volume among the programmes identified corresponds to those developed on a local level, from which we can deduce that the majority of actions being developed to promote participation takes place in contexts that are close to children and youth. However, many of the known programmes constitute isolated experiences and are not connected with each other, despite having, in many cases, common elements (Casas et al, 2008, pp 400–1).

In order to provide a brief overview of the main actions of support and promotion of child participation in the local sphere, we now focus on the most significant organisational structures existing at local level. Subsequently we will comment briefly on the performance and results of the most widespread programmes. Finally we will provide an approximation of children's views on the opportunities of participation they are offered and of those they are not.

With the advent of the first democratic City Councils in 1979, sectorial policies were re-configured to attend to the less favoured sectors of the population; Youth and Women Councils were created within this framework. The Convention on the Rights of the Child places the spotlight on the child as a subject of rights and stresses the policies that promote his or her autonomy. Until then, children were treated in the towns as pupils (Department of Education) or as individuals to protect (Social Services). Following a meeting of Mayors Defenders of Children, organised by UNICEF in 1996, and a subsequent meeting of municipalities, the child is now considered as a non-fragmented being and the need to create 'comprehensive plans' is taken into consideration for the joint action of several departments, as well as the creation of child areas in every City Council (Romero, 2003, p 63).

In 1997 the Local Network for the Rights of Children and Youth was constituted. This network has among its objectives promote the forms of Child Participation that respect the criteria of universality, representativeness, non-manipulation, being binding (as much as possible) and to treat young people as true protagonists and actors. The Network provides counselling, training, exchange of experiences and the possibility of networking together in projects in favour of children's' rights; the network is comprised of 24 municipalities.

The Spanish Federation of Municipalities and Provinces (Federación Española de Municipios y Provincias (FEMP)) was created voluntarily in January 1980 as an association of local institutions. It currently represents 7,287 City Councils, Provincial Councils, and Island Councils which speak for over 89% of Spanish local government. In its 1999 General Assembly the governing bodies of FEMP decided that the commitment of Local Institutions to their children was fundamental, and that the municipality is a key element for the promotion and protection of children's rights, considering that the administration and the local policy are an 'educational laboratory', a school of citizenship and democracy (Palacios, 2003, p 43). The FEMP promotes the development of comprehensive policies for children within the municipalities, the exchange of experiences and the participation in different areas of debate and training. The FEMP is also part of the National Observatory on Youth and collaborates with other institutions in subjects of awareness, dissemination of children's rights or training. FEMP also stresses its collaboration with UNICEF in the Child Friendly Cities programme.

The National Network of Educating Cities (Red Estatal de Ciudades Educadoras (RECE) is a movement created in Barcelona (Spain) in

1990, when a group of representatives of local governments raised the common objective of working together in projects and activities to improve the quality of life of the inhabitants. This revolves around people's active involvement in the use and development of the city itself; the city is not considered as educating children only, but all the inhabitants, children holding a special consideration therein. This network forms part of the International Association of Educating Cities which is active in 14 countries around the world, with 361 associated cities, of which 194 are located in Spain.

There is also the Platform of Organizations for Children (POI). This is an alliance of non-profit organisations, formed in 1997 to promote initiatives for advocacy, protection and promotion of the rights of children and young people. There are now 47 member institutions. Among its objectives POI includes 'to promote children's participation and association'.

Many of the programmes developed and implemented are inspired by UNICEF's Child Friendly Cities (CFC) strategy. Its Spanish application began in 1993 with the Mayors Defenders of Children initiative. Since 2000 however, an interdisciplinary and holistic approach has been adopted. The earlier version of the Child Friendly Cities initiative was redirected in 2011 into a programme that promotes the implementation of the CFC at municipal level and encourages mayors to promote children's rights. Activities undertaken include but are not restricted to:

- A biannual national competition for municipalities implementing municipal policies on child rights. There are now 54 cities with the Child Friendly Cities' Certificate (30% of the total Spanish population);
- A biannual contest for cities distinguishing themselves in different domains of child wellbeing best practices;
- Development of tools and manuals to contribute to the training of municipal partners (Belmonte, 2003; Becedóniz and Aranda, 2009; Aranda, 2009, 2010);
- A database of municipal activities, initiatives and publications for children.

Children and Youth participation is one of the selection criteria for certification in the annual competition on Child Friendly Cities. The creation of a children's council is the measure most commonly implemented by municipalities. In June 2010 the first inter-regional meeting of Municipal Councils of Child and Adolescent Participation took place. The children participants, aged between 10 and 17 years and coming from 17 municipal councils wrote a manifesto for children's participation (Manifesto de Avilés, 2010) deepening the meaning of Article 12 of the CRC from the point of view of children.

With reference to RECE (the Spanish educating cities network) any city that commits to the principles of the Charter of Educating Cities can pay the membership fee and join the International Association of Educating Cities (IAEC). There are regular meetings of national networks, and international congresses are held every two years. The Association has an International Documents Databank (BIDCE) and Thematic Networks whose purpose is to promote the exchange of ideas and good practices of members, working together around specific issues.

While the last congress of the Spanish network (RECE) held in 2011 was clearly directed at education and less to the children's participation[2], a recent publication of the thematic network Participation and Training of the Children and Youths of the Educating Cities (Malagón, 2011) goes beyond this framework. On the basis of the experiences gathered, they have established projects that cover the following areas:

- Civic education projects (in the school or outside the school sphere)
- Child and youth participation projects
- Projects of participation in the schools
- Project of participation outside the schools
- Projects of universal participation
- Projects of participation through representatives.

Likewise, this publication uses a theoretical framework based on a 'mediational' perspective. They understand that the actions promoted and/or performed by city councils to influence the types of relations that children and young people establish with society and society with them are 'social mediations'. They represent the relation between three systems: political, social and childhood, in the following way (see figure 8.2):

The Italian project *La cittá dei bambini* (The town of children) with Francesco Tonnucci as its core leader had also a significant influence in Spain. This action, which is based on the idea that children could be active and conscious elements for change in the future of the towns, aimed at changing town life through children's empowerment in the processes of knowing, planning, advising, discussing, deciding and finally acting. It is affected by 'a stress on the primacy of adult guidance, a cultural preference for education and the domination of a developmental theory approach' (Baraldi, 2003).

Figure 8.2: The relation between political, social and childhood

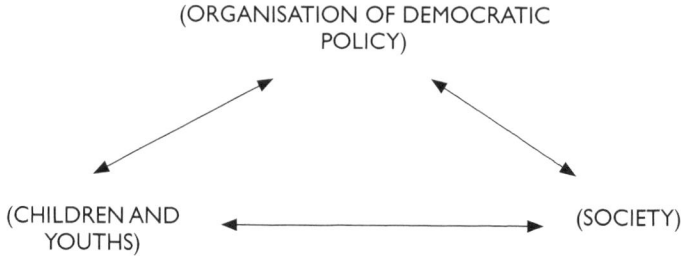

Source: Malagón, 2011, p 9

To conclude this section we will comment on children's views regarding the processes of participation designed for them. Although child consultations are frequently within the scope of local child participation policies in the majority of cases, they can be isolated actions, performed without scientific criteria and not very systematised.

Two recent studies by the Platform of Organizations for Children (Plataforma de Infancia, 2010a, 2010b) constitute an exception to this lack of systemised data; the input of young people who belong to the children's councils and other institutions has been systematised throughout the years of work in children's workshops, meetings and forums, regarding the proposals of the National Strategic Plan For Childhood and Adolescence (Plan Estratégico Nacional de Infancia y Adolescencia PENIA). The conclusions regarding participation can be summarised thus:

Information:

– That girls and boys have information about what their participation is requested.

Opinion:

– It is necessary for adults to learn to communicate with young people. Information campaigns and training on child participation for adults is required.
– Young people need to be taught to participate and encouraged to express themselves.
– Areas designated for self-organization need to be ensured, and children and youth participation needs to be grouped according to age.

Decision-Making:

- Establish the right to vote.
- Participation in the proposing and formulation of rules and laws around education and school life.
- Proposals made by young people require mechanisms that ensure that these proposals reach decision makers.

Organization:

- The creation of mini-town-councils of children and young people.
- Creation of child and youth representative in town councils.
- To create social spaces wherein young people can participate, Such sites must be accessible and comfortable for young people.

(Plataforma de Infancia, 2010a, pp 34–5; Plataforma de Infancia, 2010b, p 66)

A general view

Considering the foregone, it is obvious that children's' and youth participation does not lack support in Spain; in public policies or in NGOs. Does this mean that young people really participate in social life? It is not easy to answer this question. The existing spaces of participation are very limited for these young populations. There is an absence of solid quantifiable data with information on the different projects functioning located throughout the country; the number of young people and children involved is also unknown. A systematic evaluation of the programmes implemented is required, by applying the criteria of relevance, effectiveness, efficiency, sustainability and impact, to the opinions and demands of girls and boys (Plataforma de Infancia, 2010a, p 9).

Another question regarding children and youth: are they satisfied with their participation in the public sphere? In general, the children and young persons involved in participatory projects declare that it has been a good experience for them. The more serious and effective the project is, the more they feel that they are important for the community, and the consciousness of their rights increases; this encourages them to consider it fair to defend new spaces for participation. Although the young people and children believe that regulating participation is not enough to ensure its continuance, they consider that it is necessary to do so. They also hold the view that formal channels have to be combined with attention to spontaneous initiatives from children and young people. This is because they believe that:

> Adults have a perspective about the world very different than the one we have, we know that we have not the same words neither understand as much as you, but we also know that we have a perspective and we want it to be listened to, we have some feelings and some ideas and we want to share them. (Intervention of a girl in a seminar with adults on children's participation, VV. AA., 2004)

In new childhood studies and among the advocates of children's rights, it is common to criticise the way adults organise children's participation. If we believe that the former ways of participation (*to play to participate*) are obsolete, and the adults' formal democratic models are out of place, we have to attend to the new forms of participative democracy and the ways in which children's own feelings on participation are close to or far from these new forms of participation.

The strategies to extend children's participation rights cannot leave any pathway unexplored. None of the different forms of participation should be excluded. Among the existing participation mechanisms, the school councils presents us with a paradox: the hierarchical and formalised relationships between students and teachers made it easier to organise a system of democratic student representation and organisation (Wyness, 2005, p 16) but the difference in power benefited adults and makes a genuine participation of the children and young people difficult. Locally based councils occupy a different space, they exist outside of child control structures and participation is voluntary (although frequently induced by parents). The difficulty here is the political instrumentation of some of them, where the children are but *decorative objects* to demonstrate good intentions, and the lack of continuity of these projects, either due to changes in the policies, or because the participating children pass from an age of *childhood* to an age of *adolescence* or youth where similar activities are not facilitated.

Regarding other alternatives in line with participative democracy let us turn to citizenship and social movements. The very idea of citizenship as a condition that belongs to the people born and resident in a national state is changing and reaching into wider arenas where people are integrated within social relations. It is important for children and young people to be included in this conceptualisation. Cockburn, quoting Young, argues: 'no persons, actions or attributes of persons should be excluded from public discussion and decision-making, although the self-determination of privacy must nevertheless remain' (Young in Cockburn, 2005, p 23).

These current movements for participative democracy have not included children and young people; at least not yet. The reason is simple: as adult movements they share the same mistrust with regard to the capacity of children to think and in consequence to act regarding public matters. Therefore, children have not changed from their position of *becoming human beings* to achieving the status of full *human beings* (Qvortrup, 1994). It is not considered credible that children and young people can and do organise themselves; when they do so, there is a suspicion that they are being manipulated. That is related to the constraints to children's rights, and brings us again to the issue of a citizenship that is acquired and recognised only when the person reaches 18 years. The elimination of any form of discrimination based on age will not only allow children to vote, if they wish to do so, but it will also tear down the barriers that obstruct their participation in broader fields of the social life (Gaitán, 2008).

Notes

[1] As an example, it can be mentioned that, in Navarre, there are 118 youth clubs, to which 15,000 young people between 14 and 30 belong, as reported in a guide published in 2010, 14% of the total population aged 14–30. Activities developed are recreational (24%), cultural (22%) and walkers (11%).

[2] See http://ciudadeseducadoras.ciudadalcala.org/

References

Aranda, G. (ed) (2009) *Bases para un debate sobre participación infantil en el ámbito local* (Bases for a debate on child participation in the local level), Madrid: UNICEF Comité Español.

Aranda, G. (ed) (2010) *Guía para el desarrollo de planes de infancia y adolescencia en los gobiernos locales* (Guide for developing plans for children and young people in local governments), Madrid: UNICEF Comité Español.

Baraldi, C. (2003) 'Planning childhood: children's social participation in the town of adults', in P. Christensen and M. O'Brien (eds) *Children in the city*, London: Routledge Falmer.

Becedóniz, C., Aranda, G. (2009) *Pongamos a la infancia en la agenda política local. Manual básico para responsables políticos municipales* (Take children in the local political agenda. Basic manual for municipal policy makers), Madrid: UNICEF Comité Español.

Belmonte, C. (2003) (ed) *Una ciudad para los niños: políticas sociales de infancia* (A city for children: childhood's social policies), Toledo: UNICEF, Save the Children, Junta Comunidades Castilla-La Mancha, Universidad de Castilla-La Mancha.

CANAE, www.canae.org. Consulted in 2008.

Casas, F. and Gaitán, L. (2008) 'Spain', in *The Greenwood encyclopedia of children's issues. Worldwide*, Westport: Greenwood Press.

Casas, F., González, M., Montserrat, C., Navarro, D., Malo, S., Figuer, C. and Bertran, I. (2008) *Informe sobre experiencias de participación social efectiva de niños, niñas y adolescentes* (Report on effective social participation experiences of children and young), Madrid: Ministerio de Educación, Política Social y Deporte.

Cockburn, T. (2005) 'Children as participative citizens', *Journal of Social Sciences*, Special Issue, no 9, pp 21–9.

Consejo de la Juventud de España (1999) *Participando que es gerundio* (Participating, it does mean participating), Madrid: Consejo de la Juventud.

Consejo Escolar del Estado (2006) 'La participación en las elecciones a Consejos Escolares de Centro' (Participation in the Elections for School Boards), *Participación Educativa*, no 1, pp 15–17.

Gaitán, L. (2008) 'El ejercicio del voto en el marco de los derechos de la infancia' (The voting in the context of children's rights), *Revista de Estudios de Juventud*, no 85, Documento 5, pp 1–18. www.injuve.es/contenidos.downloadatt.action?id=597163635

Malagón, J. (2011) *Guía para el diseño y ejecución de proyectos de participación y capacitación cívica de la infancia y la adolescencia* (Guide for the design and implementation of participation projects and civic training of children and young people), Madrid: Ayuntamiento de Rivas Vaciamadrid. www.rivasciudad.es/portal/RecursosWeb/DOCUMENTOS/1/0_2307_1.pdf

Manifesto de Avilés (2010) *Manifiesto de Avilés por la Participación Infantil y Adolescente.* pdf. Observatorio de la Infancia de Asturias. www.observatoriodelainfanciadeasturias.es/foromunicipal/2011/01/manifiesto-de-aviles-por-la-participacion-infantil-y-adolescente/

Miguel, D. and Bretones, X. (2008) *Confancia: Con voz. 6 años de trabajo infantil en organizaciones juveniles,* (*Confancia:* With voice. 6 years working for children in youth organisations), Madrid: Consejo de la Juventud.

Palacios, D. (2003) 'Ciudad e Infancia. La Federación Española de Municipios y Provincias' (City and Childhood. Spanish Federation of Municipalities and Provinces), in Belmonte, C. (ed) *Una ciudad para los niños: políticas locales de infancia* (A city for children: childhood's social policies), Toledo: UNICEF, Save the Children, Junta Comunidades Castilla-La Mancha, Universidad de Castilla-La Mancha.

Plataforma de Infancia (2010a) *Sistematización de propuestas de niños, niñas y adolescentes en relación al PENIA* (Systematization of the proposals made by children and young people concerning to *PENIA*), Madrid: Plataforma de Organizaciones de Infancia.

Plataforma de Infancia (2010b) *Reinventando el PENIA. Soluciones creativas a la Política de Infancia* (Reinventing *PENIA*. Creative solutions for Children Policy), Madrid: Plataforma de Organizaciones de Infancia.

Qvortrup, J. (1994) 'Childhood Matters: an Introduction', in J. Qvortrup et al., *Childhood matters*, Avebury: Aldershot.

Romero, M. P. (2003) 'Red Local a favor de los derechos de la Infancia y la adolescencia' (Local Network for the Rights of Children and Youth), in Belmonte, C. (ed) *Una ciudad para los niños: políticas locales de infancia* (A city for children: childhood's social policies), Toledo: UNICEF, Save the Children, Junta Comunidades Castilla-La Mancha, Universidad de Castilla-La Mancha.

UNICEF/UAM (2004) *Guía de buenas prácticas sobre Planes y Consejos de Infancia en el ámbito municipal español* (Guide on good practices on Plans and Children's Councils at the municipal level in Spain), Madrid: UNICEF.

VV. AA. (2004) *III Encuentro La ciudad de los niños. ¿Qué ciudades? ¿Qué niños?* (III Meeting the City of Children. What City? What Children?), Madrid: Acción Educativa.

Wyness, M. (2005) 'Regulating participation: the possibilities and limits of children and young people's councils', *Journal of Social Sciences*, Special Issue no 9, pp 7–18.

Part Three

Extending spaces of participation

Interplay of youth culture, Web 2.0 and political participation in Europe: new reflections after the 'youth quake' in Northern Africa and the Middle East

Morena Cuconato and Natalia Waechter

Introduction

On the two shores of the Mediterranean Sea young people are actively engaged in creating or re-thinking *democracy*. On the southern shore they are risking their lives fighting to achieve it for the first time. On the northern coast they are defending it as the government ignores democratic rules, placing both freedom and equality in jeopardy. Despite social, political and cultural differences, in both regions young people are using the same methods for communicating their unease, for organising protest and for mobilising themselves by utilising the Web 2.0 for acting out their vision of the world through youth culture.

New Internet-based communication offers both the tools to facilitate a pervasive diffusion of youth culture and an arena in which young people can find free space to renegotiate and as a result reinvent their individual and collective identity as independent social, cultural and political actors. Through the Internet young people can find own lifestyles, combining cultural artifacts (cut-paste-mix) to assert their generational difference from the parental culture (Stevenson, 2001). Moreover, youth and the culture they produce no longer represent a regional or national phenomenon but a transnational experience, expressing universal networks of communication, information-sharing, teenage consumerism and identity politics. As the Internet bridges distance and language barriers, young people around the world now possess the potential to link up in collaborative online discussions and projects, using the Web 2.0 for political and social engagement.

The recent Arab youth's rebellion offers a valuable insight into new forms of online participation, alongside the role of youth culture, for political participation. In the following chapter we commence our reflection with a discussion on the relation of Web 2.0, politics and participation. We summarise the current scientific debate on the advantages and hopes as well as on the disadvantages and fears that are related to civic online participation. Following this, we present some findings from our Up2Youth project[1] and discuss *how* youth culture may be considered participative. Finally, we analyse the elements of online participation and youth cultural participation throughout the Arab Spring; questioning the media label of a 'Facebook revolution'. We conclude with some reflections on a possible new meaning of young people's participation north and south of the Mediterranean Sea, inside and outside of Europe, in the second decade of the new millennium.

Web 2.0 and political participation

In democracies throughout Europe and the world, young people seem to be more and more disconnected from conventional political modes of expression, yet at the same time there are impressive signs of young people's civic engagement in non-governmental areas, including community volunteer work, high levels of consumer activism, and strong involvement in social causes from the environment to economic injustice in local and global arenas (Lopez et al, 2006). Research has shown that the Internet has been used by young people especially for political participation, as demonstrated by the Seattle protests in 1999; however, it is predominantly used for political reasons by young people who are already engaged in politics (see Chapter 10). Furthermore, there is little evidence that the Internet could give access to major social power to the marginalised groups, who are the most involved in the digital divide, regarding those nations, groups and individuals lacking material and cognitive resources to take advantage of digital technologies. Otherwise 'politics as usual' may be altered by them, modifying the balance of resources among political institutions, reducing the costs of gathering information and communicating messages in favour of smaller and fringe groups. These minority groups and their realities have difficulties being heard through the conventional channels of traditional mass media, but are able to achieve through the Internet's flexibility, skills and innovative capacity to produce new coalitions able of arising interventions and critical engagement around specific events locally, nationally and internationally. Now, with the recent global success of the Web 2.0, the digital world permits young people to network even more easily on contingent problems and to rapidly view the effects of their action, creating a virtual circle between action and engagement.

The growing trend of civic engagement in online social networking, blogging and live journalism obliges social scientists to consider these forms of shared online activity (from blogging to conflict and protest behaviour on gaming, fan and entertainment sites) as new forms of political engagement (Coleman, 2008). The Internet is becoming a space of micro-spheres, its character is public and self-established, and at the same time it represents fundamental elements of media and politics (Häyhtiö and Rinne, 2007, p 3). Online participation shows a quantitative and qualitative improvement and is more and more interlinked with offline forms of participation. At the same time the Internet has been colonised by mainstream media, making it more difficult to distinguish between politics and leisure, as it is evident on Facebook, YouTube, Twitter and MySpace. These new Web 2.0 applications are primarily used for private networking and self-display (Subrahmanyam et al, 2008), but owing to the large number of young people's personal networks on such sites, and the semi-public character they seem to have, they could convert into a powerful tool of political mobilisation and protest, as shown by the Arabic revolution. At the moment there is still no empirically grounded answer to the question of *how* and *how much* this new way of youth participation can contribute to the development of a common aim or lead to a further segmentation of political engagement, satisfied by clicking on an online petition sent by a friend or by a friend of a friend (Rasmussen, 2007; Vatrapu et al, 2008).

Over the past ten years innovative forms of communicative design, such as blogs, wikis and social networking portals have emerged as central elements of the *net*, becoming quite widespread among young people, and often producing a mixture of personal and political expressive forms. Characteristics are the subjective affirmation (first person utterance, expression of emotions, vivacity of the exchanges), the opening of the expertise carried by individuals or by various collectives (more factual information, verifications) and new forms of discussion (commented information, collective dimension of the argumentation), often connected with techno-activist forms aiming not only at democratic self-expression and networking, but also at global media critique and journalistic socio-political intervention (Kahn and Kellner, 2004).

Concerning the connection of blogging and politics, in France the debates on the European Constitution project before the referendum in 2005 were strongly anchored in this new form of public space. Moreover, by offering a lot of details about the events in the French suburbs, the blogs represented a very important tool of expression and communication for the young inhabitants of deprived areas during the urban riots in November 2005. In its turn, the information delivered in these blogs was commented upon by the traditional media.

Growing from only a handful a few years ago, today most teenagers and young adults across Europe use *social networking sites* (SNS) such as Facebook and MySpace, or more local sites such as StudiVZ in the German speaking area for interconnecting with their peers, exchanging gossip and information, self-presenting, staying in touch with people from the past, and for keeping in contact when going abroad (Waechter et al, 2011; Subrahmanyam et al, 2008). Whereas young people have used blogs for sharing and discussing political content or for making personal diaries public, social networking sites seem to be used mainly for private not public concerns. Recent research on social networking sites has, above all, focused on identity development (e.g. Neumann-Braun and Autenrieth, 2011; Subrahmanyam et al, 2008), on cyber mobbing (e.g. Grimm et al, 2008) and data security (e.g. Goetzenbrucker, 2010; Reading, 2009). SNS were treated as important for the young people's individual development but so far, research has not seen their capacity for mobilising a sizeable proportion of the (young) population for political reasons, as there is evidence for today from the Middle East and Northern Africa. However, is it appropriate to call it a 'Facebook revolution'? Facebook, like cell phones, the Internet, and Twitter, do not have agency, a moral universe, and are not predisposed to any particular ideological or political orientation. They are what people make of them.

In general and beyond any form of determinism and rhetoric, the contribution of ICT to the creation of spaces for participation and deliberation, and to the development of new expressions of democratic citizenship is not due to the technological development alone. It should be seen as the possible result of the interactions between technology and society and at the same time, of the social construction of technology that up to now has produced a two-faced phenomenon: ICT as instrument of freedom and as an instrument of control (Rodotà, 1997), producing inclusion and exclusion.

There is currently a growing corpus of literature[2] that considers the Internet as a new arena for political participation, yet at the same time there are researchers for whom the Internet doesn't in itself reflect a fundamentally new age of political participation, only a powerful medium that people will use to fit traditional political behaviours (see Chapter 10; Jensen, 2006). Bimber et al (2005) affirm that the Internet could produce 'accelerated pluralism', modifying the structure of political power while still not giving rise to a new era of democracy (cf. Aydemir, 2007; Brlek and Turnšek, 2007).

Classifying the current literature permits us to highlight three different attitudes towards tackling this question:

- The *pessimistic* claim that the Internet reinforces the voices of the powerful, strengthening inequality for those nations, groups and individuals lacking the resources and motivation to take advantage of the new structure of opportunities (Freschi, 2009). Considering the global diffusion of new media, Norris (2001) came to the conclusion that the diffusion patterns of the Internet in various regions of the world closely reflected those of old media, but the recent Northern Africa and Middle East revolutions, where the Internet use is supposedly rare in comparison with the northern hemisphere, have introduced new inputs to scholarly and political reflections, contradicting Norris's statement yet paradoxically confirming that the Net strengthens the position of young people, who deployed high-value social and cultural capital, evidenced by the organisation and employment of well-educated Egyptians and Tunisian students.
- The *optimistic* (or hyperbolic and unrealistic) claim that the Internet transforms governance as we know it and restores former levels of mass political participation (Hacker and van Dijk 2000; Lusoli and Ward 2006; Owen 2006). It provides new forms of horizontal and vertical communication, facilitates social engagement and enriches deliberative democracy thanks to the ICT's interactive and potentially widely accessible environment where *representatives* and *represented* can get in touch without mediation. Such technologies are expected to contribute to the constantly changing nature of the communicative relations between political elites and constituencies.
- The *sceptical* claim that the Internet reflects 'politics as usual. The *interactivity*, breaking down the *one-to-many* communication model of the traditional mass media and making 'multidirectional communication' possible should have been the truly revolutionary aspect of this new medium (McMillan, 2002, p 165). However, as Castells pointed out, *neither* citizens, *nor* politicians take as much advantage of it as they could, therefore 'the Internet cannot provide a technological fix to the crisis of democracy' (Castells, 2001, p 156).

The recent online mobilisation of young people in Northern Africa and the Middle East has caused us to carefully re-think these three positions mentioned above, and to include the resulting analysis in this discussion.

Youth culture and political participation

Contemporary youth culture activities are infrequently perceived and studied in connection with political participation, whereas in the 1970s, youth culture was viewed as subversive and countercultural. Researchers (Schwendter, 1973) used the term 'subculture' to define it, pointing out that youth culture participants were different from general society in respect to attitudes, values and behaviours. In the 1990s a new approach replaced the concept of subculture: youth cultures were defined 'youth scenes'; they were regarded as being flexible, fun-oriented, short-lived, non-political, and non-rebellious (Muggleton, 2005; Ferchhoff, 2007). Even though there are scholars today who emphasise the explicit and implicit political agency of youth cultural activities (Stauber, 2001; Waechter, 2011) and others who criticise the strong focus on music and style (Shildrick and MacDonald, 2006), youth culture remains portrayed as rather disconnected from ideology and politics. In the public opinion, even youth cultural activists, who declare themselves explicitly politics-oriented, are treated not as political participants but rather as troublemakers. The young people's focus on topics and issues corresponding with institutional and traditional politics does not lead to their recognition as political actors (as squatters deal with gentrification, housing shortages, or as anti-globalisation activists criticise the financial system, capitalism, exploitation of the Third World).

In the project Up2Youth; Youth – Actor of Social Change' (funded by the European framework programme 6) we approached the concept of *participation* from different perspectives which all had in common to broaden and question the existing definitions and understanding of participation by considering young people as actors. In our understanding young people are not only affected by social structures but in turn, their agency also affects the structure. Regarding young people's *political* participation we focused on online participation as well as on youth culture. The findings of the Up2Youth project reveal that on the one hand late political movements such as the no-global enfold, a (youth) cultural activity, while on the other hand youth cultures themselves, assume in many respects a participatory aspect (use/appropriation of public space, shaping of imageries by symbolic policies, identity politics) (Pohl et al, 2007). Empirical case studies conducted in five European countries (Austria, France, Ireland, Italy, Slovakia) brought to life different forms of participation, which may appear at the margins or even in contradiction to institutional types. In addition to the explicitly politics-oriented youth cultural scenes, we analysed also youth cultures which to the casual observer are apparently just sports-, style- or fun-oriented and found that they employ 'life style politics' (Roth and Rucht, 2000), expressing political attitude through *agency*. Skateboarders who do not even share the same political beliefs combine through their common goals and their public, subversive activities. On the one hand, they connect with each other in order to gain more power in demanding the construction of a skate park or for fighting laws and restrictions against street skating (Waechter, 2011). On the other hand, above all street skaters, criticise capitalism and oppressive institutional architecture (Borden, 2011), question the ownership and rules of public space and negotiate its use by making it their "playground". In this sense, their activities may be considered intrinsic participatory.

Regarding explicitly politics-oriented youth culture, we have analysed *squatters* and alternative *media activists*. Though they are often concerned with major themes of traditional politics such as economics, housing, environmental and ethical questions, their activities are not regarded as participatory but as a danger to the existing political system. While squatters also question *who* the public space belongs to and *how* it may be used, they are concerned not only about themselves but often provide services for disadvantaged societal groups. We concluded that young people engaged in youth cultures have to be regarded as *social actors* in order to achieve a better understanding of the political meaning of youth cultures and a new, broader approach to contemporary political participation.

Social media, youth culture, and their impact on the rebellions in Northern Africa and the Middle East

The latest occurrences in the Middle East and Northern Africa can be considered a proof of the potential that youth cultures have as 'tools' for political expression and participation. As riots and protests spread throughout Tunisia, a Facebook sensation arose through a video entitled 'President, Your People Are Dying', performed by 22-year-old Hamada Ben Amor (also known as El Général). In the clip, the rapper accuses (now former) President Ben Ali for having produced the unemployment and hunger that is tormenting the country while he and his family move money abroad. The feelings of resentment about poverty, police brutality and government ills were so perfectly captured in this song that a few days later it was sung in Tahrir Square by Egyptian young people protesting against Mubarak; thereafter it was adopted by Yemen's protesting young people. This is not the first political youth protest powered by hip-hop: marginalised young people across Europe have always used hip-hop to express their unhappiness and difficulties with the political system, the (host) society and living conditions. The civil unrest in Paris in 2005 was foretold by the music of Muslim rappers in France, who had been openly speaking about racism and xenophobia in the country for more than a decade. *Hip-hop* and *rap music* were created as voices from the oppressed and although they have also been accepted and incorporated into mainstream culture during the past decades, their subversive potential has not been extinguished. Even though they seem to have lost their rebellious character, this does not mean that this rebelliousness cannot be easily reactivated. The Middle East and Northern Africa events demonstrated that hip-hop cannot only be used for self-expression, but also for mobilising the (young) masses. Youth culture seems to be a perfect tool for reaching the young population, especially when distributed through new social media such as Facebook or YouTube. We conclude that it was too early to proclaim the death of political and ideological oriented youth cultures. They are not some relict from the 1970s and '80s (indeed small sub-cultural scenes such as *punks* or *skinheads* are still alive) but still have the potential to take a leading role in a whole generation's protest.

The recent Arab revolution shows that new technology has brought an extension of the aims of participation, broadening their territorial spectrum and enabling coordination and political influence on a transnational scale. Half of the population of the Arab countries is less than 30 years old and seems to prefer the freedom that comes with democracy to political autocracy or the rule by religious conservatives.[3] All of the recent revolts against poverty, oppression and corruption on the southern shore of the Mediterranean Sea have been started by young men and women: many of them have not been activist prior to the 'Arab Spring' but all of them are active in using modern tools such as social networking sites and texting over mobile phones.

Suddenly they started using these tools to organise and amplify their apparently new emerged political protests. Apparently new, because not so long ago these young people were called the 'lost generation'. Much the same as European young people, they have been largely regarded as being uninterested in politics and unwilling to participate. For three decades Middle Eastern political and social scientists have been describing Arab young people as frustrated, disliking and distrusting their authoritarian rulers, but unable to press for change. According to this narrative, the only outlet for youthful dissent was offered by Islamic extremism, but surprisingly young people started asking for the right to choose and change their leaders, for the opportunity for employment and for social improvement.

Nevertheless, even if social media did play a leading role in driving the uprising in Tunisia and especially in Egypt, the idea of a 'Twitter revolution' or 'Facebook revolt' as spread through the media worldwide sounds hyperbolic: undoubtedly it was people who were arrested or killed on the street and it was people who fought against corrupt and authoritarian leaders.

The Facebook group 'We are All Khaled Said', founded to commemorate the violent death of a young man at the hands of the Egyptian police, assisted greatly in catalysing the protests. Prior to Said's murder there were blogs and YouTube videos on the subject of police torture, but these blogs and videos had not yet energised strong communal identity or protestation. The Facebook-based 'April 6 Youth Movement' also helped to bring people out protesting. Meanwhile, Twitter was a constant source of news from Egypt for people around the world. Thus far it seems that online social networks contributed to the cause of the protesters as an *organising tool*, as a *news source* and as a *public arena* for building a community of like-minded activists. Critically reflecting on these three functions of ICT in the Arab Spring we find that:

- As *organising tool*: social media played a powerful role in mobilising protesters onto the streets and coordinating demonstrations. The theory of *social-media-for-social-change* seems to have held true in Egypt. In Tunisia, Twitter helped a great deal in coordinating protests simultaneously in numerous cities across the country. In Egypt, the two Facebook groups mentioned earlier, the immense 'Khaled Said' (152,485 'friends') and the little 'April 6 Youth Movement' (6,625 'friends') were very active in organising the initial protests and motivating their users to demonstrate. As we have seen in Egypt, Tunisia, Yemen and elsewhere, social media can certainly be used as a mechanism for the organisation and mobilisation of would-be protesters. As soon as the Egyptian government denied access to the Internet by shutting it down, the protests gathered more momentum, suggesting that these tools are not essential; at least once protests have begun.
- As a *news source*: the idea of social media as a global source for news is easily subject to media hyperbole. It is certainly captivating to

follow what is happening on the street second-by-second. Yet this is insufficient to know what is really going on: only the power of 'independent' traditional media can reconstruct and cover the framework of events, a role performed by Al Jazeera on this occasion. On the other hand, when there is – as in Tunisia – a suppression of free press, Twitter, Facebook, YouTube and other local social media sites become essential in getting news out of the country, and mainstream media has come to depend on citizens reporting for their own coverage. We know that in some cases global awareness may protect protesters from their own government, but in others – as the Libyan case demonstrates – it does not.

- As a *public sphere* for building a community of like-minded activists: this idea that over time activists can use social media and the broader online public space to discuss and construct a shared perspective, and to connect with a like-minded subject is grounded in long-term public sphere theory (Bohmann and Roberts, 2004). This new generation of social actors in Egypt found their voice and built significant parts of their movement on Facebook. Before using Facebook to bring people on to the streets, the activists used it to articulate their political critique and to build a constituency and community around those ideas; a community which has grown up over years.

Conclusions

The recent 'youth quake' in Northern Africa and the Middle East demonstrates that we should not underestimate the political potential of the younger generation as well as that of youth culture but, at the same time, we should not overestimate the potential of social media for attracting young people into political activism. We support the sceptical claim that the Internet will be used for political participation but will not necessarily fix crises of democracy. It is a helpful apparatus, especially when employed by young people for mobilisation. However, it is just a tool and not the driving force – the driving force is the youth being fed up with their life circumstances and the governments responsible for these circumstances.

The rebellious youth attitude shows clearly that young people's participation cannot be expected to meekly follow the traditional forms of political participation provided by the older generations and government authorities. Similar to the Up2Youth project findings, which showed that young people may prefer non-traditional or even illegal practices of participation, the rebellious young people in Northern Africa and the Middle East had to put aside traditional methods of political participation. They are now being criminalised and hunted for their desire to establish a democratic system. But at this point the same question that we encountered during our research in Europe remains unanswered: Can the highly charged online North African and Middle Eastern youth movements evolve into a continuing and stable force, or are they capable of only single-event eruptions to the ultimate advantage of more structured groups?

Postscript: Since we started writing this chapter, Western Europe has experienced an outburst of youth riots in two countries, Spain (centred in Madrid) and England (centred in London). These two events differ in protest procedure. The Spanish young people have adopted the recent North African and Middle Eastern approach; embarking on a series of anti-establishment demonstrations included tactics such as Twitter calls-to-action and setting up of Tent City in Madrid's central square, thereby following the example of their Egyptians coevals in Tahrir Square. In England young people have reacted violently to the murder of Mark Duggan, a 29-year-old man who was shot dead on 4 August 2011 by police attempting to arrest him in Tottenham. In any case these suddenly outbursts represent the last straws following long years of social tension, as happened in the 2005 French suburban riots.

The two countries share a high rate of youth unemployment, especially in the regions and districts where the riots started, and also share among young people a widespread feeling of neglect from politics and exclusion from society. Without the opportunity to participate in the labour market and consumerism, youth is not able to participate in traditional politics. On the one hand, their anger about their exclusion has led to non-democratic rebellion; on the other hand, they were prevented from any other means of political participation as participation in mainstream society's institutions is predicated on participation within the democratic political system.

The riots in Western Europe and the Arab revolution both reflect youth's anger at being excluded. In both regions they used the Web 2.0 to mobilise their peers, to connect and to organise their political protest. When a British Web 2.0 provider announced an intention to provide data of potential rioters to the police, (young) hackers threatened, successfully, to harm his system.

To fully explain and analyse the differences and similarities of the Western and the Arab rebellions, other than the use of the Web 2.0 and the basic motivations for these protests, we can now see a need to conduct empirical research with these rioting young people.

Notes

[1] Up2Youth.Youth – Actor of Social Change is an international research project implemented in 2006–09. The project was conducted by the international research network EGRIS, International Group for Integrated Social Research and primarily funded by the European Union's Sixth Framework Programme. Project website: http://www.up2youth.org/.

[2] In this respect see the detailed analysis of the existing literature on this topic delivered by *Project CIVICWEB – D4 Report: Young People, the Internet and Civic Participation: State of the Art Report*, Institute of Education, London: University of London, 2007.

[3] The Annual ASDA'A Burson-Marsteller Arab Youth Survey focuses on the political, financial and social needs of the region's youth. Its second edition reports the opinions of 2,000 young people through face-to-face interviews in nine nations and highlights that the single most important priority for young people in the region is living in a democratic country, followed by infrastructure and access to the best universities. On line version: http://www.arabyouthsurvey.com/2009/downloads/highlights2009.pdf.

References

Asda'a Burson-Marsteller (2010) *Second Annual ASDA'A Burson-Marsteller Arab Youth Survey*, online version: www.arabyouthsurvey.com/downloads/highlights2009.pdf

Aydemir A. T. (2007) 'Young People, Politics and the Internet' in Institute of Education, (ed) *Young People, the Internet and Civic Participation: State of the Art Report*, online version: www.civicweb.eu/images/stories/reports/civicweb%20wp5% 20final.pdf

Bimber, B., Flanagin, A. J. and Stohl, C. (2005) 'Reconceptualizing collective action in the contemporary media environment', *Communication Theory*, no 15, pp 365–88.

Bohman, J. and Roberts, J. M. (2004) 'Expanding dialogue: the Internet, the public sphere and prospects for transnational democracy', in N. Crossley (ed) *After Habermas: New Perspectives on the Public Sphere*, Oxford: Blackwell.

Bontempi, M. and Pocaterra, R. (2007) *I figli del disincanto. Giovani e partecipazione politica in Europa* (The children of disenchantment. Young people and political participation in Europe), Milano: Bruno Mondadori.

Borden, I. (2001) *Skateboarding, Space and the City. Architecture and the Body*, Oxford and New York: Berg.

Brlek A. S. S.,Turnšek M. (2007) 'Activism and the Internet', in Institute of Education (ed): *Young People, the Internet and Civic Participation: State of the Art Report*, online version: www.civicweb.eu/images/stories/reports/civicweb%20wp5%20final.pdf

Castells, M. (2001) *The Internet Galaxy: Reflections on the Internet, Business, and Society*, Oxford: Oxford University Press.

Coleman, S. (2008) 'From Big Brother to Big Brother: two faces of interactive engagement', in P. Dahlgren (ed) *Young Citizens and New Media: Learning and Democratic Engagement*, New York: Routledge.

De Rosa, R. (2007) 'Weblog e processi di formazione dell'opinione pubblica' (Weblog and building processes of public opinion), in *Comunicazione Politica*, vol 8, no 2, pp 75–91.

Ferchhoff, W. (2006) 'Jugendkulturen im 21. Jahrhundert' (Youth Cultures in the 21st Century), *Deutsche Jugend,* vol 45, no 3, pp 124–33.

Ferchhoff, W. (2007) *Jugend und Jugendkulturen im 21. Jahrhundert. Lebensformen und Lebensstile* (Youth and Youth Cultures in the 21st Century. Ways of Life and Life Styles), Wiesbaden: VS Verlag für Sozialwissenschaften.

Freschi, A. C. (eds) (2009) *E-democracy. Il caso della policy italiana: Primo rapporto di ricerca sui progetti della seconda fase del Piano nazionale di e-government* (E-democracy. The case of Italian policy. First report on the projects of the second step of the e-government National Plan).

Götzenbrucker, G. (2010) 'Beyond Impression. Riskante Formen der Selbstpräsentation auf Sozialen Netzwerkseiten am Beispiel von StudiVZ' (Beyond Impression. Risky ways of self-presentation on social networking sites by the example of StudiVZ), in J. Fuhse and C. Stegbauer (eds) *Kultur und mediale Kommunikation in sozialen Netzwerken* (Culture and Media Communication in Social Network), Wiesbaden: VS Verlag.

Grimm, P., Rhein, S. et al (2008) *Gewalt im Web 2.0. Der Umgang Jugendlicher mit gewalthaltigen Inhalten und Cyber-Mobbing sowie die rechtliche Einordnung der Problematik* (Violence in the Web 2.0. How young people handle violent content and cyber mobbing as well as how understand the legal context), Berlin: Vista.

Hacker, K. L. and van Dijk, J. (eds) (2000) *Digital Democracy. Issues of Theory and Practice*, London: Sage Publications.

Häyhtiö, T. and Rinne, J. (2007) 'Little Brother is watching. Reflexive civic watch through ICTs', paper presented at the ICS Symposium *Changing Politics through Digital Networks*, Firenze, October 5–6.

Hill, K. and Hughes, J. (1998) *Cyberpolitics: Citizen Activism in the Age of the Internet*, New York: Rowman and Littlefield.

Jensen, J. L. (2006) 'The Minnesota E-democracy project: Mobilising the mobilised?', in S. Oates, D. M. Owen, and R. K. Gibson (eds) (2006) *The Internet and Politics: Citizens, Voters and Activists*, London: Routledge.

Kahn, R. and Kellner, D. (2004) 'New media and Internet activism: from the "Battle to Seattle" to blogging', *New Media and Society*, no 6, pp 87–95.

Katz, J. and Rice, R. E. (2002) *Social Consequences of Internet Use. Access, Involvement, and Interaction*, Cambridge: MIT Press.

Lopez, M. H., Levine, P., Both, D., Kiesa, A., Kirby, E. and Marcelo, K. (2006) *The 2006 Civic and Political Health of the Nation: A Detailed Look at How Youth Participate in Politics and Communities*, CIRCLE, online version: www.civicyouth.org/PopUps/2006_CPHS_Report_update.pdf

Lusoli W. and Ward S. (2006), 'Hunting protestors: mobilization, participation and protest on line in the Countryside Alliance', in S. Oates, D. M. Owen, and R. K. Gibson, *The Internet and Politics: Citizens, Voters and Activists*, New York: Routledge, pp 52-71.

McMillan, S. J. (2002) 'Exploring models of interactivity from multiple research traditions: users, documents, and system', in L. A. Lievrouw and S. Livingstone (eds) *Handbook of New Media: Social Shaping and Consequences of ICTs*, London: Sage, pp 163–82.

Muggleton, D. (2005) 'From classlessness to clubculture: a genealogy of post-war British youth cultural analysis', *Young*, vol 13, no 2, pp 205–19.

Murdock, G. and Golding, P. (2004) 'Dismantling the digital divide. rethinking the dynamics of participation and exclusion', in A. Calabrese and C. Sparks (eds) *Toward a Political Economy of Culture. Capitalism and Communication in the Twenty-First Century*, Boulder: Rowman and Littlefield, pp 244–60.

Neumann-Braun, K. and Autenrieth, U. P. (eds) (2011) *Freundschaft und Gemeinschaft im Social Web. Bildbezogenes Handeln und Peergroup-Kommunikation auf Facebook and Co.* (Friendship and Community in the Social Web. Screen-related agency and peer-group communication on Facebook and Co), Baden-Baden: Nomos.

Norris, P. (2001) *Digital Divide: Civic Engagement, Information Poverty, and the Internet Worldwide*, Cambridge: Cambridge University Press.

Oates, S., Owen, D. M. and Gibson, R. K. (2006) *The Internet and Politics: Citizens, Voters and Activists*, New York: Routledge.

Owen D (2006) 'The Internet and youth civic engagement in the United States', in S. Oates, D. M. Owen, and R. K. Gibson, *The Internet and Politics: Citizens, Voters and Activists*, New York: Routledge, pp 17-33

Pohl, A., Stauber, B., and Walther, A. (2007) *Youth – Actor of Social Change. Theoretical Reflections of Young People's Agency in Comparative Perspective*, Interim Report (D12) of the FP7-project Up2Youth.

Project CIVICWEB – D4 (2007) *Report: Young People, the Internet and Civic Participation: State of the Art Report*, London: Institute of Education, University of London.

Rasmussen, T. (2007) 'Two Faces of the Public Sphere. The Significance of Internet Communication in Public Deliberation', paper presented at the ICS Symposium *Changing Politics through Digital Networks*, Florence, October 5–6.

Reading, A. (2009) 'The Playful Panopticon? Ethics and the Coded Self in Social Networking Sites', in K. Nyiri (ed) *Engagement and Exposure. Mobile Communication and Ethics of Social Networking*, Wien: Passagen Verlag, pp 93–101.

Rodotà, S. (1997) *Tecnopolitica. La democrazia e le nuove tecnologie della comunicazione* (Technopolitics. Democracy and new communication technologies), Roma-Bari: Laterza.

Roth, R. and Rucht, D. (eds) (2000) *Jugendkulturen, Politik und Protest: vom Widerstand zum Kommerz?* (Youth Cultures, Politics, and Protest: From Resistance to Commerce?), Opladen: Leske & Budrich.

Sartori, L. (2006) *Il divario digitale. Internet e le nuove disuguaglianze sociali* (The digital divide. The Internet and the new social inequalities), Bologna: Il Mulino.

Schwendter, R. (1973) *Theorie der Subkultur* (The Theory of Subculture), Köln: Kiepenheuer and Witsch.

Shildrick, T. and MacDonald, R. (2006) 'In defence of subculture: young people, leisure, and social divisions', *Journal of Youth Studies*, vol 9, no 2, pp 125–40.

Stauber, B. (2001) 'Junge Frauen und Männer in Jugendkulturen – gewandelte Bedeutungen in der späten Moderne und Konsequenzen für die Jugendforschung' (Young Women and Men in Youth Cultures – The change of meanings in late modernity and the consequences for youth research), *Deutsche Jugend*, vol 49, no 2, pp 62–70.

Stevenson, N. (ed) (2001) *Culture and Citizenship*, London: Sage Publications.

Subrahmanyam, K., Reich, S., Waechter, N. and Espinoza, G. (2008) 'Online and offline social networks: use of social networking sites by emerging adults', in K. Subrahmanyam and P. M. Greenfield (eds) *Journal of Applied Development Psychology, Social Networking on the Internet – Developmental Implications*, vol 29, no 6, pp 420–33.

Vatrapu, R., Robertson, S., Dissanayake, W. and Jeedigunta, A. (2008) 'Are Political Weblogs Public Spheres or Partisan Spheres? A Virtual Ethnographic Study of Online Participations and Implications for Civic Participation in the Internet Age', paper presented at DEMO-net research workshop *Empowerment and e-Participation in Civil Society: Local, National and International Implications*, Örebro University, Sweden, May 9–10.

Waechter, N. (2011) 'Partizipation und Jugendkultur. Zum Widerstandscharakter von Jugendlichen am Beispiel von SkateboarderInnen und HausbesetzerInnen' (Participation and Youth Culture. About the resistance of young people using the example of Skate boarder and squatter), in A. Pohl, A. Walther, et al (eds) *Jugend als Akteurin Sozialen Wandels. Übergänge in Arbeit, Elternschaft, Citizenship* (Youth as actor of social change. transitions to work, parenthood and citizenship), Weinheim and München: Juventa, pp 263–86.

Waechter, N., Triebswetter, K., et al (2011) 'Vernetzte Jugend online: Social Network Sites und ihre Nutzung in Österreich' (Linked youth online. Social networking sites and how they are used in Austria), in. K. Neumann-Braun and U. Autenrieth (eds) *Freundschaft und Gemeinschaft im Social Web. Bildbezogenes Handeln und Peergroup-Kommunikation auf Facebook und Co* (Friendship and Community in the Social Web. Screen-related agency and peer-group communication on Facebook and Co), Baden–Baden: Nomos, pp 55-78

Young people and online civic participation: key findings from a pan-European research project

Shakuntala Banaji and David Buckingham

Introduction

Over the past two decades, there has been widespread concern across Europe and in many other industrialised countries about an apparent decline in civic and political participation. Commentators point to long-term reductions in voting rates, declining levels of trust in politicians and waning interest in civic affairs; and these phenomena are frequently seen as evidence of a broader crisis in democracy (e.g. Putnam, 2000; Scheufele and Nisbet, 2002; Gibson et al, 2003; Galston, 2004). These issues are generally seen to be most apparent among the young: it is often asserted that young people are increasingly apathetic and reluctant to exercise their civic responsibilities. In this context, some have looked to the Internet as a means of re-engaging young people. The Internet is seen to have greater appeal and relevance for young people than 'older' means of civic participation; and to have the potential for creating new, networked forms of communication and democratic political culture (Bennett, 2003; Lenhart et al, 2004; Coleman, 2005, 2008; Kann et al, 2007). These possibilities have been addressed by growing numbers of researchers in recent years (e.g. Bachen et al, 2008; Bennett, 2008; Bennett et al, 2009; Dahlgren, 2007; Loader, 2007; Gerodimos, 2008).

The CivicWeb project

In this chapter, we present some key findings from a pan-European research project that attempted to put some of these arguments to the test. CivicWeb was a three-year research project funded under the European Commission's Framework 6 programme for targeted socioeconomic research (2006–09). It set out to analyse the potential contribution of the Internet to promoting civic engagement and participation among young people aged 15–25. It focused specifically on the range of youth-oriented civic sites created by organisations, interest groups and individuals, ranging from small-scale, local initiatives to national and international projects.

The research used both quantitative and qualitative methods, and focused on three key dimensions of this new online civic sphere:

- the nature and characteristics of such sites, in terms of their content and formal features (design, mode of address, structure), and the extent to which they invite active participation among their users;
- the production of the sites, including the motivations, working practices and economic models of the producers;
- the uses and interpretations made of such sites by different social groups of young people, and the relationship between this online activity and their civic participation 'offline'.

In framing our research, we adopted a deliberately broad and open conception of 'civic participation'. The kinds of sites and activities we examined included:

- initiatives on the part of government (including the EU) or political parties (for example via their youth 'wings') to secure greater civic participation;
- those based on 'single-issue' campaigns (e.g. around globalisation, discrimination, opposition to hunting, homelessness);
- more open forums, in which young people from particular social groups (disabled people, refugees, gays and lesbians) come together to define and debate their own agenda of issues;
- sites promoting social activity or participation based on religious beliefs;
- those encouraging volunteering and social or political activism;
- those designed for specific minority ethnic communities or geographically isolated groups;
- sites addressing areas that might be seen as problematic, such as political violence or xenophobic hatred.

We explored how the civic potential of the Internet varies across the different political cultures of seven European member states or applicant nations: Hungary, the Netherlands, Slovenia, Spain, Sweden, Turkey and the UK. The partner countries each represented very different cultural and political histories, different political systems and different relationships with the EU.

Our research therefore addressed several pressing questions: Can the Internet in fact deliver on this promise of re-engaging young people in the public sphere, and of creating new forms of political and civic culture among young people? How far does participation online result in greater participation offline? Are some kinds of young people more likely to respond to such invitations than others? Are some groups more likely to stay within more traditional forms of civic participation, or to resist them altogether? What are the obstacles to such new media initiatives? How far does the model of 'networked citizenship' actually correspond to the everyday practices and motivations of the majority of young people? And how do these developments vary across the different political cultures of European member states? This chapter presents a brief overview of our responses to these questions.

Methods

Our approach involved several distinct but overlapping forms of investigation, which were described in a series of reports as the research proceeded (see www.civicweb.eu). We began by reviewing existing research, and then mapping the field of young people's online civic culture. Our study at this point was largely descriptive: we selected and classified approximately fifty civic/political websites and thirty youth-specific sites in each country, making a total of 560 sites. These were categorised in terms of their topic, stated purpose and aims, use of applications, layout, interactivity, network features and mode of address, as well as their pedagogic approach and ideological outlook. We then went on to develop in-depth case studies of a range of civic websites (just under 50 in total), examining interconnections between the pedagogy, design, mode of address, ideological stance and aims of the site. Overlapping with the survey of websites and the case studies were in-depth interviews with producers of civic websites in each partner country (n=85). For these more detailed case studies, we sampled sites and producers from a range of organisations and contexts, from national and local governmental bodies and large NGOs through to 'grassroots' youth activists.

Finally, in considering the users or potential users of these sites, we conducted a broad survey alongside in-depth qualitative analysis. We used an online questionnaire with over 3,300 participants in the seven participating countries, to gather basic quantitative data about young people's uses of the Internet, and the extent to which they were engaging in civic activities both online and offline. This was followed by a series of in-depth focus group interviews with young people: around 10–12 such groups were convened in each country, covering a range of demographic groups, and involving young people who were civically active and inactive, Internet-savvy and excluded. These groups enabled us to explore young people's online practices within different sociocultural contexts; their motivations for political and/or civic engagement, and how the Internet helped them to pursue their interests in this field; their responses to civic content online; and the role of civic/political education.

Towards empowerment?

In general, our research supports the view that young people feel alienated or disconnected from traditional forms of politics. Most of the focus group respondents across all our national samples said they saw politicians as corrupt, boring or hard to understand, only working for their own interests, and far removed from the everyday needs and realities of common citizens. A large proportion of respondents felt that things needed to change – and they spoke at length about issues such as inequalities, corruption, lack of housing and job opportunities, high prices, religious, ethnic or regional discrimination, police harassment of civil protest, and government censorship of the media. However, they generally felt that they themselves were unable to change these things. This perceived lack of efficacy was related both to their general feelings about the unresponsiveness, untrustworthiness and distance of politicians and to actual experiences of having participated (for example, in schools councils, e-petitions or demonstrations), and of not having been listened to or not managing to change anything. In some instances, it also related to fears about how active participation or political critique might impact on them as individuals and make them targets of the state, the police or other aggressive citizens with opposing views.

For many of the web producers whom we interviewed, this perceived lack of efficacy was the central problem. The rhetoric of 'youth empowerment' and 'youth voice' was particularly prominent here. These discourses typically see young people as lacking a voice, or at least the skills to make their voice heard: when they are given a voice online, it is argued, they will be empowered to express their own concerns in a safe environment, and this can then be transferred offline to provide them with greater control of their own lives. While some producers saw this as a more or less spontaneous consequence of gaining access to the technology, many working within more activist and/or charitable organisations felt that there should be more opportunities and training for young people, to help them develop the skills necessary for making their voices heard in the public sphere. Ironically, however, many of them were aware that their users tended to be mostly those youth who were already engaged or skilled in civic participation. The challenge for all concerned was to find ways of reaching 'hard to reach' and disadvantaged young people, those most at risk of exclusion from civil society and politics. Those with most experience of working with such young people had found that the Internet was not in fact a particularly good means of doing this: they argued that traditional offline approaches such as via youth workers and local youth groups are still the main means of contact for economically and socially disadvantaged young people.

These perceptions were reinforced by the findings of our research with young people. Unsurprisingly, we found that social factors such as class, ethnicity, age and religion significantly affected the ways in which they approached and used the Internet. In our survey, the interest in civic and political websites appeared to be stronger among older respondents (19- to 25-year-olds rather than 15- to 18-year-olds), those not living with their parents, those who identified themselves as religious, and girls and young women. This contradicts some commonly held perceptions, for instance that girls and young women are less motivated to participate politically than boys and young men. However, the factor showing most clear patterns in relation to Internet use and civic participation across most of the countries was that of socioeconomic class. There was evidence here of a continuing digital divide along socioeconomic lines, both in the quality and level of access to technology, and in the extent of civic engagement.

Perhaps unsurprisingly, the Internet appeared to be an important tool for young people who were already engaged in civic or political activities offline. In focus groups with young people who were active in global or local political, religious or identity-based groups, the Internet was consistently presented as a major 'hub' for political activities. This appeared to be the case for groups as diverse as political parties' youth organisations, various kinds of established activist networks and communities of civic interest. The Internet was also an important resource for minorities – political, sexual, ethnic, regional or religious – and, in some notable instances, seemed to offer young people from such communities a space to question and explore identity, to challenge traditional views, to discuss the meaning of culture and citizenship, and to debate methods of participation and protest (Bognar and Szakács, 2010).

However, it is important not to homogenise the content and loci of the discussions that do take place online. The respondents to our survey were overwhelmingly interested in websites on entertainment and lifestyle issues: only a fairly small proportion (around 10%) reported having visited civic or political sites. However, this does not necessarily mean that they have not participated in civic discussions online: we found some evidence that such discussions (between people of all ages) may be found within the forums of entertainment and social networking sites of various kinds (Farrelly, 2008). Furthermore, not all young people who are civically active offline participate in such discussions online; and the ones who do participate most often may do so sporadically.

Using the Internet

The Internet seems to be regarded by a number of civic and political organisations as an inexpensive and effective method of disseminating information and making contact with young people. However, our research suggests that this is by no means always the case. Several producers pointed out that for a site to be known there needs to be considerable thought given to marketing and publicity, both online and offline. Most civic website producers have neither the time nor the money to publicise their sites adequately and hence the core of users remains relatively small. Indeed, a majority of the websites surveyed across the project functioned with a combination of one or two part-time paid employees and several voluntary staff. Others went for months without being updated, because initial grants only funded the building of the site and not its maintenance, which is crucial to success. We found that there was a high turnover of volunteer staff at many of the civic websites surveyed which sometimes led to the stagnation or closure of a site.

Despite the availability of more or less interactive applications such as blogs, wikis, message boards, forums, video uploading, podcasts and so on, static websites composed primarily of written text and a few visual images still appear to be the norm. Out of potentially ten interactive applications, most youth civic websites in our larger survey offered only an average of 2.5 (and this included photographic content and embedded YouTube videos). The possibility for young people to post their own content or question content on the sites was rare; although since 2009 such sites are increasingly including social bookmarking buttons. However, the issue of interactivity on youth civic sites is not straightforward. Some funders appear to think that complex and more expensive sites are automatically 'better' than their simpler counterparts. However, our interviews suggested that offering interactive facilities does not automatically mean that young people participate. We found several instances of websites that have forums, user content upload facilities and message boards, especially on general themes relating to European or more global issues, that were under-utilised or full of spam.

Claims about the Internet being a completely safe and equal space for participation were also challenged by responses from producers and users. Several producers were aware that dealing with controversial issues of social justice could provoke strong and negative responses from some members of the public. Some young people described being 'attacked' online, a phenomenon that was particularly apparent with sites concerned with sexuality and, in the case of Sweden, gender. In the Netherlands and the UK most notably, young first- and second-generation immigrants are forming civic organisations online to challenge prejudice both within and outside their communities. Many of them are subjected to fierce and sometimes racist critique and flaming, often by organised right-wing groups online. In Hungary, we found Roma sites that were attempting to avoid this situation by having closed membership or censoring posts from racist users (Bognar and Szakács, 2010).

As this implies, the use of forums and other interactive applications has to be carefully explained, encouraged, motivated and managed. Young people are sometimes disappointed by the lack of possibilities for giving comments or interacting online; but they can equally be intimidated by what they view as a 'requirement' to contribute original content. The skills for using applications such as RSS feeds, videocasts or podcasts have to be taught, rather than being taken for granted; and specialised jargon has to be avoided or explained. This again requires planning, time and money for personnel that most youth civic organisations surveyed simply do not have. As a result, several of the producers we interviewed felt it was better to offer a clear, helpful but static site with the possibility for emailing the organisation than to offer potentially off-putting or even dangerous opportunities for 'interaction'.

For producers of political and civic websites, our research therefore suggests that much more thought needs to go into how they spend their money. Significant amounts of funding are sometimes allocated to website design – and especially to interactive features – without a clear conception of their function. While such features might conceivably make the organisation look good for their funders, a large and complex site is not necessarily better for users. As some of the young people in our research suggested, it was important that sites were 'fit to purpose'. This meant looking beyond the latest gimmicks and beyond some politically correct sense that an organisation lives or dies by its website.

Motivating civic and political participation

It is often argued that amusing and entertaining young people (on the Internet as well as elsewhere) is the best way to attract their attention and thence encourage them to become engaged in civic initiatives. However, we found few cases of attractive website design or the latest interactive features motivating civic engagement and participation in themselves. For the participants in our focus groups, civic and political engagement tended to focus predominantly on issues of immediate proximity to their everyday lives (Gerodimos, 2008, 2009): individual and group identities and local experiences are key. Thus, civic and political interests are related, in a number of cases, to having a family and/or close community of relatives or friends that is interested in the same issues and concerns.

A further key issue here is the sense of efficacy. In a number of cases, local civic achievements, the experience of being active together and of group solidarity, the feeling of having organised an event or campaign which received positive feedback from peers or older adults generates a sense of efficacy that encourages and motivates further participation. On the other hand, the results of offline active citizenship were frequently and emphatically called into doubt by young people who had experienced governments' failure to respond, for example when they had demonstrated in large numbers against rising university tuition fees and for better housing provision, or against the war in Iraq. Yet while such seemingly 'unsuccessful' protests might sap the motivation to participate, for some the resulting anger led to further participation. In most of our focus groups, when young people were involved in civic activities that were related to their immediate contexts (both on- and off-line) they seemed to feel more confident in their capacity to bring about change.

From young people's perspectives, civic participation often appears to be most successful when it is *both* peer-to-peer *and* enables opportunities for reciprocal engagement with those in power (Coleman, 2008). Most youth civic organisations tend to offer one or the other, and the engagement with politicians is most often not reciprocal. This can be seen as a disincentive for young people to engage with formal politics online – as one young woman in our focus groups put it, 'why should we speak if no-one is listening?' However, in the context of our cross-national study, this aspect took on a different form in different countries. For example, in both Hungary and Slovenia the sphere of politics is generally seen as dirty and corrupt, and civic organisations often work hard to detach themselves from politics. This means, ironically perhaps, that voting is not generally encouraged by youth civic sites in these countries, and that even party sites attempt to steer clear of connections with politics.

By contrast, most of the civic or political participation and engagement, in particular sustained engagement, described and identified across our focus groups appeared to begin and end offline in real communities or communities of interest and identity, even if the Internet has provided a space, a tool, or a focal point for aspects of this engagement. Of course, some civic sites may be set up as a short-term solution to a problem rather than being integrated into other activities – for instance to prevent the demolition of a skate-park or to gather support for a neighbourhood campaign. Such sites are often not heavily used over an extended period of time, unlike ones that have more diffuse motivations such as the coming together of a community of young people who are linked by common bonds. In line with this, websites formed by 'specialist' groups (based on religious, cultural or subcultural identity or locality), aimed at a very specific audience amongst young people and produced by members of that specific group, or particularly by young members, tend to support a stronger sense of belonging and community and are more likely to be used.

Saliently, a majority of civic website producers in our sample did not see the Internet civic sphere as a replacement for offline civic and political actions, but as a complement to them. For many, engagement still begins and ends offline, with the Internet sustaining and contributing to this. The notion that online civic action and offline civic action reside in separate realms with separate participants was much debated, yet was ultimately regarded by many as untenable. Many of the producers we interviewed were at pains to connect online and offline politics and civic action explicitly, suggesting that they were never quite convinced about the status of actions that took place solely online.

Nevertheless, signing online petitions, or forwarding letters to big corporations – termed 'one click activism' by one producer and 'feel good activism' by another – are not necessarily seen as the be-all and end-all of the things that young people are motivated to do online. Most civic producers view the information gathering necessary for making up one's mind about a particular cause or the meeting up, discussion and protest offline as being supported and enhanced rather than replaced by the online actions offered in polls or forums. This is confirmed by focus group discussions with young people who connected their offline and online participation, and who saw the Internet as feeding into offline organisation in the areas of formal politics, music, environmentalism or other campaigning. As this implies, offline civic-based or politically sympathetic friendships and comradeship can be strengthened and complemented online.

Conclusion: new politics online?

Despite these points, we emphatically do not wish to suggest that there is nothing new in the forms of political and civic engagement that are taking place online. On the contrary, there is evidence that civic websites for young people are tapping into newer forms of participation. This is perhaps most apparent in the case of so-called 'ethical consumption' or socially conscious shopping – which obviously plays on the Internet's qualities as a medium of shopping and marketing *par excellence*. Questions remain, however, about whether and how such activities are linked to traditional or more activist forms of political participation (Banaji and Buckingham, 2009). We have found further interesting exceptions, where the Internet did seem to make a clear difference to individuals or groups of young people in terms of engagement with a wider civic and political sphere. For example, in a number of our partner countries, the Internet was used by groups of young people as an alternative to mainstream media, and a means of accessing perspectives and information not found in traditional press or broadcasting. Although, here again, there is a question of how this relates to action, the significance of having a freer flow of information and a less rigid hierarchy in terms of who can express and broadcast political ideas online should not be downplayed. In countries where the authorities have begun to censor and regulate the online sphere – such as Turkey – the loss of this freedom highlights its importance still further.

We have also found evidence that the Internet can enable young people to take on and refine their role as monitorial citizens – for instance, by tracking elections, keeping abreast of privacy issues, discussing, photographing and publicising police behaviour, debating civil liberties and getting behind the scenes in conflict situations. In special cases such as file-sharing and the free downloading of music – as with the Swedish 'Pirate Party' (Miegel and Olsson, 2008) – the Internet itself can be the focus of and reason for civic action. Significantly, young people who take part in such civic actions are not always those who are already active in civic or political campaigns offline.

Our research was designed in the age of what is now commonly known as Web 1.0, with a general idea of the world wide web as a matter of individual or linked sites that would be put up largely by organisations, groups or campaigns. Since then, more interactive and 'social' networks have emerged. While we can certainly be sceptical about an overly celebratory and decontextualised view of the possibilities of 'Web 2.0', it is clear that instant messaging and social networking sites like Facebook and Twitter, as well as Wikis and other kinds of 'social software' do represent a significant addition to face-to-face activism, and offer different possibilities for participation. This has certainly been evident in North Africa and the Middle East in the opening months of 2011; although here too, we would caution against any simplistic technological determinism – these uprisings were no more 'caused' by Twitter or Facebook than it was MTV that brought down the Berlin Wall (Morozov, 2011).

Finally, there is a danger here also of assuming that participation is always a good thing in itself – that it is necessarily better than non-participation, and that young people are somehow automatically at fault if they choose not to participate (Coleman, 2005, 2008). Yet if we consider some of the more confrontational and abusive ways in which people interact online, and how governments and corporations censor expression and invade people's privacy – and the offline consequences of these things – can we really be so sure (Banaji, 2008)? There may be some very well-founded reasons for non-participation; and more generally, it is important to avoid normative assumptions here about what responsible young people *should* be doing. In light of this, perhaps the fundamental question that informed our research – and the wider debate in this area – needs to be rephrased. It is not so much a matter of whether the Internet can re-engage young people, or enable them to participate when they were not participating before. Rather, it is a question of how the Internet might engage with other movements within society, or how those other movements might use technology, to bring about egalitarian, anti-authoritarian change. It becomes a question not about technology, but about social and cultural processes.

Acknowledgements

The research discussed in this article was made possible by funding from the European Commission, under the Framework 6 programme. We would like to thank the website producers in our seven countries who participated in our research and also the young people whose insights and input made the research so interesting. The overall findings discussed in this paper are the collective work of our seven teams in the UK, the Netherlands, Slovenia, Hungary, Spain, Turkey and Sweden. All the reports referred to are available for download from www.civicweb.eu.

References

Bachen, C., Raphael, C., Lynn, K. M., McKee, K. and Philippi, J. (2008) 'Civic engagement, pedagogy, and information technology on web sites for youth', *Political Communication*, vol 25, no 3, pp 290–310.

Banaji, S. (2008) 'The trouble with civic: a snapshot of young people's civic and political engagements in twenty-first century democracies', *Journal of Youth Studies*, vol 11, no 5, pp 543–60.

Banaji, S. and Buckingham, D. (2009) 'The civic sell: young people, the Internet and ethical consumption', *Information, Communication and Society*, vol 12, no 6, pp 1–27.

Bennett, W. (2003) 'New media power: the Internet and global activism', in N. Couldry and J. Curran (eds) *Contesting Media Power: Alternative Media in a Networked World*, Lanham Md.: Rowman & Littlefield Publishers Inc, pp 17–36.

Bennett, L. W. (ed) (2008) *Civic Life Online: Learning How Digital Media Can Engage Youth*, Cambridge, MA: MIT Press.

Bennett, L. W., Wells C. and Freelon, D. G. (2009) *Communicating Citizenship Online: Models of Civic Learning in the Youth Web Sphere*, Report for the *Civic learning online project*, Centre for Communication and Civic Engagement. Available at www.engagedyouth.org/blog/wp-content/uploads/2009/02/communicatingcitizeshiponlinecloreport.pdf (accessed August 2009)

Bognar, E. and Szakács, J. (2010) 'Making Sense of Zhoriben: The Story of a Romani Social Networking Site in Hungary', *International Journal of Learning and Media*, Winter, vol 2, no 1, pp 67–80.

Coleman, S. (with Rowe, C.) (2005) *Remixing Citizenship: Democracy and Young People's Use of the Internet*, London: The Carnegie Trust Young People's Initiative.

Coleman, S. (2008) 'Doing it for themselves: management versus autonomy in youth e-citizenship' in L. W. Bennett (ed) *Civic Life Online: Learning How Digital Media Can Engage Youth*, Cambridge: MA: MIT Press, pp 189–206.

Dahlgren, P. (ed) (2007) *Young Citizens and New Media: Learning Democratic Participation*, London: Routledge.

Fairlie, R. (2006) *Crossing the Digital Divide: Immigrant Youth and Digital Disparity*. Santa Cruz: Centre for Justice, Tolerance and Community, University of California, Santa Cruz, www.ctjsc.edu/docs/esdigital.pdf (accessed: October 2008).

Farrelly, G. (2008) Does Rotten Tomatoes Spoil Users? Examining the Effects of Social Media Features on Participatory Culture. In *Stream: Culture, politics, technology / A graduate journal of communication*. Online at: http://journals.sfu.ca/cpt/index.php/stream/article/viewFile/13/11. Last accessed 26.4.2012.

Galston, W. A. (2004) 'Civic education and political participation', *PSonline, The Journal of the American Political Science Association*.

Gerodimos, R. (2008) 'Mobilising young citizens in the UK: a content analysis of youth and issue websites', *Information, Communication & Society*, vol 11, no 7, pp 964–88.

Gerodimos, R. (2009) 'New media, new citizens: youth attitudes towards online civic engagement', in *Proceedings of the websci'09: society on-line*, 18–20 March 2009, Athens, Greece.

Gibson, R., Nixon, P. and Ward, S. (eds) (2003) *Political Parties and the Internet*, London: Routledge.

Kann, M., Berry, J., Gant, C. and Zager, P. (2007) 'The Internet and youth political participation', *First Monday*, vol 12, no 8, accessed at: www.firstmonday.org (30 August 2009).

Lenhart, A., Fallows, D. and Horrigan, J. (2004) 'Content creation online. The Pew Internet and American Life Project', www.pewInternet.org/pdfs/PIP_Content_Creation_Report.pdf (accessed 1 August 2008).

Loader, B. (ed) (2007) *Young Citizens in the Digital Age,* London: Routledge.

Miegel, F. and Olsson, T. (2008) 'From pirates to politicians: the story of the Swedish file sharers who became a political party', *Democracy, Journalism and Technology: New Developments in an Enlarged Europe*, pp 203–15.

Montgomery, K. et al (2004) *Youth as E-citizens: Engaging the Digital Generation. Executive summary*, Center for Social Media. American University www.centerforsocialmedia.org/ecitizens/execsum.pdf (accessed: October 2008).

Morozov, E. (2011) *The Net Delusion: How Not to Liberate the World?*, London: Allen Lane.

Olsson, T. (2007) 'An indispensible resource: the Internet and young civic engagement', in P. Dahlgren (ed) *Young Citizens and New Media: Learning for Democratic Participation*, London: Routledge, pp 187–204.

Putnam, R. D. (2000) *Bowling Alone: The Collapse and Revival of American Community*, New York: Simon & Schuster.

Scheufele, D. and Nisbet, M. (2002) 'Being a citizen online: new opportunities and dead ends', *Press/Politics*, vol 7, no 3, pp 55–75.

Warschauer, M. (2003) *Technology and Social Inclusion*, Cambridge, MA: MIT Press.

Westheimer, J. and Kahne, J. (2004) 'Educating the good citizen: political choices and pedagogic goals' in PSOnline at www.democraticdialogue.com/DDpdfs/WestheimerKahnePS.pdf (accessed 3 August 2009).

ELEVEN

Young people and mental health: when ICT becomes a tool of participation in public health in Finland

Camilla Granholm

Introduction

Owing to increased use of information and communication technologies (ICT), concepts such as health, wellness and participation in life have gained a new and wider meaning. The Internet and mobile devices provide access to virtual opportunities for information seeking, real-time interaction, relationship building and collaborative involvement. This chapter supports research (Zimmerman, 1995; Christensen et al, 2011) suggesting that (community) participation has a positive effect on psychological empowerment. Psychological empowerment is defined as a mechanism that gives individuals greater mastery and control of their lives (Perkins and Zimmerman, 1995).

Participation is defined as taking personal action in issues that concern one's own wellbeing; it also include a social dimension of a striving towards the common good (Anttiroiko, 2003). The concept of participation in this text is very closely related to the concept of social support. Social support has been defined as an exchange of knowledge, emotional or evaluative support. Social support is mediated in social networks and relationships through human interaction (Heaney and Israel, 1997). The online participation described in this chapter includes the mentioned features of social support. The participation is in fact sharing information and knowledge, sharing experiences and offering emotional support.

The aim of this chapter is to give an insight in how participation through ICT and particularly the Internet can and is used for maintaining and promoting mental wellbeing by young people in Finland by providing an overview of recent research and literature describing the current situation in Finland. The focus is on university students; they are a group of young people that have been socialised into using this new technology since the early days of the Internet. Another reason for concentrating on this specific group of young adults is because of the interesting literature and research available.

These Finnish university students have their own national healthcare system: the Finnish Student Health Service (FSHS). This service provides general, mental and oral healthcare for undergraduate students of universities and other institutions of higher education. To ensure quality of service the employees at FSHS continuously carry out research. Research is conducted on topics directly connected to medicine and healthcare and also on related topics such as the students' mental wellbeing and students' electronic communication with healthcare professionals (http://www.yths.fi/en).

The chapter consists of five sections. The first section gives a short general overview of ICT use among these young adults and is based on recent statistics. In the following two sections questions on mental health among young adults in Finland are examined. These give a brief overview on recent research concerning university students' mental health issues and e-health in Finland. In the fourth section the Nyyti Student Support Centre (www.nyyti.fi) and its virtual services will be used to example how the Internet can serve both as a channel for support seeking and as a mechanism for participating in giving support to peers in need. The chapter concludes with a summarising discussion and suggestions on how ICT could, in the future, be utilised to an even greater extent.

Finnish youth and young adults on the Internet

For young people and young adults the Internet has become a natural part of everyday life. Young people in Finland spend a lot of time hanging out in virtual spaces. Information and communication technologies are primarily used to keep in touch with friends but also for sharing thoughts, ideas and supporting peers in anonymous arenas, or for finding information on available services such as healthcare. Studies show that Finns and especially young people in Finland are frequent users of the Internet. The most recent statistics describing the situation (spring 2010) show that 76% of all Finns aged 16–24 use the Internet several times a day. Among the age group 25–34 the percentage is two points higher (Tieto- ja viestintätekniikan käyttö –tutkimus, 2010, Statistics Finland).

The most popular categories of Internet use for young Finns aged between 16 and 34 are e-mail and reading online newspapers, or following the web pages of TV channels. Additionally, the Internet is frequently used for searching for information about products and services, and for banking. Over 80% of young people aged 16–24 and 76% of the young adults aged 25–34 are registered users of some social media site (such as Twitter or Facebook). Among the younger age group 67% are daily users of social media; the figure drops slightly among the elder age group to 60% (Tieto- ja viestintätekniikan käyttö –tutkimus, 2010, Statistics Finland).

Young people also use the Internet in searching for health, illness and diet information. Almost two thirds of young people aged 16 to 24, and nearly three quarters of the Finnish population aged 25 to 34, use the Internet for this purpose. Eighty-six per cent of all Finns aged 16 to 34 employ the Internet to search for information and for learning and increasing knowledge (Tieto- ja viestintätekniikan käyttö –tutkimus, 2010, Statistics Finland).

Mental wellbeing among university students in Finland

Since 2000 the Finnish Students Health Services have conducted three nationwide comparable survey studies (Kunttu and Huttunen, 2001, 2005, 2009) on Finnish university students' health. The latest survey was conducted in 2008 among students at Finnish universities and universities of applied sciences. The questionnaire was mailed to almost 10,000 students, aged under 35. The response rate was 51.1%. The report's results have been compared with the results of the previous two studies.

Among the respondents 42% were single and living in their own household. Cohabitation was the second most common way of living, as roughly one third of the students reported living together with their spouse but without children. Less than 10% were living in a commune or a shared household. A total of 74% of the respondents spent time with friends during their leisure time on a weekly basis. Slightly more than half of the students participated in different student association activities. Even so, only 55% of the students felt that they belonged to a study-related group. Various measures indicated that 5–6% of the students considered themselves to be lonely. Nearly one in three of the male students reported experiencing having too few or no people, to talk to.

The results of the study indicate that 27% of respondents had problems with their mental health. The most common problems included continuously experienced overstrain, feeling unhappy and depressed, having difficulties in concentrating on the tasks at hand, and inability to sleep because of worries. Mental health issues seemed to be more common among female students. These problems occurred among 32% of the women and 19% of the men.

The results of the mental health screening showed that 27% of all students experienced considerable stress. The stress was most frequently related to public performance and difficulties in getting a grip on studies. Almost 20% of the students had a negative perception concerning their mood. They also felt pessimistic when thinking of the future, and of their own resources and capabilities. Empowering factors included social relations and sexuality. The experienced mental problems and stress were similar among students in both types of universities. The results of the survey done in 2008 indicates that, among those studying at the university, the mental health problems were broadly as common as they were in 2004.

University students and e-health

The Internet has opened up new ways for the authorities to implement health promotion and share health-related information. For citizens and service users the Internet has led to new opportunities for independent action in healthcare issues. Among other things people can now renew prescriptions and choose an appropriate time for making appointments with doctors. The Internet has also opened up new ways of communicating with healthcare professionals, as Internet communication with healthcare professionals gives patients more freedom to choose when, what and how they interact with service providers (McGeady et al, 2008).

The endless amount of information that is available online has also changed the relationship between patient and doctor. The patient has become a consumer and the doctor a service provider. In this new relationship the patient and doctor can meet on a more equal level giving the patient more power and more possibilities for action. The patient has (presumably) already looked up his or her symptoms on the Internet and hence, will have an idea of what might be wrong. The negative effect of this development is that the expectations of both healthcare practitioners and patients increase. Patients expect to get care that is more than the diagnosis available on the Internet. In turn the healthcare professionals expect their patients to be able to find out information by themselves and not to make unnecessary appointments (McGeady et al, 2008).

The opportunity to independently seek information and to communicate with physicians electronically appears to suit university students very well. Students often live an irregular life, combining studies with part-time work and hobbies. This means that it can be difficult for them to communicate or make appointments with doctors and other healthcare professionals during ordinary office hours. The Internet has therefore become an important means of communication between the students and healthcare professionals. The results of a recently published dissertation (Castrén, 2008) show that both physicians and patients at the FSHS have a positive attitude towards using email for communication.

Sharing and caring

The following section reviews the Nyyti Student Support Centre (www.nyyti.fi) and its services. The aim here is, using Nyyti as an example, to demonstrate how young people in Finland use the Internet both as a channel for seeking support and help for themselves, and as a mechanism for participating in providing support to peers in need. Many studies (Kraut et al, 1996; Thulin, 2004; Subrahmanyam et al, 2008) show that, when online, people predominantly communicate and interact with people they already know in real life. The example below indicates that communicating with strangers can empower people who share difficult life situations. It serves also as an example of how contacts on the Internet can lead to the formation of face to face acquaintances and interaction.

Nyyti is a registered association established in 1984. Nyyti develops and produces services that promote mental wellbeing among students at Finnish universities and art academies. It is a non-governmental organisation that employs about ten people with degrees in psychology, social psychology, theology and nursing. There are also about 40 voluntary workers engaged in the organisation as assistants in the face to face groups and engaged in marketing the services at different student events.

The support centre offers face to face and web-based group counselling. Both face to face and online groups are supervised by professional therapists and/or employees at Nyyti. The topics dealt with in both types of groups are partly selected from the results of the student health surveys done by FSHS. The face to face groups are available in the Helsinki area only. These groups gather people with common concerns and problems. The face to face groups deal with topics such as social anxiety, performance related anxiety, breaking up, and coping lifeskills. The virtual services provided by Nyyti also include a wide range of online material; articles on different topics regarding situations and problems that occur in the lives of young adults, exercises and tests and links to useful information and other services.

Online groups have been available on the Nyyti website since autumn 2005. At first there were two online counselling groups available; one aimed at Finnish exchange students leaving to study abroad, being abroad or returning home from a period of exchange studies and a second one aimed at students having problems with living to busy lives called 'From stress to balance'. The feedback from the online groups was positive and therefore Nyyti continued developing the service (Nyyti ry, 2010).

At the moment (in autumn 2011) there are three online groups dealing with different topics. One group is for people who have just ended a relationship; seeking support and sharing their experiences. The second group is for single people wanting to share their experiences concerning problems with establishing relationships. Finally, there is a group for people suffering from a more general feeling of loneliness; seeking support and sharing their feelings on this difficult topic (http://www.nyyti.fi/palvelut/nettiryhmat/).

The online groups are open for discussions during the academic year only, from the middle of September to the middle of December and from the middle of January to the end of May. During the summer of 2011 an experiment was conducted through keeping the group for people suffering from loneliness open during summertime, in-between the semesters. These discussion groups can be found on the Nyyti webpage with the messages being openly accessible: they can be read by anyone. Those who wish to join in the discussion need to register as users on Nyyti's webpage. Registration is free and open to all interested parties (http://www.nyyti.fi/palvelut/nettiryhmat/).

Every online group has its own supervisor who also acts as the discussion moderator, reading through the messages before they are posted on the discussion. The online counselling groups are supervised by Nyyti employees and every group has its own supervisor throughout the semester. The supervisors intervene in the counselling group a couple of times per week. They welcome new members and summarise the discussions, sometimes picking up on a theme or topic that has got lost in the discussion. Moreover, they suggest useful exercises sometimes, or reading connected to the themes that are under discussion. The supervision and moderation makes the atmosphere in the discussion groups safer as it eradicates inappropriate and offensive comments from participants. If a participant posts a message indicating that he or she is experiencing an acute crisis the supervisor can answer the message privately without posting it to the ongoing discussion.

Although these online discussion groups are moderated and supervised they still give the participants the freedom required for independent decision making and action. The purpose of the discussion groups is to provide space for these young adults, in similar life situations, to share their experiences and support each other. A concrete example of the potential outcomes of an online group actively acting to collectively make things better is the 'Friday hangouts'. These hangouts became real due to the initiative taken by the discussion group for people suffering from loneliness. Some of the participants in this online discussion group started talking about the possibility of meeting face to face to continue getting to know each other. Nyyti provided the facilities for the first ever hangout evening held in Helsinki in 2006. Now, five years after the first hangout evening was held, these evenings have become a regular event and are arranged all over the country, facilitated by the student unions in the different university cities. The Friday hangouts are free of charge and offer an alcohol-free alternative for university students to socialise and meet new people.

In November and December 2010 Nyyti did a user survey on the virtual services provided. The survey was open on the www.nyyti.fi web site and there were 502 responses. The results of the survey showed that the main purpose of people visiting the website is to garner information regarding their actual life situation. People also looked up the pages to read articles on different topics and to follow the discussion groups (http://www.nyyti.fi/uutiset/nyyti.fi-kavijatutkimus/).

These results correlate with the results from the national statistics referred to earlier in this chapter, which show that the young people commonly use the Internet in search for health, illness and diet information.

The users who participated in the survey felt that the online groups were important channels through which they could anonymously share their experiences. The counselling groups are an important source of support from people in similar situations and with similar experiences. The answers given also indicated that the people participating in the discussion groups felt that it was a great relief and helpful to get the chance to write about and share their experiences. The people read and wrote to the online counselling groups in order to get help, and to gain new perspectives and advice on their current situation. The results from the survey showed that the users regard the discussion groups as both interesting and helpful (http://www.nyyti.fi/uutiset/nyyti.fi-kavijatutkimus/).

The preliminary analysis of messages posted to the online counselling group on the topic of loneliness supports the results of the survey[1]. The conclusions drawn from the 58 reviewed messages strongly indicate that the opportunity for participation and sharing that is given in the counselling group is an empowering experience. As the quotations below show, the participants support each other by sharing similar experiences:

> I have always been actively participating in different activities at the university and I talk to several people every day. These people at the university are more like acquaintances and not my friends. I don't even feel comfortable with these people and I don't enjoy the same kind of living they do. Constant partying and gossiping about other people are not the most important things in my life! M2[2]

> That's exactly how I think and feel. When I came to the university I was excited and had high expectations on the new environment and interesting, people with common interests. I was shocked to find out that the social interaction was on the same level as it was in high school. I don't have the energy to awe about peoples clothing and who-did-what-with-who at the latest party. M3

Giving out advice on coping strategies and telling each other about the sorts of actions they have taken to improve their situations is a further method of sharing and supporting. Many participants wrote that they had been following the discussions in the counselling group for a long time before deciding to write a message themselves. For these silent readers finding out that there are other students with similar experiences was a great relief in itself.

> I have problems with my self-esteem. Even writing here feels a bit scary. I have been following this group for some time and even read the archives with discussions from previous years and now I wanted to contribute by writing. M14

> I am happy that this group is in action again. It is a relief to read about other people's thoughts and experiences.

Many of them are very familiar and it is easy to identify
with them. M21

The participants also report on the feelings of community and
fellowship they have found in the online group. People writing to the
counselling group expressed a desire to establish contact with each other
outside the group and even to meet face to face. The opportunity to
get acquainted online before meeting face to face is greatly appreciated
by the socially insecure or shy people that participate in the online
counselling group.

By the way is it possible to get in touch with other people
writing here? Can I post my e-mail address to the group
or is there a better way to do it? M4

It is possible to exchange contact information among
participants. As I recall from earlier years there has at least
been one private board game-evening arranged among
participants in this group. Publishing ones e-mail address
has been found out to be the easiest way to get in touch
with each other. We recommend that the address you share
is an informal one. S[3]

The primary function of the counselling group is not to match people,
but to offer a place to write about and share their burden of loneliness.
As the group is supervised and moderated in advance there is no danger
that the discussion can become indecent or off-topic.

Several studies (Reeves, 2000; Eysenbach et al, 2004; Josefsson, 2005)
show that online communities for people facing similar difficulties
and situations are an important source of social support. These online
discussion groups give people the opportunity to share experiences
concerning both the practical or technical details on symptoms
and treatments, and to also exchange thoughts and feelings such as
uncertainty, fear and anxiety. Furthermore, helping a fellow patient can
be both an empowering experience, and the opening up and writing
has, in itself, therapeutic features (Wright and Bell, 2003). Another
advantage of these online groups is that the participants themselves
choose how they want to use the support offered. They may just be the
silent readers of other people's experiences but can, if they feel like it,
contribute with their own experience and expertise (Josefsson, 2005).

Potential problems also exist, and participants in online discussion
groups need to be aware of these. Concerns about privacy and the

inappropriate use of messages posted to online discussion groups, and the risk of unreliable information have to be taken into consideration. The difficulty inherent in finding the most appropriate information among often tremendous amounts of text can entail difficulty in locating support online (Heaton, 2011). An added issue that needs to be taken account of is that not all people are able to make use of online support. For example people suffering from severe mental health problems are primarily in need of face to face support and care. These people might benefit from using online services but only as a complement to other forms of care (Granholm, 2006, 2010).

Discussion

This article has presented some changes in the way people seek help, participate, interact, build relationships and collaborate in health-related issues through the use of ICT. The boundaries of time and place no longer place limits on people's access to health-related information, help and care. The Internet offers an abundance of health information; it is easy to get information on any medical condition both from professionals and people with their own personal experiences. The information available online makes it easier for people to perform their own preliminary diagnosis on their condition and draw inference on whether or not they need to consult a physician. This can, at best, reduce unnecessary doctor visits but, at worst, it may put people's health at risk as a diagnosis based on information from the Internet can easily be incorrect.

The Internet also offers the possibility for people to consult physicians online. This opportunity has made it easier for people with busy schedules or people unable to travel owing to disabilities or other conditions to get in touch with health professionals. The Internet further provides people living in the countryside or otherwise far from a doctors' surgery the opportunity to stay in contact without having to make a lengthy journey for minor healthcare issues.

The Internet also offers an arena for anonymous interaction between people who might never be able to come together face to face. Online discussion groups offer people the chance to share experiences they might be too ashamed to talk about in real life. In online groups peers and professionals can offer the participants support and advice. Online discussions that are openly available on the Internet can be of help to more people than the active participants as there are often a large number of people silently following the discussion. This is a quality that is characteristic to online group interaction and a feature that cannot be realised in face to face groups.

The theoretical approach used as a starting point of this chapter indicated that participation can lead to psychological empowerment and increased wellbeing. For students, online communities provide excellent arenas for participating in order to improve their own wellbeing, and to support each other. As the examples presented above show, turning to the Internet to seek information, professional help and peer support occurs naturally for university students. But young adults are also eager to share their experiences on virtual arenas and to support others in need. The Internet is rapidly becoming a part of everyday life for every Finnish citizen, and a growing number of people around the world. The children and young people growing up today are socialised into communication and interacting on the Internet. Participation in an online community is for these digital natives (Prensky, 2001) as natural as participating in a real life community.

Modern information and communication technologies possess enormous as of yet untapped potential for exploration and development. The Internet will probably provide many more opportunities for including people in taking action on matters concerning their own wellbeing and health. New and innovative means for people to support and help each other virtually will, presumably, be discovered.

Yet even though the Internet is a dimension with unlimited opportunities there still are a number of people who for one reason or another cannot be part of the virtual society, and take advantage of the services provided. Reasons for not being able to participate in the virtual world can, for example, be a lack of equipment and/or computer skills, a lack of interest in things happening 'out there', or inability to participate because of ill health or other reasons. Therefore it is important that alongside the virtual services we also keep developing face to face and trans-boundary services that enable people to act freely in choosing the arena that best suits their own situations.

Notes

[1] The analysis presented here is done on messages posted to the counselling group discussing loneliness during the first two weeks of October 2010. A more thorough analysis on all messages posted to the counselling group during the autumn semester 2010 is under process. The results are presented in a separate article as a part of a doctoral dissertation estimated to be ready the end of 2013.

[2] The quotations have been translated literally from Finnish by the author. The messages (M) are given numbers according to the order in which they occur.

[3] 'S' denotes a supervisor.

References

Anttiroiko, A.-V. (2003) 'Kansalaisten osallistuminen, osallisuus ja vaikuttaminen tietoyhteiskunnassa' (Citizens' participation, involvement and influence in the information society.), in P. Bäcklund (ed) *Tietoyhteiskunnan osallistuva kansalainen – tapaus Nettimaunula. Helsingin kaupungin tietokeskuksen tutkimuksia*, p 5.

Castrén, J. (2008) 'Sähköinen viestintä ja verkkoneuvontapalvelu osana yliopisto-opiskelijoiden terveydenhuoltoa' (Email in patient communication and a web-based health advice service as a part of health care services among Finnish university students), *Acta Universitatis Tamperensis,* Tampere: Tampere University Press, p 1367.

Christensen, B. D., Peterson, N. A. and Speer, P. W. (2011) 'Community participation and psychological empowerment: testing reciprocal causality using a cross-lagged panel design and latent constructs', *Health Education and Behavior*, vol 38, no 4, pp 339–47.

Eysenbach, G., Powell, J., Englesakis, M., Rizo, C. and Stern, A. (2004) 'Health related virtual communities and electronic support groups: systematic review of the effects of online peer to peer interactions', *British Medical Journal*, vol 328, no 7449, p 1166.

Granholm, C. (2006) 'Nedstämda studerandes berättelser på en virtuell arena: Nyyti rf:s Virtualskuldra som en ny kanal för självreflektion' (The narratives of depressed students on a virtual arena: The Virtual Shoulder as a new channel for self reflection), Master's thesis in Social Work at the Department of Social Science at University of Helsinki. Unpublished.

Granholm, C. (2010) 'Virtuaalinen auttamisympäristö voimaannuttavan vuorovaikutuksen ja sosiaalisen tuen tarjoajana' (Social support and empowering bonding in supporting online environments), in a. Pohjola, A. Kääriäinen and S. Kuusisto-Niemi (eds), *Sosiaalityö, tieto ja teknologia (Social Work, Knowledge and Technology)*. Jyväskylä: PS-kustannus, pp 157–81.

Heaney, C. and Israel, B. (1997) 'Social networks and social support', in K. Glanz, F. Marcus Lewis and B. K. Rimer (eds) *Health Behaviour and Health Education, Theory, Research and Practice*, 2nd edn, San Fransisco: Jossey Bass, pp 179–203.

Heaton, L. (2011) 'Internet and health communication', in M. Consalvo and C. Ess (eds) *The Blackwell Handbook of Internet Studies*, Chichester, West Sussex: Wiley-Blackwell, pp 212–31.

Ilolakso, A. (2005) *Nyyti 20 vuotta. Yhteisöasumisesta virtuaaliolkapäähän* (Nyyti 20 years. From cohabiting to a Virtual Shoulder), Helsinki: Nyyti ry.

Josefsson, U. (2005) 'Coping with illness online: the case of patients online communities', *The Information Society*, vol 21, no 2, pp 133-41.

Kraut, R., Scherlis, W., Mukhopadhyay, T., Manning, J. and Kiesler, S. (1996) 'The HomeNet field trial of residential Internet services', *Communications of the ACM*, no 39, pp 55–63.

Kunttu K. and Huttunen, T. (2001) *Korkeakouluopiskelijoiden terveystutkimus 2000* (Student Health Survey 2000: a national survey among Finnish university students), Sosiaali- ja terveysturvan katsauksia 45, Helsinki: Kansaneläkelaitos.

Kunttu, K. and Huttunen, T. (2005) *Yliopisto-opiskelijoiden terveystutkimus 2004* (Student Health Survey 2004: a national survey among Finnish university students) Ylioppilaiden terveydenhuoltosäätiön tutkimuksia 40, Helsinki: Ylioppilaiden terveydenhuoltosäätiö.

Kunttu, K. and Huttunen, T. (2009) *Korkeakouluopiskelijoiden terveystutkimus 2008* (Student Health Survey 2008: a national survey among Finnish university students) Ylioppilaiden terveydenhuoltosäätiön tutkimuksia 45, Helsinki: Ylioppilaiden terveydenhuoltosäätiö.

McGeady, D., Kujala, J. and Ilvonen, K. (2008) 'The impact of patient–physician web messaging on healthcare service provision', *International Journal of Medical Informatics*, vol 77, no 1, pp 17–23.

Nyyti ry (2010) *Nettiauttamismalli* (The online support praxis), www.nyyti.fi/nyyti-ry/materiaalipankki/julkaisut/

Perkins, D. D. and Zimmerman, M. A. (1995) 'Empowerment theory, research, and application', *American Journal of Community Psychology*, vol 23, no 5, pp 569–79.

Prensky, M. (2001) 'Digital natives, digital immigrants Part 1', *On The Horizon,* vol 9, no 5, pp 1–6.

Reeves, P. M. (2000) 'Coping in cyberspace: the impact of the Internet use on the ability of HIV-positive individuals to deal with their illness', *Journal of Health Communication*, vol 5, no 1, pp 47–59.

Subrahmanyam, K., Reich, S. M., Waechter, N. and Espinoza, G. (2008) 'Online and offline social networks: use of social networking sites by emerging adults', *Journal of Applied Developmental Psychology*, vol 29, no 6, pp 420–33.

The Pew Internet and American Life Project (2000, May 10) *Tracking Online Life: How Women Use the Internet to Cultivate Relationships with Family and Friends.* www.pewInternet.org/reports/

Thulin, E. (2004) *Ungdomars virtuella rörlighet. Användningen av dator, Internet och mobiltelefon i ett geografiskt perspektiv* (The virtual mobility of youth. A geographic perspective on the use of computers, Internet and mobile phones), Göteborg: Kulturgeografiska institutionen vid Handelshögskolan vid Göteborgs universitet.

Tieto- ja viestintätekniikan käyttö -tutkimus 2010 (Inquiry on the use of information and communication technology 2010) Statistics Finland www.stat.fi/til/sutivi/2010/sutivi_2010_2010–10–26_fi.pdf

Wright, K. B. and Bell, S. B. (2003) 'Health-related support groups on the Internet: linking empirical findings to social support and computer-mediated communication theory', *Journal of Health Psychology*, vol 8, no 1, pp 39–54.

Zimmerman, M. A. (1995) 'Psychological empowerment: issues and illustrations', *American Journal of Community Psychology*, vol 23, no 5, pp 581–599.

Internet resources

www.nyyti.fi
www.nyyti.fi/palvelut/nettiryhmat/
www.yths.fi/en

Part Four

Participation and learning

TWELVE

Learning to participate or participating to learn?

Andreas Walther

Introduction

> State Parties shall assure to the child who is capable of
> forming his or her own view the right to express those
> views freely in all matters affecting the child, the views of
> the child being given due weight in accordance with the
> age and maturity of the child. (United Nations Convention
> on the Rights of the Child, Art. 12, 1)

Article 12 of the 1989 United Nations Convention on the Rights of
the Child (1989) remains a key reference to initiatives, programmes
and studies concerned with children's and young people's participation.
However, it also contains one of the central constraints to child and
youth participation; in order to participate children and young people
are expected to acquire specific skills, competencies and knowledge.
This corresponds with research into inequalities in youth participation
in education as well as to policies aimed at reversing an apparent decline
in youth participation by means of information and education; these
policies and assumptions share implicit assumptions on the relationship
between education, learning and participation (Fahmy 2006; Spannring
et al, 2008; Thomas and Percy-Smith, 2010).

This chapter aims to question these assumptions. It suggests that
making youth participation conditional upon education, learning
and personal development (or 'maturity') reproduces and legitimises
existing, institutionalised meanings, contents and forms of participation
rather than contributing to the empowerment of children and young
people. Reconstructing the societal function of youth and education as a
life phase characterised by preparation for the rights and responsibilities
connected to the status of adulthood (for a definition of 'citizenship',
see Marshall, 1950) illustrates the relationship between education,

learning and participation as one of conditionality and postponement: first learn, then participate (Walther, 2010). This approach neglects the reality of learning as a subjective process which requires participatory educational settings – unless learning is intentionally conceptualised as a one-way process of adaptation and normalisation of the younger generation to the values, norms and institutions established by the older generation.

As a first step, the relationship between education, learning and participation will be assessed by means of comparative analysis of how participation is dealt with in formal and non-formal education in different European countries: Austria, France, Ireland, Italy and Slovakia. Comparative analysis will address the meaning of civic or citizenship education and the role and scope of student councils. In a second step, this is complemented by comparing different models of youth work in these countries as a potential space of participation in non-formal education. These two sections are based on a chapter of the thematic report on young people's agency and participation produced in the context of the EU-project *Youth – Actor of Social Change (UP2YOUTH)* (Machacek and Walther, 2008; Loncle and Muniglia, 2008; Walther et al, 2009). Section three aims at deepening the insight into the relationship between education, learning and participation by referring to some qualitative studies concerned with both young people's reflections on subjective meanings of participation as well as their participation experiences in formal and non-formal learning environments. Section four will conclude by relating these research findings to education and learning theory.

Participation in formal and non-formal education

School: learning for participating – later?

School is *the* institution expected to ensure the transfer of knowledge, skills and competences representing the cultural, economic and political foundation of society from one generation to the next – or more precisely: the societal functions of school are allocation (to unequal social positions), qualification (of the labour force) and integration (internalising norms and values) (Fend, 1974). Viewed as a universal right and responsibility, children and young people's public education attendance is an effective institution for both empowering and controlling these children and young people. Consequently, actors concerned with democracy building and youth participation place emphasis on the role of the school: '... the education system may be regarded as the most important medium through which to impart and demonstrate the principles of equity, inclusion and cohesion' (Eurydice, 2005, p 7).

The following overview over participation in school relates to civic education and student councils and is based on reports commissioned by the EU's former education agency, Eurydice, and the Council of Europe (Dürr, 2004; Birzea et al, 2004; Eurydice 2005).

Citizenship has its place somewhere in the curriculum of all EU countries in terms of *civic education* or *citizenship education* (see table 12.1). In some cases it has the status of a separate mandatory subject, especially at secondary level, while being more integrated during primary education. In other contexts it is integrated with either history or social sciences, or dealt with as a cross-curricular subject. It is revealing to see the age at which children engage with the subject and for how many years. From the countries involved in the overview, *Austria* is the country where it is addressed for the lengthiest period, partly in a cross-curricular fashion and partly as a subject combined with history. In *Slovakia* it is being taught over five years as a separate mandatory subject, yet for only one hour per week. The Slovak case is of particular interest inasmuch as civic education is both a symbol for the transformation process and a reflection of the expectation that democracy can be built through education. As regards form and content, in all countries citizenship education at school is taught and assessed similar to other school subjects in examinations and/or tests. The implied risk is that it is viewed and experienced by pupils as a mere school subject which is to be studied to achieve competence and/or grades but not in terms of subjectively relevant learning (Cockburn, 2010). This hypothesis, for which empirical data is thus far lacking, is supported by the reality that civic education plays only a minor role in teacher training. In some cases (Italy and Slovakia), it is only provided by in-service teacher training while in France and Ireland it is at least addressed by specific initial teacher education programmes. In Austria it is a compulsory component in secondary education teacher training (Eurydice, 2005, p 48).

Apart from through regular teaching, participation and civic education are subjects of extraordinary school projects which follow a learning-by-doing approach (Krätzl-Nagl and Zartler, 2010). These projects tend however to be separated from regular teaching. In sum, civic education appears to play a marginal role in school across Europe. The fact that it is largely dealt with as a normal subject reflects that it is primarily intended as preparing students for participation in their

Table 12.1: Organisation of civic education in school

Country	Terminology	Education level	Approach	Time and assessment
Austria	Civic education History and civic education	Primary Secondary (ISCED 2 and 3)	Cross-curricular principle New statutory subject	No data
France	Living together, Civic education Civic, legal and social education	Primary and lower secondary Upper secondary	Separate mandatory subject Separate integrated core	Formal national examination 3-4 hours/week
Ireland	Social, personal and health education Civic, social and political education Leaving certificate applied/ transition year	Primary Lower secondary Upper secondary	Integrated Separate mandatory subject Part of special programmes	Examined in junior certificate
Italy	Social studies History and civic education	Primary Lower/upper secondary	Integrated Separate and integrated subject	Exams in connected subjects
Slovakia	Civics education social science	Primary (6–9) Secondary (9–11)	Mandatory separate subject	I hour/week

Source: Eurydice, 2005

later lives as adults – outside school – rather than affecting participation within school.

Another aspect of participation in school is student involvement in decision making at individual level, classroom level, through student councils at school level, or in local, regional or national bodies. Student participation may concern individual and peer issues, class affairs, school life and extracurricular activities. Organisational and staff affairs, curricular and didactic issues are only rarely open for student participation. Recently, in the context of the increasing phenomena of mobbing and bullying in school, in most countries students have been trained and become active as mediators in case of conflicts among students in the classroom or at school level.

As regards participation on the individual level, Austria is the only country wherein individual participatory rights (largely consultation) are established by law. In all of the countries, student councils are established, yet to different extents, at different levels and with different competencies (see table 12.2). While some countries have rudimentary elements starting from primary level, student participation in a narrower sense starts with secondary education.

Table 12.2: School and students' councils

	Official term	Creation	School level	Competencies	**Degree of power**
Austria	Pupil/student representatives	In 1990s	All levels	School life, partly co-decision	Medium
France	Student representatives' councils Councils of secondary school life	1989 1995	Mainly secondary	School life, partly co-decision	Medium
Ireland	Student councils	1998	Primary, Secondary	School life	Weak
Italy	School councils, Provincial student councils	1999	Secondary	School life	Weak
Slovakia	School students' councils	2003	Secondary	School life, partly co-decision	Medium

Sources: Dürr, 2004; Eurydice, 2005; Loncle and Muniglia, 2008

In Ireland, student councils are a strategic goal of the National Children's Strategy. However, the initiative appears to be very much a matter of choice for the schools.

In Italy, student councils are mostly established at the level of province (local district) covering several schools involving a place to meet and a small budget for student activities. The main functions of the councils are promoting dialogue among students, organising extra-curricular activities (normally involving several schools), representing student interests to school authorities and organising student counselling. At national level, province councils are organised in an umbrella organisation.

In France, in secondary education each class elects two representatives who participate in the class council representing students in relation to teachers and school management. Apart from this, each school has a 'council of secondary school life' chaired by the headteacher and composed of ten student representatives. It must be consulted on issues affecting the organisation of school life, projects, and on health and security issues. Students are also represented in the school board where most decisions are taken. Finally, each school has a health and citizenship education committee in which students are represented together with parents and teachers. With mainly advisory functions (similar to national bodies) the regional council of secondary school life draws half of the members from students.

In Austria, students' participation rights are legally fixed in terms of student representatives at class and school level and at federal state and national level. A particular Austrian element is the school committee with one student member elected from class representatives or directly by the student community. In the student assembly, class representatives discuss issues concerning student interests. At federal state and national level, Austrian student participation primarily means student representation towards the educational authorities.

In Slovakia student councils represent the hope for an increase in young people's interest in public issues and democracy. Students are expected to express their views in relation to educational issues, to participate in the creation and application of school rules, to represent students to school management, to elect representatives for the School Council and to engage in non-formal education. Not all schools have student councils yet, but their share is rapidly increasing (Machacek, 2006).

To summarise, it appears that the scope of student participation is most strongly established in Austria, encompassing both primary and secondary education. It includes individual and collective rights and connects classroom, school, regional and national levels. In France student participation is established but restricted to secondary education. In Italy and Ireland it is less strongly institutionalised but developing. Slovakia, with the youngest tradition of student councils, represents a dynamic field of societal development. Beyond this, comparative analysis is limited by a lack of more differentiated and representative data. However, comparative research on young people's school-to-work transitions has shown that the individual status of young people within education systems varies across different *transition regimes* (see Chapter 2). In the Nordic countries, in the *universalist* transition regime, students enjoy the most pronounced status as co-citizens which is reflected by individual education plans, a supportive infrastructure including for example counselling within school, as well as social rights including educational allowances, at least for those above the age of 18 years. In the UK and Ireland, representing the *liberal* transition regime, participation tends to be market driven in terms of free school choice while students may get involved in school evaluation. In the *conservative* or *employment-centred* transition regime in continental countries, students are subject to selective procedures placing them on different tracks of secondary education according to performance in primary education whereby individual choice is rigidly restricted (France is an exception in this respect). Finally, in the *under-institutionalised* regime of the Mediterranean countries, the structural deficit with regard to youth policies reflects a paternalistic approach towards young people in public institutions – including the education system (Walther et al, 2006).

Youth work: learning through participation?

One of the most prominent settings for non-formal learning is the sphere of open youth work. Youth work in most countries starts from young people's own interests and progresses to (ultimately) providing open space where they can develop their own activities and initiatives.

This principle results both from the fact that young people attend on a voluntary basis and from a 1968-influenced movement turning (open) youth work into a public infrastructure for young people (in contrast, associative youth work in most cases restricts itself to specific social and cultural milieus). Youth work exemplifies settings wherein young people engage in leisure activities, performing arts, sports and/ or political action, with many different types and forms co-existing; ranging from 'open youth work' (e.g. youth centres) to associative youth work addressing particular milieus or focusing on specific activities, projects for young people at risk or holiday camps.

While participation seems much more articulated in youth work than in school, it also displays contradictory aspects while explicit references to learning and education vary (Banks, 1999; Jeffs and Smith, 1999; IARD, 2001; ISS, 2007; Burgess and Herrmann, 2010). Often participation is reduced to one method among others – and then rejected by youth workers as an additional demand on top of their normal workload – instead of an integral principle of everyday practice. This is also reflected by such as the 'ladder of participation' (Arnstein, 1969; Hart, 1992) which – while criticising limited or tokenistic participation – suggests that participation can be 'done' in terms of a technique. Youth work conceptionalised as general prevention is often also difficult to distinguish from selective prevention such as social youth work in Germany and Flanders. Especially when it comes to integration of immigrant youth, unemployed youth or early school leavers, non-formal learning tends to be more compensatory than participatory (Walther et al, 2006; Coussée, 2008). Based on different sources, national constellations of youth work can be mapped as in table 12.3.

Table 12.3: Constellations of youth work

	Concept	Legal basis	Dominant forms	Qualification of youth workers
Austria	Youth work	Yes	Open and associative youth work	Social workers, social pedagogues, volunteers
France	Sociocultural animation	No	Open and associative youth work	Social workers, social educators, volunteers
Ireland	Youth work	Yes	Open youth work and social inclusion	Youth workers, volunteers
Italy	Sociocultural animation	No	Youth information, extracurricular activities	Social educators, volunteers
Slovakia	Youth work	No	Associative youth work, extracurricular activities	Social workers, volunteers

Sources: IARD, 2001; Lauritzen et al, 2005; ISS, 2007

In Austria, the idea of youth work as a space of non-formal learning is widespread, yet not always spelled out explicitly. While in open youth work aspects of social learning are addressed through moderating open spaces, associative youth work also involves learning through voluntary engagement. Mobile youth work is an outreach service following a 'low threshold' approach for young people not engaged by other forms of youth work, revealing that youth work also contains a control aspect. Apart from learning objectives, this is prominent in French youth work which is strongly characterised by the function of getting young people off the streets to do something '*reasonable*' (Loncle, 2009).

In Ireland, professional youth work was traditionally seen more as preventative work with marginalised young people. However, the shift of political responsibility for youth work into the Department of Education symbolised that modern youth work is more and more understood as an instrument of (non-formal) learning and competence-building. The effects of the more recent (2010) transfer of Irish youth affairs into a new Department of Children and Young People is not yet clear (see Chapter 7).

In Italy, the origin of youth work in municipal 'youth projects' refers more to a welfare approach aimed at providing young people access to public spaces rather than to an educational approach. At the same time, qualifications have been developed inside educational sciences and thereby contributed to an 'educational turn'.

In Slovakia, the development of youth work is still quite recent and influenced by the decentralisation process. While at national level European programmes are used to develop a modern youth work profile, at local level paternalistic forms of youth work with minimal participatory opportunities coincide with afternoon clubs in schools connected to school subjects (Lauritzen et al, 2005). The relationship between learning and participation in youth work obviously depends on the degree in which non-formal education follows concrete, pre-defined objectives. Contrary to the Slovakia situation, where youth work prioritises clearly defined extra-curricular activities, youth work in Austria and Ireland largely accepts that outcomes of participatory learning cannot be planned but are uncertain.

Moreover, these lines of differentiation can be related to the comparative model of youth transitions which distinguishes general representations of youth as well as different relations between formal and non-formal education.

In Austria, the employment-centred transition regime is characterised by differentiated systems of school and youth services; youth work is institutionally strictly separated from both youth welfare and school. This results in a low status on the one hand but a non-formal and participatory space on the other hand.

In France this openness appears to be more limited, reflecting a more protectionist state approach to youth in general. A further cultural legacy in these countries may be the paternalistic influence of the Catholic Church. In Ireland the prevalence of a social inclusion agenda reflects the dominant 'youth as a problem' approach in the liberal regime. This is also visible in the Italian case where (as in France) youth work is being referred to as 'cultural animation'. The structural deficit typical for the under-institutionalised regime type is addressed at municipality level by developing a professional youth sector through the tool of youth information. Slovakia, as a post-socialist country, aims at reconstructing a national identity as a democratic society while at the same time coming under pressure from transnational actors such as the European Union and/or the Council of Europe in building infrastructures in line with the current agendas of these actors such as lifelong learning. While this comparison has not involved countries from the universalistic model, according to international research reviews, youth work in Finland is a powerful actor following a thoroughly participatory approach while in Denmark youth work is more marginalised. Here, school offers both non-formal learning and possibilities of individual choice (IARD, 2001; Williamson, 2002; Walther et al, 2006).

The sections above have shown that across national contexts participation in school is limited, while voluntary involvement in non-formal learning, especially youth work, ensures larger opportunities. However, because of a lack of recognition, non-formal learning and participatory learning does not necessarily contribute to the social integration and empowerment of young people. Available comparative information suggests that the institutional contexts of education, welfare and youth policies have an impact on the relationship between education, learning and participation. Therefore, more differentiated data are needed to explain the reasons and consequences of cross-country difference; these data need to include young people's own accounts of participation.

Young people's experiences of participation and learning

This section aims at differentiating the picture by drawing on some qualitative studies on young people's biographical experiences of getting involved (or not) and on the role education and learning play in their participation biographies. Because of the lack of qualitative data in this respect, the presentation does not cover all of the countries referred to above.

As regards experiences of participation in school, a German study combining quantitative and qualitative methods has analysed the relationship between participation in different school types within the differentiated German school system and students' political socialisation (Helsper et al, 2006). It identifies different cultures of students' participation according to how students feel recognised as individuals and as co-decision makers in school life and by teachers in particular. Low levels of recognition in school relate with student vulnerability towards extreme right-wing, nationalist and xenophobic orientations, mirroring the double-bind situation of school participation in which civic education restricts participation to later in life while student rights and the competencies of student councils are limited.

Conversely, a British action research by Yamashita and Davies (2010) shows how student councils are experienced positively if 'all students' are involved, if 'serious issues' such as staff selection are included, and if students are given recognition as 'professionals' for the students' perspective – regardless of their level of information and training. Beyond this, the experience of participation can contribute to a more reflexive and differentiated perspective towards the own learning biography (Bloomer and Hodkinson, 2000).

The requirement for an advance of trust and responsibility also emerged from the EU-funded study *Youth Policy and Participation* (YOYO) on the relationship between the possibilities of participation and so-called 'disadvantaged' young people for engaging actively in transitions to the labour market (Walther et al, 2006). The research redefined participation in terms of biographical self-determination: individuals engage if it is subjectively meaningful for their own biographies. On the one hand, biographical interviews with young people revealed that alongside experiences of failure a lack of choice with regard to education and training undermines subjective motivation. On the other hand, project case studies revealed that measures that combine 'hard' and 'soft' aspects – qualifications, skills, jobs or income as well as choice, experimentation, responsibility or trust – succeeded in re-motivating young people who had already given up. While such measures represented the exception rather than the rule (the sample consisted of 28 case studies across nine countries), this was more often the case at the margins of the transition system (e.g. where youth workers engaged in supporting youth in their transitions to work) than in mainstream (pre)vocational schemes. The Danish case studies showed that in the context of the universalistic transition regime disadvantaged young people experience more possibilities of choice and intrinsic motivation.

The need to take a biographical perspective in understanding participation of disadvantaged youth emerges also from a qualitative study of von Schwanenflügel (2011) in Germany. By reconstructing the biographies of young people from disadvantaged social backgrounds who engaged as volunteers in youth centres, she found that the choice of content and form of participation largely depended on the moment(s) in their lives when these young people came into contact with youth work in general and the possibilities of participation in particular. Engagement remained either limited to the realm of the individual youth centre or expanded whereby young people experienced the youth centre as a bridge into larger society, for example by representing their peers in a local youth council.

These perspectives are confirmed by findings of a European study on the life histories of adults concerning learning for active citizenship which located three key aspects of learning for citizenship: developing a sense of agency and ability to make change happen; social issues corresponding to an individual challenge; and reflexivity with regard to the connection between oneself and the social context (Holford and van der Veen, 2003, p 50): 'Active citizens usually learn their citizenship skills through trying to solve a problem or to fulfil a mission, rather than by setting out to "learn to be good citizens" ... Learning ... is interactive and deeply embedded in specific contexts' (Holford and van der Veen, 2003, p 8).

In sum, a key question is whether or not young people are taught to accept practices and meanings of participation as given, or if they can interpret them according to own needs and interests.

Discussion and conclusions

The observations and reflections concerning learning for participation made so far suggest that the public discourse primarily problematises the skills and competencies of young people with regard to the demands of formally acknowledged forms and contents of participation. In fact, reference to young people's skills and knowledge is used to legitimise limitations rather than possibilities for participation. The majority of youth participation programmes intend to inform, educate and teach young people how to participate in predefined ways in regard to predefined issues whereby they risk missing what is subjectively relevant and attractive for these young people. At the same time, young people themselves undergo a variety of learning processes with regard to participation – in school, in youth work and in public space. Implicitly, they learn from their involvement in these practices that participation rarely relates to issues which are relevant for their lives but is limited to formally delineated themes and social fields – or that participation in subjectively meaningful forms, fields and contents is not recognised.

This discrepancy relates to a pedagogical misunderstanding according to which participation can be learned through education regardless of the asymmetrical structure of educational arrangements. Most pedagogical practice implies a causal relationship between intentional education and learning processes of the learners, neglecting the complexity of learning as an individual activity embedded in inter-subjective relationships. Activity psychology, in contrast, conceives of learning as a process by which an individual explores and appropriates its social and natural world in order to develop its own agency (Leontjev,

1981; Holzkamp, 1993). Relying on the pragmatic thinking of Dewey and Mead, Lave and Wenger (1991) have reconstructed learning as 'legitimate peripheral participation'. This implies that learning is both situated and social. Legitimate peripheral participation means that the learner is accepted as a member of a 'community of practice' (Wenger, 1998) – and therefore recognised as an individual – irrespective of his or her actual competencies. It implies that learners learn (only) what they identify subjectively as relevant, what they can actively appropriate and integrate with their subjective identity, what provides them experiences of recognition – or where they experience possibilities of participation (Freire, 1972).

In German, the concept of education has a double meaning: on the one hand it means the intentional instruction of learners through educators (*Erziehung*), on the other hand it means the formation of an individual towards becoming a subject of his or her own life (*Bildung*), a concept developed during the Enlightenment. In the institutionalisation of public education the difference between these two meanings has been increasingly blurred resulting in a functional understanding of education as qualification, integration and allocation (Fend, 1974). Social pedagogy is interested in the social aspects of education and consequently criticises the dominance of a functional understanding of learning as reproducing both social disadvantage and the alienation of learners. It implies that the social (re-)embedding of learning and education requires integration into biographically meaningful social spaces such as in open youth work where the provision of (largely unstructured) space for self-determined appropriation allows for (non-formal) learning (Deinet and Reutlinger, 2004; Kornbeck and Jensen, 2009). At the same time (intentional) education can only support processes of subjective appropriation if it succeeds at least partially in suspending the inherent hierarchy between educators and learners: participation (Winkler, 2000).

In sum, research and theoretical reflections of the relationship between participation and learning suggest reversing the order or learning first and participating later. This suggestion has two fundamental consequences: firstly, it is not only the forms of participation that need to be renegotiated but also the contents; secondly, it means (re-) accepting the contingencies of learning and education: 'Learning cannot be designed, it can only be designed for – that is facilitated or frustrated' (Wenger, 1998, p 229).

Percy-Smith (2006) suggests shifting from 'making youth participate', which in most cases means little more than consultation, which young people need to be trained for in order to be listened to and which tends to be both unattractive and ineffective, towards a model of 'dialogic social learning' within the community. This is reminiscent of Dewey's work on education in (and not for) democracy based on the assumption that: 'democracy is more than a form of government; it is primarily a form of associated living, of conjoint communicated experience' (Dewey, 1963, p 87). Inter-subjective *recognition* can therefore be seen as the missing link between learning and participation on the one side and subjective identity and social integration on the other. Education which does not recognise learners as subjects of their learning biographies tends to miss the intra-individual process of learning as well as the process through which experiential learning turns into subjective reflexivity (or *Bildung*, see Fitzgerald et al, 2010). From this perspective learning to participate implies participatory learning – that is experience of participation.

References

Arnstein, S. (1969) 'A ladder of citizen participation', *Journal of American Institute of Planners*, vol 35, no 4, pp 216–24.

Banks, S. (ed) (1999) *Ethical Issues in Youth Work*, London: Routledge.

Birzea, C. (ed) (2004) *The All-European Study on Pupils' Participation in School*, Strasbourg: Council of Europe.

Bloomer, M. and Hodkinson, P. (2000) 'Learning careers: continuity and change in young people's dispositions to learning', *British Educational Research Journal*, vol 26, no 5, pp 583–98.

Burgess, P. and Herrmann, P. (eds) (2010) *Highways, Crossroads and Cul de Sacs. Journeys into Irish youth and community work*, Bremen: Europäischer Hochschulverlag.

Cockburn, T. (2010) 'Children and deliberative democracy in England' in B. Percy-Smith and N. Thomas (eds) *A Handbook of Children and Young People's Participation*, London: Routledge, pp 306–18.

Coussée, F. (2008) *A Century of Youth Work Policy*, Gent: Academia Press.

Deinet, U. and Reutlinger, C. (eds) (2004) *'Aneignung' als Bildungskonzept der Sozialpädagogik* ('Appropriation' as concept of education in social pedagogy), Wiesbaden: VS-Verlag.

Dewey, J. (1963) *Democracy and Education*, New York: Macmillan.

Dürr, K.-H. (2004) *The School: A Democratic Learning Community. The All-European Study on Pupils' Participation School*, Strasbourg: Council of Europe.

Eurobarometer (2007) *Young Europeans. A Survey Among Young People Aged Between 15–30 in the European Union. Analytical Report*, Brussels: Eurostat.

Eurydice (2005) *Citizenship Education at School in Europe.* National descriptions, Brussels: Eurydice, online: www.eacea.ec.europa.eu (accessed 10 May 2011).

Fahmy, E. (2006) *Young Citizens, Young People's Involvement in Politics and Decision Making,* Aldershot: Ashgate.

Fend, H. (1974) *Gesellschaftliche Bedingungen schulischer Sozialisation (Societal conditions of school socialisation),* Weinheim: Beltz.

Fitzgerald, R., Graham, A., Smith, A. and Taylor, N. (2010) 'Children's participation as a struggle over recognition: exploring the promise of dialogue', in B. Percy-Smith and N. Thomas (eds) *A Handbook of Children and Young People's Participation,* London: Routledge, p 293–306.

Freire, P. (1972) *Pedagogy of the Oppressed,* Harmondsworth: Penguin

Hart, R. (1992) *Children's Participation: From Tokenism to Citizenship,* Florence: Unicef Innocenti Centre.

Helsper, W., Krüger, H.-H., Fritzsche, S., Sandring, S., Wiezorek, C., Böhm-Kasper, O. and Pfaff, N. (2006) *Unpolitische Jugend. Eine Studie zum Verhältnis von Schule, Anerkennung und Politik (Unpolitical youth. A study on the relationship between school, recognition and politics),* Wiesbaden: VS-Verlag.

Holford, J. and van der Veen, R. (2003) *Lifelong Learning, Governance and Active Citizenship in Europe.* Final Report of the ETGACE Project. Guildford: University of Surrey.

Holzkamp, K. (1993) *Lernen. Subjektwissenschaftliche Grundlegung (Learning – subject-oriented foundations),* Frankfurt am Main, New York: Campus.

IARD (2001) *Study on the State of Young People and Youth Policy in Europe. Final report.* Milano: IARD.

ISS (Institut für Sozialarbeit und Sozialpädagogik) (2007) *The Socioeconomic Scope of Youth Work. Study commissioned by the youth partnership between Council of Europe and European Commission,* online: www.youth-partnership.net (accessed 10 May 2011).

Jeffs, T. and Smith, M. (1999) 'The problem of youth for youth work', *Youth and Policy,* no 62, pp 45–66. www.infed.org (accessed 10 May 2011).

Kornbeck, J. and Jensen, N. R. (2009) (eds) *The Diversity of Social Pedagogy in Europe,* Bremen: Europäischer Hochschulverlag.

Kränzl-Nagl, R. and Zartler, U. (2010) Children's participation in school and community: European perspectives', in B. Percy-Smith and N. Thomas (eds) *A Handbook of Children and Young People's Participation,* London: Routledge, pp 164–74.

Lauritzen, P., Hansen, B. J., Azzopardi, A., Walther, A., Raykova, A. and Baenziger, D. (2005) *Youth Policy in the Slovak Republic*, Strasbourg: Council of Europe Publishing.

Lave, J. and Wenger, E. (1991) *Situated Learning. Legitimate Peripheral Participation*, Cambridge: Cambridge University Press.

Leontjev, A. N. (1981) *Problems of the Development of the Mind*, Moscow: Progress Publishers.

Loncle, P. (2009) 'Youth work and policy in France', in G. Verschelden, F. Coussée, T. Van de Walle and H. Williamson (eds) *The History of Youth Work in Europe*, Strasbourg: Council of Europe, pp 131–51.

Loncle, P. and Muniglia, V. (2008) (eds) *Youth Participation, Agency and Social Change. UP2YOUTH Thematic report*, online: www.up2youth. org.

Machacek, L. (2006) 'Student school councils: an impulse for non-formal education for Democracy in Slovakia', *Kultura i Edukacja*, no 4, pp 36–45.

Machacek, L. and Walther, A. (2008) 'Participation and learning', in: Loncle, P. and Muniglia, V. (eds) *Youth Participation, Agency and Social Change. UP2YOUTH Thematic report*, online: www.up2youth.org, pp 62–80.

Marshall, T. H. (1950) *Class, Citizenship and Social Development*, Chicago: University of Chicago Press.

Percy-Smith, B. (2006) 'From consultation to social learning in the community: participation with young people', *Children, Youth and Environment*, vol 16, no 2, pp 153–79.

Reutlinger, C. (2005) 'Unsichtbare Jugend und verdeckte Engagementstrukturen' ('Invisible youth and hidden structures of engagement'), in Austrian Institute for Youth Research (ed) *Die Jugend ist die Zukunft Europas, aber bitte noch nicht jetzt! Möglichkeiten der Integration und Partizipation von Jugendlichen in Europe, (Youth is the futur of Europe but please not yet! Possibilities of integration and participation of young people in Europe)*, Vienna: OEIJ, pp 155–73.

Spannring, R., Ogris, G. and Gaiser, W. (eds) (2008) *Youth and Political Participation in Europe. Results of the Comparative Study EUYOUPART*, Opladen: Barbara Budrich.

Thomas, N. and Percy-Smith, B. (2010) 'Introduction', in B. Percy-Smith and N. Thomas (eds) *A Handbook of Children and Young People's Participation*, London: Routledge, pp 1–9.

von Schwanenflügel, L. (2011) '"… dass ich ja doch was ändern kann." Biographische Relevanz für benachteiligte Jugendliche in der Jugendarbeit' ('"… that I can really change things." Biographical relevance of participation for disadvantaged youth in youth work'), in A. Pohl, B. Stauber and A. Walther (eds) *Jugend − Akteurin sozialen Wandelns* (Youth − the changes for social actors), Weinheim, München: Juventa, pp 237–63.

Walther, A. (2010) 'Partizipation oder Nicht-Partizipation? Sozialpädagogische Vergewisserung eines scheinbar eindeutigen Konzepts zwischen Demokratie, sozialer Integration und Bildung' ('Participation or non-participation? Social pedagogical reflection on an apparently unambiguous concept between democracy, social integration and education'), *Neue Praxis*, vol 40, no 2, pp 115–37.

Walther, A., du Bois-Reymond, M. and Biggart, A. (eds) (2006) *Participation in Transition. Motivation of Young People in Europe for Learning and Working*, Frankfurt a.M.: Lang.

Walther, A., Stauber, B. and Pohl, A. (2009) *Youth Actor of Social Change. Final report*, online: www.up2youth.org.

Wenger, E. (1998) *Communities of Practice. Learning, Meaning and Identity*, Cambridge: Cambridge University Press.

Williamson, H. (2002) *Supporting Young People in Europe: Principles, Policy and Practice*, Strasbourg: Council of Europe.

Winkler, M. (2000) 'Diesseits der Macht. Partizipation in Hilfen zur Erziehung - Annäherungen an ein komplexes Problem' ('Not beyond power. Participation in public care − approaching a complex problem'), *Neue Sammlung*, vol 40, pp 187–209.

Yamashita, H. and Davies, L. (2010) 'Students as professionals: the London secondary school councils action research project', in B. Percy-Smith and N. Thomas (eds) *A Handbook of Children and Young People's Participation*, London: Routledge, pp 230–40.

THIRTEEN

Pupils' participation in French secondary schools: the interplay between tradition and innovation

Valérie Becquet

Introduction

The analysis of youth participation in France, whether directed towards political, associative or protest practices (Roudet, 2004; Becquet, 2009b; Muxel, 2010) or towards institutional programmes (Becquet, 2005a, 2006, Loncle, 2008) often leaves aside participation in schools. Yet school participation involves a wide range of young people: the pupils in secondary schools. These young people often combine in school participation with out-of-school participation, or move from one to the other (Becquet, 2005b; Guillaume and Verdon, 2007). Moreover, opportunities for participation have been developed in school since the 1990s, principally through the increase in pupils' rights and in the number of pupils' representative bodies. These different levels of interest in pupil participation reflect the historical conception of the school's role in citizenship training.

First of all, in France, and particularly since the Revolution, the ambition of school has been to form future citizens through a model of political socialisation aiming at the transmission and achievement of knowledge to be used once voting age is attained. Secondly, at the same time and over the centuries, all of the informal upper secondary school pupils and students participation practices (associations, think-tank, congregation, newspapers, folk parade, etc.) were and are either controlled or prohibited by the school authorities. Two reasons are advanced for this state of affairs. On the one hand, informal participation was considered more as a problem for authorities than as a contribution to daily school life. Restricting it was a means of preventing the pupils from getting out of hand (Caron, 1991; Legois et al, 2007). On the other hand, pupils were not considered to be active participants in their schools, thus informal participation had no place in school and was not encouraged.

This lasting conception of the role of the school and the place of the pupil explains the resistance that goes hand in hand with the development of pupil participation in secondary school, the minor legitimacy it is granted, and the preference for formal participation. Consequently, while political discourse concerning school makes widespread use of the notion of citizenship, the schools themselves have difficulty in allowing it to be exercised. This chapter deals with the link between school, citizenship and participation. Firstly, it will show that there are three models of citizenship coexisting in secondary education: educational, juridical and political. Why do they exist and to what social and political developments do they refer? On what definition(s) of citizenship are they based? This chapter illustrates that citizenship in school is expressed through formal participation which is often supervised by adults. Secondly, the implementation of the political and juridical models will be analysed. How concerned are pupils and how are they involved? Do they face limits and problems? Does the reality of differing definitions of citizenship and tools to make pupils be and become citizens have negative effects on adult and pupil involvement in school?

Citizenship as a subject of training

In France, citizenship training, that is the acquisition of knowledge and skills required to exercise the future role of citizen, lies within an intellectual tradition linking education with access to citizenship and more generally with the training of the individual. This training favours a transmission model based on a process of internalisation of social and civic norms. Moreover, this definition of the school's role is also linked to French political history. During the revolutionary period, citizenship crystallised the debate and become a central reference. It constituted at the same time the foundation and the future perspective of the new regime, using school to legitimise the principles of political sovereignty and prepare its future actors. School, henceforth compulsory, had to afford the challenges of bringing individuals into the 'community of citizens', leading them to recognise themselves as members of the nation (Schnapper, 2000) and emancipating them from traditional socialisation spaces such as family and Church.

From this perspective the Civic Education Plan, ratified in an Act on 28 March 1882 (Act n°11 696 on Compulsory Primary School), was of vital importance. Inspired by Enlightenment philosophy and the ideas of Condorcet, this school subject aimed to develop in children a 'love for the Republic, France, the Fatherland and the State'. Civic education was based on the transmission of knowledge relating to institutional functioning, the rights and duties of citizens, and their expected moral and political behaviour (Deloye, 1994). According to these political preferences, from then on school was in the position to contribute to 'the moral training of the country', as Emile Durkheim emphasised in *Education and Sociology* (1922). As a 'little society' (Durkheim, 1925), school is the place of education, that is of preparation for generations 'not yet ripe for social life'. While the choices made during the Third Republic asserted the school's role in training citizens and clarified this in terms of format and content, many changes have since been made, concerning both the level of interest accorded to this mission and to its implementation. Consequently, while the question of citizen training is always present in educational policies, the contexts of mobilisation for this objective, the political and social expectations expressed on the subject, and the public structures involved have become distinctly more complex.

Contemporarily, the reference to citizenship echoes social phenomena that are relatively heterogeneous yet all point to problems in regulating how secondary schools operate and how pupils behave.

On the one hand this issue considers the deterioration of the climate in schools, the increase in incivility and school violence, and the weakening of teachers' authority; on the other hand it takes into account participation by the pupils, the assertion of their rights and their demands for dialogue, involvement and justice expressed in their protests. The legal texts, the 1989 Orientation for School Act followed by the 2005 Orientation and Programme for the Future of the School Act continue in line with the republican project, conferring on the school the mission to prepare the child for 'the exercise of his/her responsibilities as a (wo)man and a citizen', but the practices of citizenship in schools have become more and more diversified. Citizenship is no longer simply defined in terms of the evolution and the future of the individual but now arouses 'expectations in the present' (Barrère and Martucelli, 1998). This results in different conceptions of citizenship and along with the transmission approach, the introduction of a participative method favouring practice as a way of constructing civic knowledge and skills, and as a means of regulating pupils' behaviour. At present there are three approaches to citizenship in secondary education. These have specific objectives and are organised around particular methods, but they all lie within a dual temporality: the present time of school life and the future time of voting age.

Citizenship: three models to the same concept

The first model is disciplinary and based on the transmission of knowledge. The introduction of civic and moral education by Jules Ferry at the end of the 19th century laid the foundations of the citizenship-training programme. Though it was perpetuated by successive political regimes, the disciplinary model changed its name and organisation. It either gave rise to a separate subject or was included in the history/geography syllabus. In France today citizenship training exists throughout school education. In primary and lower secondary schools it forms part of the 'common base of knowledge and skills' introduced in 2006 and refers mainly to the acquisition of a 'humanist culture' (history, geography, literature and arts) and of social and civic skills (topics such as rights, duties, responsibility, freedom, principles of the state and institutions).

In upper secondary schools it comes under civic, juridical and social education (ECJS) and is taught by history/geography teachers. ECJS content deals with topics such as the state, the public institutions, political and social life, armed forces and security, and ethical questions. The disciplinary model shows two dimensions: a behavioural dimension which is central in the first stage, conveying the notion of 'living together' (Raveaud, 2006) and a cultural dimension focused on the transmission of the formalised knowledge concerning the existing social, economic and political order, and also on the will to take account of current events. Active teaching methods such as debating and discussion are increasingly given preference.

The second model is grounded on a juridical approach, rooted in school rules. Transmitting the rules of common life implies measures regarding teaching organisation, school discipline, pupils' rights and obligations and so forth. The juridical model has achieved a growing role in regulating the running of schools. This development reflects the demand for law and order expressed by teachers and principals due to the increasing school violence and the difficulty in exercising authority. It also reflects a more global change in the position of the school towards the law. Up to the end of the 1980s, disciplinary measures taken by schools were regarded as 'internal measures'; however, legal problems regarding the wearing of religious signs and the application of the principle of secularity have linked the school to general legal principles. In order to pride itself on being a space of rights and duties, justifying the pupils' respect of these, school could no longer remain a space ruled by customary law. School rules were therefore changed and their legality monitored more strictly. Together with the regulation of duties and sanctions the rights of pupils have been gradually promoted and incorporated in law. These rights have been growing since the early 1990s. Changes were facilitated due to the 1989 Orientation for School Act, and the International Convention on Children's Rights adopted by the United Nations in 1989 and subsequently ratified by France in 1990. These texts define the 'rights' enjoyed by pupils and 'children'. In continuity with this and following an upper secondary school protest movement, the rights of publication, association and meetings were recognised in 1991. When these public rights entered upper secondary schools, some limits were set in consideration of the specific features of schools. In July 2000, in order to bring previous choices into coherence and recall the importance of this text in school life, the secondary schools rules were revised (Merle, 2005). The juridical model thus frames the school community while focusing on the status of the pupils within it. It states the nature of the legal relations between pupils and institution by defining duties, rights and norms of justice.

The third model is political and sprang from the concept of 'school life' that appeared after the Second World War. In October 1945 a circular stipulated the existence of 'class leaders representing pupils in the permanent sections of the councils and administrative offices'. It took some twenty years for the second stage to be reached with the creation of the role of class delegate, and pupils' clubs in 1968. The admission of pupils to staff meetings provoked opposition from teachers and school principals fearing a loss of power. The creation of the Établissement *Public d'Enseignement Local* (local state school) in 1985 included a reassertion of the role of the class delegate on school boards. The 1989 Orientation for School Act proposed the creation of pupils' delegate council, an assembly of all class delegates; this last assembly did not come into existence until November 1990. The first stage of consultation with pupils was later completed through a series of texts. In 1991 the academic upper secondary school committee was created, then in 1995 the national upper secondary school council. The final implementation took place at local level: the Upper Secondary School Pupils' Life Council was created in 2000 and the Pupils' Delegates Committee was replaced by the Pupils' Delegates' Conference, followed in 2004 by the General Assembly of Pupils' Delegates. The political model is fully developed in upper secondary schools. In lower secondary education it is restricted to pupil representation in staff meeting and in the school board. The political model is based on a definition of the school as a political city to which its members are committed. Via school, pupils come to be granted the status of citizens.

This presentation of the three models highlights the coexistence of different approaches to citizenship and the role of the school in building civic behaviour. The disciplinary model meets the traditional objective of citizen training, citizenship being exercised at voting age. The other two models regard the pupil not as a citizen in evolution but as a fully active citizen. The pupil is duty-bound to act within a legal framework of rights and duties, and can exercise political power through voting or eligibility. Thus citizenship is exercised without 'preparation'. However, this distinction between the three models does not mean that the borders between their respective aims are clear. Civic education was actually relaunched with the purpose of improving the atmosphere in schools. Successive governments assumed that learning about institutions and behaviour had to have a direct impact on the everyday school life. The existence of three identifiable models raises the question of their interaction, and with their adequacy concerning the school's operation and the pupils' place in it. Pupil participation is seen primarily within the juridical model which allows them to publish newspapers, carry out projects in the socio-educational club or pupils' club, or to create in-school associations, and within the political model which allows the pupils to represent their classmates and execute projects via the pupils' councils or via the health and citizenship education committees.

Participation through the juridical and/or the political model is grounded in the idea of formal participation. It always takes place in an institutional framework that allows school principals to monitor activities if they so wish. Consequently, it is quite difficult for secondary school pupils to develop informal participation. For example, if they want to organise a carnival, a year-end party or a concert, they have to submit the project to the Pupils' Delegates' Committee in order to obtain authorisation. This procedure is not only related to issues of liability and safety but it also reflects an approach of pupil's participation.

In reality, if the development of those opportunities in response to present-day school evolution can be considered as a positive orientation for pupils, the way they are framed and implemented also shows a certain ambiguity. Anne Barrère and Danilo Martucelli (1998) underline the tension between the logic underlying the models of citizenship and the youth experience in school life. They stress the existence of a form of 'expressive individualism' and school utilitarianism in a state of tension with school integration and collective action. Pupil participation is apparently all the harder to develop as it is based on the gap between the highly valued standards of action and the pupils' real experience. Pupils are supposed to behave like autonomous, responsible individuals, but at the same time they are maintained in an infantilising position: they should behave like citizens without being treated as such (Xypas, 2003). This hiatus is clearly evident in surveys on pupil participation in secondary schools.

Being a citizen at school: conditions and limits of participation practices

In 2004 a quantitative survey, carried out by the French Ministry of Education among final year upper secondary school pupils, aimed to measure participation practices in and outside schools (Guillaume and Verdon, 2007). This survey is important because there was no national quantitative measure of pupils' participation. Most of the surveyed pupils (84%) had taken part in at least one activity in 2003–04: four in ten (43.6%) had partaken in activities both inside and outside their schools; one in three (35.2%) in external activities only, while a small minority (4.9%) was only active inside their school. Nevertheless, almost half of the pupils participated in group activities in school, either in the socio-educational club, the pupils' clubs and the representative bodies. Only 13% of them have experienced responsibility, the others are participant simply by being there. The Ministry of Education survey shows that there is consistent pupil participation but other qualitative studies are more critical towards participation conditions and the practices that ensue.

In relation to formal participation appropriate to the political model, even if the pupils are informed and vote in the class delegate elections at the beginning of school year, their interest in this kind of participation is different. Upper school pupils express unequal desire to participate or else justify their defection by mentioning study requirements or extra-school activities. The lack of desire reflects the declining importance attributed to the representative's role, while study requirements echo the amount of schoolwork and the need to pass the baccalaureate examinations. Pupils elected as delegates also put such arguments forward.

Surveys highlight six reasons to stand for election. There are three main reasons: the 'vocation', the 'continuity', the 'distinction'. The other three are secondary reasons: the 'integration', the 'curiosity'; the 'sacrifice' (Becquet, 2005c, 2009a). Concerning 'vocation', pupils insist on their interest in this function. They think they are 'made for' being pupils' delegates who can represent the other pupils. They also explain their candidacy through their wish to help pupils and solve problems in their classroom.

> Actually, I repeated my second (first year of upper secondary school) and last year I was in a quite chaotic class … Pupils' delegates did not do their job very well … Actually, the class was really … it was really a shame … the whole year long. It was really a disaster. You know, I wanted to stand for election to try and solve problems that may arise in the classroom.

> What I like most about the position of delegate is that you can attend the class council. There we get to know what they think of us, what they dare not tell us and what they say between teachers. … It is mainly to defend the class and compare our viewpoints. To come, discuss and try and reach an agreement.

'Continuity' concerns pupils who have a genuine interest in the position and whose first experience becomes part of a continuous process. Each year they stand for election because they have the 'vocation' and are not disappointed with their previous experience. 'Distinction' is eventually referred to the specific position in the classroom gained from being a delegate. Pupils insist on their proximity with adults and their access to information on the school's management.

> Actually, it's because I'm curious. I like to know what's going on in my upper secondary school. Yes because we do not know everything. Students do not know everything and for me it was a kind of curiosity at the beginning. Then I grew more and more interested by the school board. And there are the adults. They talk a lot about positions, budget. I'm interested in this. I like all that stuff out there, all they can do for us. It's true that I enjoy taking part into this.

The three other reasons that explain standing for election are less present in pupils' interviews but show how they use this function. First, pupils refer to 'integration' when becoming a delegate helps them discover their new school and meet the other pupils. Second, they quote 'curiosity' when they were not interested in this function during lower secondary school, but grow more interested when arriving in upper secondary school. Reference to curiosity is also linked to the creation of the pupils' delegates committee in 2000. Some pupils who were not interested in being pupils delegates in the classroom decided to join this new council. Third, some pupils compare their candidacy to a 'sacrifice' because on election day nobody wanted to become pupils' delegate. As a consequence, they decided to stand for election.

When they stand for election, they declare a wish to be useful to others, a certain taste for responsibility, a desire to have a relationship with the adults in the school other than educationally, and having access to information (Guillaume and Verdon, 2007; Becquet, 2009a). They hold a genuine interest in the position and in some cases the experience becomes part of a continuous process.

Despite this, the work of François Dubet (1991) and Patrick Rayou (1998) came to a relatively pessimistic conclusion on formal participation. They insist on the hazardous or even unlikely nature of the interplay between roles, the role of pupil and that of pupils' delegate, wherein outlines are blurred. They describe a school experience characterised by tension and trials, in which delegates are placed in uncomfortable situations leading to conflict or renouncement. Class delegates are in a difficult position owing to three conflicting aspects. The first concerns the definition of the pupils' delegate mandate. Pupils' representatives in a class council or on a school board often stress the vagueness of their role and the consequent difficulty in knowing what exactly their activity involves. Many difficulties emerge among schools, ranging from the single transmission of information to representation of pupils demands (Becquet, 2002).

> Yes, it's a little bit discouraging. I'm involved in this council for three years. We must persevere or we'll never succeed. By dint of trying we get there a little more. In spite (of setbacks) there's an improvement. Anyway, he [the principal] will have to adapt. And even if it doesn't please everyone, we try to move forward. We try to do things. Even if we do not succeed, you have to convince that it works. We mustn't give up.

> If there was something concrete, we could say we had done something for the school. We have to stop talking and do something concrete. Two years that it exists. There is nothing. It's hard. We worked but it was unsuccessful.

When pupils describe their function, they point out different types of activities (Becquet, 2005c). Pupils' delegates' work in class council is organised around three phases: first, before the class council meeting, delegates try to grab information from pupils about the atmosphere of the classroom, their teachers and, individually, on personal situations that can help them to defend pupils; second, during the class council meeting, they take notes on individual assessments made by each teacher and they try to intervene to explain pupil's specific situations; third, they give collective or individual feedback to pupils of their classroom. In the other councils where pupils are represented, the work is quite different. In the school board, meetings deal with administrative and financial issues. Pupils' delegates attend meetings and are present only to give the 'pupils' point of view'. In the pupils' delegates committee, which is focused on everyday school life, during official meeting delegates communicate pupils' demands and suggest facilities to improve pupils' life and organise different projects. Between two meetings, they also work together on projects (Becquet, 2002, 2005c).

> Right now for example, I make them fill individual sheets for the class council in relation to their personal problems or school work problems. There are many pupils who don't write anything on the form but who come to me and tell me things. But they do not necessarily want me to speak about this during the class council meeting.

> During the meeting, the teachers ask me what I think about the class. I say what I think about the pupils who have problems, about the scholar level of the pupil. And then, when they examine the case of each pupil, well I say what I think, if I agree or not with teachers and after I write all the information I have, what the teachers say about each pupil and I fill a sheet for each pupil with what they think about his behavior.

> They usually come to me after the class council meeting. When I see our teacher, she exposes everyone's problems in public. Everyone in the class does not like that. For example, there are two that have behavior warnings and she told people names. Everyone said it's nobody's business, that was personal, but she really insisted and she said it.

The second concerns the possibility of speaking in representative bodies and asserting the pupils' point of view. While the inequality in pupils' expression is linked to their personalities, it also relates to the contexts in which they speak. Because of the formal nature of the meetings and the difficulty in defining the subjects to debate, pupils sometimes fail to speak (Becquet, 2009a). Thus in class councils dealing with examination results and pupils' behaviour, defending the pupils is not easy; and in upper school councils, many subjects are bypassed in order to avoid conflict. Consequently the pupils' delegates have difficulty in expressing their points of view, a difficulty that increases in case of disagreement with adults' opinion (Becquet, 2002).

> Especially we have a principal that, he leaves us talk ... well let's say that. We decide but sometimes we feel that he would like to influence us a little bit and it's sometimes a little unpleasant. We would like to be able to decide alone among pupils. And it happened once that a delegate told him 'listen is up to us and ...' Politely I mean ... But sometimes it's a bit annoying because the principal is still ... He represents the authority. It's not easy to get in front against the principal.

> During the class council we can speak but I don't do it often. I'm intimidated by all the teachers and as the other delegate is not present ... But if there is anything that seems important to me I am telling it. When all the teachers are talking I prefer not to take the floor.

The third relates to the risks run by pupil delegates, who often fear of receiving poorer marks or negative feedback by their teachers. Delegates with poor or average results in schoolwork, or who criticise school and campaign for improvements in study conditions particularly feel this. The sense of risk also concerns relationships with other pupils in the class, who sometimes consider class delegates as allies of the adults against their peers. This dual discredit does not always encourage pupils to participate in representative bodies, especially in becoming class delegates. These three aspects clearly raise the issue of the legitimacy of institutional participation by pupils. It is encouraged by the Ministry of Education yet not given equal support in schools. Between a school where the principal and teaching staff are in favour of it and one where they are not, there is a real contrast in terms of participation dynamics and activities performed.

Regarding the juridical model, the analyses throws light on the concepts of the law working in schools, particularly the primacy of respect for teaching and public order over the expression of individual rights, and the persistence of a hierarchical relationship among the actors in the school community. They also point out the gap between the reality of a right and the pupils' poor awareness of it, even the existence of a discrepancy between this reality and the pupils' idea of their own rights within the school. Thus when the school's rules seem out of keeping with the experience of pupils in lower and upper secondary education, they question the honesty and therefore the legitimacy of these rules. They don't reject the principle of the right but the way it is put into practice (Merle, 2005). Such disparities between formal and actual rights are seen in studies handling the experience of upper school journalists, who are not always acquainted with the texts governing the right of publication. They complain about the impossibility of covering certain topics such as everyday school life or politics, and about acts of censorship. Their judgement of the fairness of such decisions is erratic because these are explained insufficiently and without reference to the law. These disagreements show a difficulty in understanding the freedom of expression granted to pupils and a fear that this freedom may be exercised against teaching staff. The problem relates more generally to issues about how the respective positions of the actors are perceived and about conceptions of order in school, rather than to strictly legal questions (Becquet, 2003). As with institutional participation, the question arises from the legitimacy of pupils' participation via the publication of a magazine. The right of self-expression, exercised within the framework of a representative body or in writing, clashes with a school organisation struggling to position itself and accept this right in all its dimensions. For example, in school pupils' newspapers, discussions concerning politics or the running of the school are not always allowed. On the one hand, pupils decide to leave politics alone to comply with the editorial line of their newspaper; however, it is also because they do not want to share their personal opinions as they fear reaction the school's reaction:

> ... at the beginning we did not have a particular ideology in the newspaper. We said that we did not want to do something political, we do not want controversy. So it was at the political level, addressing the news but remaining, giving his opinion but I mean not drawing the crowds. It's not that this is not a political paper, but we did not want that there were really specific ideas linked to a political movement.

Pupils refuse to talk about school life and, in particular about teachers, because they find it uninteresting or because they fear accusations of defamation:

> ... it's not our type to talk about teachers, making fun for example. If I want to make fun of a teacher, I do it in class,

not in the newspaper. While it is true, pupils expect it a little bit. But this is not our goal. (Becquet, 2003)

It is hardly surprising that pupils fail to see their school as a living space, where they can take part in associations. On this point, although practices in schools have not been extensively studied, pupils have access to activities, mainly sports and cultural, but only rarely do they help to develop these activities. They often prefer to be involved in associations outside of school.

Surveys do not analyse the relations between those different models of formal participation but findings show that there are not in actuality linked to each other. Pupils' participation is based more on these three ways of defining and implementing citizenship in school than on an integrated mode.

These models are complementary however or, at least in some aspects, overlapping. The school experience is mainly structured by the juridical and political models through the application of school rules and the presence of pupils' representatives. Through them, pupils face situations that contribute to their political socialisation and build opinions and behaviours concerning citizenship. If the implementation of these models is not consistent, or gives rise to inconsistencies between the models, the legitimacy of the reference to citizenship may be invalidated. For example, if on the one hand, pupils have a right of expression integrated in the school rules and, on the other hand, pupils' delegates are unable to express their demands or their discontent, they highlight the gap between principles and reality and reveal that the right of expression is a formal rather than a tangible right, or that the election of class representatives is unnecessary because they possess a minimum prospect of performing their function from the pupils perspective. Therefore, through such a situation, several of the principles and mechanisms of citizenship are weakened. Examples of tension between the juridical and the political models can be multiplied. The risk of inconsistency becomes more important when the disciplinary model is taken into account. Indeed, the situation described refers to principles and practices that civic education promotes. As the aim of this programme is to provide standards of behaviour, pupils must be convinced of the value of rights and duties and of the benefits of the democratic model and, for example, of the need to vote to choose their representatives. However, if the school fails to implement the standards they value, pupils may question their legitimacy. Various media have already provided them with knowledge of political and social life, and to show a certain distrust of politicians and political institutions. If the encountered situations and their implementation contradict (perhaps) the principles that they are expected to endorse as citizens, they also question pupils' positions. In the disciplinary model, pupils learn how to become a citizen and have a rather passive attitude. In the juridical and political models; they exercise their citizenship and are encouraged to be active. The transition from one posture to another, from the pupil who receives information to the pupil who has to speak, express opinion or defend the other pupils, is not always obvious. It takes place in a similar context, the school environment, but in a different situation, one side a teaching situation (the class), the other a political situation (the class board council for example).

The discrepancies between the three models also result from the existence of different conceptions of the role of school in building citizens and the means to achieving this conception. These disagreements, when expressed inside the same school, do not promote the legitimacy of the three models, nor do they facilitate pupils' participation. Nevertheless, the lack of an integrated model of citizenship is the result of the political choices that frame the references to citizenship in school. As stressed in the description of the three models, the different tools have been implemented more often than not through problem-solving logic rather than through the logic of building civic skills and the integration of pupils in daily school life. In many ways, the notion of citizenship was gradually manipulated and the tools and practices required are now segmented.

The implementation in 2006 of the 'common base of knowledge and skills' in primary and lower secondary education can be seen as a means to foster an integrated approach to citizenship in schools. Indeed, three skills refer to the training of citizens and can be compared with the three models: 'humanistic culture' that 'contributes to the formation of judgment, taste and sensitivity and can acquire markers', 'the social and civic competences' which aim 'to master, as an individual and as a citizen, the basic rules of social life and to implement them in schools' and 'autonomy and initiative' skill which aims towards independence and then carrying out of projects across the school. However, the skills approach is not easy to implement in an educational system that values sheer knowledge above all else. It involves thinking about the relationship between knowledge and skills and the process of acquiring these skills and the evaluation of these processes. In addition, the school promotes some implicit social skills and excludes others that are structuring youth experiences, such as rituals and rules between pupils that adults unevenly master (Gasparini, 2008) or external practices. An integrated approach to citizenship needs to build a bridge between the three models, youth life and the acquisition of common base skills in order to highlight their continuity. This work requires a reflection on the contribution of school education for citizenship and its relationship to out of school civic practices and to supposed collaboration among and between educational professionals.

Conclusion

The analysis of pupils' participation in schools clearly highlights that the way in which French public secondary schools define and implement citizenship and pupil participation introduces various misunderstandings concerning pursued goals and the degree of pupil participation. Firstly, it seems that there is a contradictory positioning of the school towards pupil participation, participation that is simultaneously encouraged and discredited. If training citizens is part of school goals, the way the numerous measures and programmes were integrated and used in daily-life school progressively made principals, teachers and pupils either more suspicious or less interested in those opportunities. Moreover, the frequent references towards citizenship as a vehicle in solving school problems and the confusion between citizenship and civility have weakened its signification. Secondly, the coexistence between three models of citizenship raises two problems. On the one hand, the implantation of each one is not easy because the school's organisation, rules, standards, and the adult and pupil positions are tested and there is not necessarily any agreement on these elements. One the other hand, as there is no integrated model of citizenship in secondary school, tensions or contradictions between them can arise. Thirdly, the varying degrees of legitimacy granted to pupil participation have repercussions on pupils' interest and involvement. It can be noted that pupils' expression is more often transferred to areas outside schools. The recurring upper secondary school protests are evidence of this. Although they are organised in reaction to proposals for educational reform and addressed to national government, pupils' claims are also linked to daily school life (study conditions and relationships with teachers for examples). They could be expressed beyond the scope of pupils' representative bodies but it seems to be more difficult to be heard in them. Pupils, like young people in general (Becquet, 2009b; Muxel, 2010), prefer using direct means of expression such as demonstrations, strikes (which are 'prohibited' because pupils are not considered to be workers), or sit-ins. On this point, school participation seems to be disconnected from other forms of participation, which young people regard as more legitimate. All those elements should be taken into account because participation in schools is a contribution to political socialisation. In surveys among voluntary workers or militants, primary experiences in school are frequently spotted. Such experiences, when they occur in good conditions, leave visible traces in personal biographies. It is highly likely that discrediting them will have the opposite effect and nourish mistrust of commitment to the community.

References

Barrère, A. and Martucelli, D. (1998) 'La citoyenneté à l'école: vers la définition d'une problématique sociologique' ('Citizenship in school: toward the definition of a sociological problem'), *Revue française de sociologie*, vol 34, no 4, pp 651–71.

Becquet, V. (2002) *Mise en place et fonctionnement des conseils de la vie lycéenne (The implementation of high secondary school councils)*, Ministère de la Jeunesse, de l'Education nationale et de la Recherche.

Becquet, V. (2003) 'Les journaux lycéens entre droits et infractions' ('Students' newspapers between rights and offences'), in G. Hénaff and P. Merle (eds), *Le droit et l'école. De la règle aux pratiques (Law and school. From rule to practices)*, Rennes: Presses Universitaires de Rennes.

Becquet, V. (2005a) 'Dialoguer avec les jeunes: un engagement réciproque? Les conseils de la vie lycéenne et les conseils de la jeunesse' ('Dialogue with young people: a reciprocal engagement? The high secondary school councils and the youth councils'), in V. Becquet and C. de Linares (eds) *Quand les jeunes s'engagent. Entre expérimentations et constructions identitaires (When young people engage themselves. Between experimentations and identity buildings)*, Paris: L'Harmattan, pp 107–26.

Becquet, V. (2005b) *Les conseils de la jeunesse à Paris. Atouts et difficultés d'un dispositif de démocratie participative (Paris youth councils. Assets and difficulties of an attempt of participative democracy)*, Rapport de recherche, Paris: CAFI.

Becquet, V. (2005c) 'Les délégués des élèves: contenus et effets d'une fonction représentative' ('Pupils' representatives: content and effects of a representative function'), in *Les dossiers de l'Observatoire de la vie lycénne*, Caen, Rectorat de l'Académie de Caen, pp 8–23.

Becquet, V. (2006) 'Participation des jeunes: regards sur six pays' ('Youth participation: analysis in six countries'), *Agora Débats Jeunesses*, no 42, pp 14–29.

Becquet, V. (2009a) 'Se saisir du conseil de la vie lycéenne: des principes à l'exercice de la fonction de délégué' ('To use the high secondary school council: from principle to reality'), *Carrefours de l'éducation*, no 28, pp 65–79.

Becquet, V. (2009b) 'L'engagement des jeunes dans l'espace public' ('Young people's engagement in public space'), in B. Roudet (ed) *Regard sur les jeunes en France*, (Analysis on young people in France), Laval: Les Presses de l'Université Laval, pp 103–22.

Caron, J.-C. (1991) *Générations romantiques. Les étudiants de Paris et le quartier latin (1814–1851), (Romantic generations. Paris' students and the Quartier Latin (1814–1851))*, Paris: Armand Colin.

Deloye, Y. (1994) *Ecole et citoyenneté. L'individualisme républicain de Jules Ferry à Vichy: controverses, (School and citizenship. Republican individualism from Jules Ferry to Vichy: controversies)*, Paris: Presses de la FNSP.

Dubet, F. (1991) *Les lycéens (High secondary school pupils)*, Paris: Seuil.

Durkheim, E. (1922) *Education et sociologie (Education and Sociology)*, Paris: Presses Universitaires de France.

Durkheim, E. (1925) *L'éducation morale, (Moral education)*, Paris: Presses Universitaires de France.

Gasparini, R. (2008) 'Compétences sociales des élèves' ('The social competencies of pupils'), in A. van Zanten (ed), *Dictionnaire de l'éducation (Dictionary of education)*, Paris, Presses Universitaires de France.

Guillaume, J.-C. and Verdon, R. (2007) *Pratiques citoyennes des lycéens dans et hors de l'établissement (High secondary school pupils' citizenship practices in and out school)*, Les dossiers Insertion, Education et Société, Paris: Ministère de l'éducation nationale, de l'enseignement supérieur et de la recherche.

Legois, J.-P., Monchablon, A. and Moder, R. (eds) (2007) *Cent ans de mouvements étudiants (A century of students' movements)*, Paris: Syllepse.

Loncle, P. (2008) *Pourquoi faire participer les jeunes? Expériences locales en Europe (Why should young people participate? Local experiences in Europe)*, Paris: L'Harmattan.

Merle, P. (2005) *L'élève humilié. L'école, un espace de non droit? (The humiliated pupil. School as a lawless space?)*, Paris: Presses Universitaires de France.

Muxel, A. (2010) *Avoir 20 ans en politique, (Being twenty years old in politics)*, Paris: Seuil.

Raveaud, M. (2006) *De l'enfant au citoyen, (From the child to the citizen)*, Paris: Presses Universitaires de France.

Rayou, P. (1998) *La Cité des lycéens (The city of high secondary school pupils)*, Paris: L'Harmattan.

Roudet, B. (2004) 'Entre responsabilisation et individualisation: les évolutions de l'engagement associatif' ('Between responsibility and individualisation: the evolutions of associative engagement'), *Lien social et politiques*, no 51, pp 17–27.

Schnapper, D. (2000) *Qu'est-ce que la citoyenneté? (What is citizenship?)*, Paris: Gallimard.

Xypas, C. (eds) (2003) *Les citoyennetés scolaires (School citizenship)*, Paris: Presses Universitaires de France.

Part Five

Outlook and conclusions

Participation or non-participation? Getting beyond dichotomies by applying an ideology-critical, a comparative and a biographical perspective

Andreas Walther

A common thread connecting the contributions gathered in this volume relates to the observation that public as well as scientific discourses tend to measure young people's political and social participation one-dimensionally and against the standards of formally institutionalised and acknowledged contents and forms of participation. Consequently, the assessment of youth participation tends to be reduced to a quantitative measure of 'more' or 'less' both in historical perspective and across different social and educational backgrounds; or to a qualitative distinction between 'real' and 'false' participation from both affirmative and critical viewpoints. Both perspectives imply a secure and shared knowledge that allows distinction between participation and non-participation. This chapter builds on the previous chapters. However, rather than summarising them, it aims to extract three core perspectives which seem promising in overcoming this dichotomy: (1) an ideology-critical perspective analysing the meaning and function of current participation discourses; (2) a comparative perspective transcending assumptions of normality regarding the participation of young people which in national contexts appear to be held as self-evident or even natural; and finally (3), a biographical and cultural perspective which conceptualises participation as individual agency that flows consequently from the subjective perspective of individual actors.

Beyond discourses

> The young human capital needs to be nourished and
> nurtured ...Youth needs to be prepared for profiting from

the chances of participation. (European Commission, 2009, p 1)

Both classical critical theory as developed by Adorno and Horkheimer and modern discourse analysis following the work of Foucault have repeatedly pointed out that there is no single concept within concrete societal discourses which does not fulfil specific functions, that is not embedded within grown power relationships and that is not related to the interests of particular actors. The same applies for the concept of participation which has been increasingly referred to, starting from the last decade of the 20th century, and triggered by documents such as the *United Nations Convention on the Rights of the Child* or the EU White Paper *A New Impetus for European Youth* (European Commission, 2001). The historical and societal context can be denoted by late or reflexive modernity characterised by the acceleration of individualisation and the de-standardisation of institutionalised life courses. This means, on the one hand, that individual choice has become a cultural good on which individuals rely as almost natural (Beck, 1992). On the other hand, this also means that national welfare states no longer succeed in providing their citizens equal opportunities for a 'good life' based on employment and consumption (Jessop, 2002; Taylor-Gooby, 2004; Held, 2006).

The quote above on the relationship between participation and human capital is extracted from a youth policy document of the European Commission (2009) with the telling title *Investing and Empowering*. It reveals that the meaning of participation in current discourses is far from restricted to the perspective of democracy and individual autonomy but expands to the dimensions of economic competitiveness and welfare restructuring. In fact, there is more than casual analogy between the concepts and discourses of participation and activation (van Berkel and Hornemann-Møller, 2002). Both refer to the active individual and the need to remove institutional restrictions from individual agency. The fact that activation implies not only limiting social rights and imposing sanctions on school leavers, job seekers and welfare recipients in case of ascribed passiveness, but goes along also with increasing the mechanisms of state control (Rose, 2000) suggests that it interprets the idea of the autonomous individual not in terms of democracy and participation but of flexibility and self-responsibility – or the concept of '*homo economicus*' making rational choices. Moreover, if the specific concept of participation emerges from different conceptual backgrounds and normative assumptions, the discursive context needs to be taken into critical consideration. Masschelein and Quaghebeur

(2003) have pointed out the potential of the participation discourse in serving as a 'strategy of immunisation' whereby it prepares the cultural ground for a positive connotation of self-responsibility while discrediting the notion of solidarity as inhibiting individual agency.

This means that securing both the analytical and the normative potentials of the concept of participation for youth research and youth policy requires a critical 'reading' of societal contexts and the hegemonic conditions framing both its use and reference (Gramsci, 1975) and distinguishing participation which simultaneously secures individual autonomy with rights and resources from the one-dimensional demands of self-responsibility.

Beyond national normalities

While the current discourse on participation has evolved globally and connects to trends of transnational governance it remains rooted in national traditions, pathways and connotations of (active) citizenship. Citizenship implies specific sets of rights and responsibilities and reflects assumptions of normality regarding the legitimacy of individual and collective claims and demands. These normalities – or discourses – are cultural patterns which are interwoven with public institutions as well as with individual biographies whereby they are endowed with considerable normative power. The regulative potential beyond state institutions – encompassing even participation structures in the Internet (see Chapters 8 and 9) – as well as their normalising power justify referring to them as 'regimes'. Comparative research on welfare as one of the key institutions of modern nation states therefore distinguishes welfare regimes as different rationales in regulating the relationships between the individual and society (Esping-Andersen, 1990). These works have been also applied in comparing youth policies (IARD, 2001), school to work transitions (Walther, 2006) or structures of the life course (Mayer, 1997; Heinz, 2001; Walther, 2011).

International comparison in these contexts serves as a means of deconstructing normalities that have been institutionalised nationally. In the following, a comparative analysis of constellations of participation will be outlined for the countries involved in this volume: Austria, Finland, France, Ireland, Italy, Slovakia and Spain. It needs to be repeated that available data allow only for a very tentative overview which in a second step will be related to the model of youth transition regimes (see Chapters 3 and 11).

The information on youth participation collected with regard to the seven countries derives from European statistics (EUROSTAT), the Young Europeans Study (Eurobarometer, 2007), the Council of Europe's All-European Study on Participation in School (Dürr, 2003; Birzea, 2004) and European research projects such as EUYOUPART (Spannring et al., 2008), the IARD study (IARD, 2001), information provided by the Knowledge Centre of the Youth Partnership between European Commission and Council of Europe (www.youth-partnership.net) and the YOYO study on participation in young people's transitions to the labour market (Walther et al., 2006). The information covers the areas of youth and student councils, civic education and youth work, rates of membership in organisations, and relates them to contextual factors of national youth policy structures and to comparative typologies such as welfare and transition regimes.

Austria provides a relatively sustainable context of young people's participation compared with other countries. Youth and student councils benefit from a legal framework which prioritises representative forms of participation and, to some extent, includes forms of co-decision making. Every second young person is a member of an organisation, usually in leisure time and recreational activities while every fourth is involved in voluntary activities. Apart from voting, taking part in online forums is the preferred political activity. Civic education is a mandatory school subject although it remains unclear as to what extent its cross-curricular establishment is a strength or weakness. Professional youth work relies on a distinct social work profile in open youth work while associative youth work depends largely on volunteers. In sum, youth participation in Austria seems well organised, which facilitates and restricts engagement at the same time within institutional boundaries at national and regional level. Local possibilities of participation depend on the political priorities of local governments.

In Finland, youth councils or youth parliaments have traditionally been closely connected to politics and administration at municipal as well as national level, with elections of representatives held in schools. Sometimes these structures coincide with student councils, sometimes both structures exist independently. While this system ensures that young people's voices are heard and that they are involved in decision making – and evidences that young people enjoy some citizenship status –, the limitation of activity to an official (adult) agenda has led to a decline in young people's involvement. In many municipalities, new developments have arisen either replacing or complementing these councils through flexible youth forums, action groups and Internet-based structures. Similarly, civic education is partly integrated, and partly taught as a separate subject. Around two in five young people are members of organisations. Apart from unconventional forms of participation such as signing petitions, membership in trade unions is much higher in Finland than in any other EU country, which suggests that formal social rights still seem to be relevant for Finnish young people.

In France, youth councils are established at local, department and national level although less sustainably so than in Austria and in a less reflexive fashion when compared with Finland. Student councils are restricted to secondary school and have minimal impact on the organisation of school life. The presence of school principals in council sessions suggests a paternalistic approach, which is also reflected by legal instruction as a part of civic education or by a youth work model of sociocultural animation in which traditionally the organisation of 'positive' leisure activities dominated over the provision of open spaces. In analogy, participation often simply means involvement of professional youth workers in decision making at local level where youth participation strongly depends on political priorities. Only one fourth of young people are members of any organisation, mainly in culture and arts, one in eight is engaged in voluntary activities. Preference for demonstrations can be interpreted either as a resentment against a dominating paternalistic approach ('participation' as concept for alternative forms of political activity) or as an expression of a specific French interpretation of 'the public'.

In Ireland youth participation is implemented both nationally and locally. Despite the title 'youth parliament' recruitment occurs through membership in organisations rather than through elections. Where student councils do exist, they are weak with limited competencies. Civic education in school is conceptualised under the title of personal, social and health education which suggests a more individualised than institutionalised approach. Youth work is professionalised, provided mainly through youth or social organisations with open approaches standing alongside more targeted preventive practices aimed at the social inclusion of young people deemed to be at risk. Slightly more than one fourth of young people declare themselves as members of an organisation and one out of every six is engaged in voluntary activities. NGOs are the most trusted and used means of political articulation. Corresponding to the central role of youth and social organisations, youth participation is often referred to in terms of social capital while also consumerism is interpreted as a form of social participation.

Youth participation in Italy is facilitated neither legally nor through infrastructures at national level apart from funding for youth-oriented projects. Youth policies and youth work depend exclusively on the socioeconomic and political climate at local level without any national legislation. In some municipalities, youth councils exist; however the most widespread local youth policy is youth information relying on concept of participation of 'users' of public services. Apart from this, youth work (or sociocultural animation) focuses on extra-curricular activities rather than open spaces. As a reaction to this, a movement of self-organised youth centres has developed. Similarly, participation is primarily interpreted in terms of alternative political engagement such as participating in demonstrations as a preferred form of political activity. Few young Italians are members of an organisation: these few are mainly found in social and political NGOs, and in cultural or arts associations. In school, student councils exist in secondary education, yet only at provincial level, while civic education is integrated into other subjects such as social sciences, law and economics, and/or history.

In Spain the implementation of structures of youth policy is a bit more advanced than in Italy. Yet, participation is limited to formal structures, civic education is not a separate subject and youth work is largely interpreted in terms of education for the labour market. This is reflected by a low rate of young people in organisations or engaged in voluntary activities.

Slovakia needs to be viewed from the perspective of an ongoing process of transformation and democratisation. In principle, a version of the Austrian model is envisaged through implementing youth councils at local, regional and national level sustained by legal framework. This applies also to student councils and to the inclusion of civic education as a mandatory subject in the school curricula. This top-down approach is mirrored in the close relationship between the National Youth Council and national youth policy. At the same time, many towns or cities neither encourage the development of youth councils nor undertake major investment in any youth policy at all. A profile of professional youth work is still in the making, with a rather weak focus on open youth work and a stronger emphasis on youth associations and the organisation of extra-curricular activities in school. Young people themselves are rarely members of organisations; when they are they prefer organisations with a focus on young people. While almost one fourth are engaged in voluntary activities, many young people prefer the discretion of online forums for expressing political views.

The comparative analysis of structures, meanings and forms of youth participation in these countries is obviously limited by lack of sufficient and solid data. Apart from this, an international comparison of youth policy suffers from the lack of information regarding the relationships between the national and local levels where youth policies tend to be delivered. In effect, the differences between single municipalities may be greater than between nations.

In order to explain the differences between institutional forms of youth participation it is necessary to analyse them in relation to the wider social contexts in which they are embedded and through which they are endowed with specific functions and cultural meaning. As a second step, we will therefore relate the indicative national configurations displayed above with comparative models regarding regimes of welfare, youth policies and youth transitions. The regime typologies refer to developmental pathways and configurations resulting from the interaction of socioeconomic, institutional and cultural factors (Gallie and Paugam, 2000; IARD, 2001; Walther, 2006; see also Chapter 2).

According to existing models, Austria and France belong to a cluster of nations characterised by a *conservative* welfare state securing employment or family status rather than individual citizenship status. Youth policies are referred to as paternalistic and protectionist in the interpretation of children and young people's rights, with the exception of Austria where individual participation rights are more explicitly established. Apart from this, the differences between local contexts are bigger in France than in Austria because there youth policies are administered on national and regional levels and therefore are more standardised across municipalities. The way in which transitions are regulated in this context can be characterised as employment-centred, as youth is primarily addressed in terms of allocation and socialisation for occupational positions. The well-organised form of participation in Austria corresponds to the corporatist structures of this regime type which is best characterised by the rather selective education system containing limited individual choices and close boundaries on the scope of youth participation and youth work. In France corporatist structures are weaker; however, the (still) centralised model of governance and the fact that youth policies have never been organised in a strong sectoral way results in a more paternalistic participation model.

The *liberal* welfare and transition regime is characterised by a strong emphasis on individual responsibility and early economic independence. In the Irish case this seems less visible with regard to youth policy and youth participation because it is balanced by the Catholic legacy of voluntarism. Another explanation is the community-based approach in youth policy with the key role of NGOs, a strong social capital discourse and participation being less strongly facilitated by institutional and legal structures (see Chapter 7).

Interestingly, youth work was the responsibility of the education department until recently (2010); it now belongs to a new Department of Children and Young People. Non-formal education and youth participation are being promoted in the context of activation policies aimed at mobilising human capital.

The cases of Italy and Spain are indicative of a structural deficit in youth policy, reflecting a rudimentary or *under-institutionalised* welfare state in which the family has a central role as 'social *amortisator*'. The relevance of informal channels and structures for welfare and youth transitions also applies in regard to youth participation. The lack of youth policy structures implies a lack of recognition of young people as co-citizens. While this has led to the emergence of a dynamic third sector in which young people do express and articulate themselves, these forms are rather unsustainable and precarious. Youth information centres represent the widest spread tools to close the gap, yet youth work is only developing slowly (see Chapters 5 and 7).

Finland belongs to the *universalistic* welfare, transition and youth policy regime of the Nordic countries. Here, youth primarily entails the personal development that is included in citizenship status, secured by social rights and individual choice. The high relevance of young people's individual social rights is also reflected by high public concern regarding the attractiveness of mechanisms of participation and a clear political will to improve them according to young people's interests and preferences (see Chapters 4 and 10).

In Slovakia the redefinition and restructuring of the relationship between the individual and society are still in progress. In various areas, policies for young people seem to orientate towards the conservative or employment-centred model – yet under different contextual conditions, for example higher youth unemployment and a segregation of Roma young people. The extent to which current policies actually match the needs of the contemporary youth population is not clear; how they fit into the overall institutional framework, whether the historical legacy is sufficiently taken into account, and to what extent the rapid decentralisation process leaves spaces for a cooperation between local, regional and national level remain unanswered questions (cf. Lauritzen, et al, 2005).

The comparative perspective adds two important aspects of differentiation to the ideology-critical perspective: firstly, it qualifies

Table 14.1: Configurations of youth participation in selected EU member states

	Austria	Finland	France	Ireland	Italy	Slovakia	Spain
Dominant meaning	Youth councils/ organisations	Youth councils, co-decision making	Political participation, youth workers	Youth, social capital, consumerism	Political participation, youth information	Youth organisations, youth councils	Youth councils
Youth councils							
name	Youth representation	Youth council	Youth council	Youth parliament	Youth council	Youth council	Youth council
level	All	All	All	Local, national	Local	All	All
legal frame	Yes	Yes	Yes	Yes	No	Yes	Yes
access	Variable	School	Variable	Organisations	Variable	Organisations	Variable
Student councils							
name	Pupil/student representation	Student councils, student union	Councils of secondary school life	Student councils	Provincial student councils	School student councils	Student councils
level	Primary, secondary	Primary, secondary	Mainly secondary	Primary, secondary	Mainly secondary	Secondary	Primary, secondary
issues	School life, co-decision making	School, co-decision making	School life	School life	School life	School life, co-decision making	School life
sustainability	Medium – high	High	Medium	Weak	Weak	Medium	Medium
Civic education							
name	Civic education	Social studies	Civic, legal and social education	Social, personal and health education	Social studies	Civic education	Social studies
school level	Primary, secondary	Primary, secondary	Primary, secondary	Primary, secondary	Primary, secondary	Primary, secondary	Primary, secondary
subject	Integrated, mandatory	Integrated, mandatory	Separate, mandatory	Separate, mandatory	Integrated, mandatory	Separate, mandatory	Integrated, mandatory
Youth work model							
name	Youth work	Youth work	Socio-cultural animation	Youth work	Socio-cultural animation	Youth work	Youth policy, animation
legal basis	Yes	Yes	No	Yes	No	No	Yes
main forms	Open/associative youth work	Open/associative youth work	Open youth work, Associative youth work	Open youth work, Social inclusion	Youth information, extra-curricular activities	Associative youth work, extra-curricular activities	Associations, labour market education, youth information

continued

Table 14.1: continued

	Austria	Finland	France	Ireland	Italy	Slovakia	Spain
professional qualification	Social worker/social pedagogue	Youth worker	Social worker	Youth worker	Social educator	Social worker/ social pedagogue	Social educator
Young people's membership in organisations, voluntary and political activity (Eurobarometer 2007)							
Total ...				28%	13.4%	11.5%	11.9%
mostly ...				Hobby-related	Cultural, artistic	Youth	Social
voluntary				17.6%	15.8%	24.8%	9.3%
political				NGO	Demonstration	Online forum	Demonstration
Context factors of youth policy, welfare and transition regimes							
Governance	Comprehensive	Comprehensive	Comprehensive	Fragmented	Fragmented	Comprehensive	Fragmented
Age range	0–25		0–25	5–18	15–30	15–25	
Youth policy	Protectionist	Universalistic	Protectionist	Community-based	Familistic	Post-socialist	
Transition reg.	Employment-centred	Universalistic	Employment-centred	Liberal	Under-institutionalised	Post-socialist	Under-institutionalised
Welfare reg.	Conservative	Social-democratic	Conservative	Liberal	Sub-protective	Post-socialist	Sub-protective

the critical view of a universal trend towards participation as cultivating the colonisation of individual subjectivity in the context of the activating welfare state by showing that activation and participation develop differently in different contexts with different scopes and consequences of autonomy for young people; secondly, it nourishes a critical perspective by the knowledge that broader scopes of individual autonomy and participation exist and are possible.

Beyond predefining young people's agency?

The third perspective which may help in transgressing institutionalised dichotomies between 'real and false' or 'more and less' participation is taking young people's subjective views as a point of departure following a biographical perspective. This does not necessarily exclude expressed collective perspectives, such as youth cultures for example (see Chapter 9), provided that they are subjectively relevant for a young person.

A biographical perspective is necessary because of social change in relation to the late modernisation and individualisation which has also affected the meaning and forms of participation and which implies taking subjective meanings into account when theorising and defining participation. Isin and Wood (1999) interpret the shift from conventional towards non-conventional forms of participation (see Chapter 3) as a change in the relationship between subjective identity and citizenship in late modernity. One key element in this is the *de-standardisation of life courses* (Walther, 2006). Prolonged and fragmented transitions between youth and adulthood imply – depending on the context of the respective regime type – that full citizenship status is suspended, especially one's access to social rights. Beyond the guaranteed attainability of a standard biography and the validity of full citizenship status, the 'fit' between subjective biography and collective action in the community needs to be justified in each situation anew as much as public institutions need to prove their trustworthiness (cf. Giddens, 1991). Thereby the relationship between individuals and the public or the collective is being biographised with situative factors gaining in relevance comparative to long-term factors. Engagement also needs to be reconciled with transitions to work as well as with youth cultural self-experimentation and self-presentation. Pais describes the participation of young men and women in late modern societies as 'trajective citizenship' characterised by fluidity and networking rather than by formalised commitment (Pais, 2008, p 238). The de-standardisation and biographisation of life courses implies that universal meanings of participation can no longer be assumed. Instead, processes of how participation is being constructed need to be addressed – including construction by individual citizens. In their longitudinal study in Britain, Smith et al. (2005) found that young people constantly shift between a formalised model of 'citizenship as status' and a more constructivist model of 'citizenship as practice' (cf. Lister, 2003). Individualised construction of participation is however affected by the fact that public space is being segmented and fragmented whereby possibilities for deliberative negotiation are decreasing (Sennett, 1977; Bauman, 2000; Cockburn, 2010). From the view point of a social geographer, Reutlinger (2005) contrasts conventional participation programmes that are normally situated in spaces detached from young people's everyday lives – 'containers' – with young people's everyday life 'maps of coping'. He outlines in a heuristic manner the spaces in which their subjective lives take place and in which they try to achieve meaningful goals. Individual and collective construction of participation therefore includes the creation – or re-appropriation – of public space (Habermas, 1992).

The biographical meaning of participation was also at the centre of the European research project *Youth – Actor of Social Change* (UP2YOUTH) on the relationship between young people's agency and social change (see Chapter 2). One problem affecting the joint work was a lack of existing research on young people's subjective views of participation, another was the constantly arising question of the boundary between participation and non-participation with the result of a constantly broadened concept of participation which can be illustrated by two cases and the debates whether these were to be seen as participation – or not:

• The youth riots in the suburbs of French cities in 2005 resulted from a conflict with the authorities in which young people felt powerless. The subsequent violent rebellion against this feeling was subsequently reinforced by repression and misrecognition from the state. In turn, young people provided a double '*mise en scene*' of the riots: on the one hand, a competition of violence (burning cars) documented on the Internet playing with double standards of public morality on the other hand, claiming to be seen and treated as citizens of the French Republic (Lagrange and Oberti, 2006; Lapeyronnie, 2006).
• Skaters are a primarily leisure- and fashion-oriented youth culture for which performing in public spaces is central; public performance which often results in conflicts with other citizens and/or the authorities. In Cork, Ireland, these constant conflicts motivated

young skaters to candidate for the municipal elections, yet without transforming into long-term political engagement.

In neither of the cases, neither the institutional actors nor the young people described themselves and their actions as political – at least in the beginning. They neither referred explicitly to the common good nor were they characterised by organised collective consciousness. In both cases, public institutions did not take them seriously but criminalised their actions, stigmatised their issues as particular or superficial and their claims as illegitimate. At the same time both cases stand as public attempts towards articulating needs and for claims to negotiate these needs in public space. They represent different forms of representation, yet forms in which the political notion of 'us and the others' is present. Pais describes youth cultural activities such as skating in public space – following Deleuze and Guattari (1993) – as transformation of striated into smooth public spaces (Pais, 2008, p 233). In fact, young people participate in constructing social space by making hegemonic spaces public. A basic need of young people in late modernity, which is expressed by burning cars as much as by skating in public areas, is *visibility.* Feeling seen and perceived is both a prerequisite and a result of social recognition and – especially under conditions of uncertainty – central for subjective identity (Giddens, 1991; Honneth, 1996):

> Speaking of citizenship means speaking of 'faces', identities. Individual identities (of a person, a voice, a position, a subjectivity) and group identities ('us'), people like ourselves, in relation to 'others' (who differ from us). But citizenship has traditionally referred to a universalised person, to an impersonal 'face'. Can citizenship exist without recognition of the identity of a 'face'? To what extent can the universalist attributes normally associated with the notion of citizenship accommodate claims for subjectivities and group identities? Does the citizenship ideal start and finish with the claim of equality or can it also recognise difference? (Pais, 2008, pp 228–9)

Both examples not only represent youth-specific forms of articulation, subcultural styles or a lack of participation competence but also – perhaps rather generational- than age-specific – claims for a right of visibility as a key component of a biographically relevant citizenship status. If one broadens institutional concepts of participation consequently towards a biographical understanding potentially all action becomes participatory (Sörbom, 2010). The aim of these reflections however is not so much laying grounds for a radicalised participatory theory of democracy (although not at all contradicting what is intended) but overcoming dichotomies between participation and non-participation, between politically relevant and irrelevant issues resulting from power relationships and assumptions of normality while hiding the everyday life and biographically relevant engagement of young people. Therefore the question *participation or non-participation?* can only be solved heuristically by referring to all actions of young people in or directed to the public as potentially participatory – provided that there is no communicative validation of the underlying subjective needs and interests and the consciousness of the collective and the public.

Outlook

If the analysis and the reflections regarding the inadequacy of dichotomising participation and non-participation along institutionalised forms and definitions of participation undertaken in this book deserve consideration this necessarily has consequences for practice, policy and research. With regard to policy this may imply the strengthening of young people's individual rights – including social rights – in order to increase their autonomy and power in negotiating needs and interests with other co-citizens and institutions. Rather than designing participation programmes, political action needs to ensure the accessibility and openness of the public sphere as a social space where individual and collective views are expressed, recognised and exchanged. In regard to practice, the fundamental requirement appears to be a practice of recognition which avoids subjecting young people to conditions and procedures of adaptation but is inventive in finding methods of understanding individual expressions which move beyond institutionalised conventions. This links to the role of research, which until now has focused on measuring young people's behaviour against institutionalised scales of participation without analysing potential new meanings and issues of the public and the collective inherent to whatever young people's actions imply. It has also concentrated on the input and output of youth participation – orientations, attitudes and values on the one hand, decisions and actions on the other – while neglecting the processing of participation, that is the complexity of negotiation and decision making involved. This in turn depends on the extent to which youth research succeeds in emancipating itself from a paradigm according to which the function of youth research is defined from the viewpoint of existing institutions rather than dynamic societies.

References

Bauman, Z. (2000) *Liquid Modernity*, Cambridge: Polity Press.

Beck, U. (1992) *Risk Society: Towards a New Modernity*, London: Sage.

Birzea, C. (ed) (2004) *The All-European Study on Pupils' Participation in School*, Strasbourg: Council of Europe.

Cockburn, T. (2010) 'Children and deliberative democracy in England' in B. Percy-Smith and N. Thomas (eds) *A Handbook of Children and Young People's Participation*, London: Routledge, pp 306–18.

Deleuze, G. and Guattari, F. (1993) *A Thousand Plateaus: Capitalism and Schizophrenia*, Minneapolis: University of Minnesota Press.

Dürr, K-H. (2003) *The School: A Democratic Learning Community*, Strasbourg: Council of Europe.

Esping-Andersen, G. (1990) *The Three Worlds of Welfare Capitalism*, Cambridge: Cambridge University Press.

Eurobarometer (2007) *Young Europeans. A Survey Among Young People Aged Between 15–30 in the European Union. Analytical Report*, Brussels: Eurostat.

European Commission (2001) *White Paper. A New Impetus for European Youth*, Brussels: European Commission.

European Commission (2009) *An EU Strategy for Youth – Investing and Empowering. A Renewed Open Method of Coordination to Address Youth Challenges and Opportunities. A Communication from the Commission*, Brussels: European Commission.

Gallie, D. and Paugam, S. (eds) (2000) *Welfare Regimes and the Experience of Unemployment in Europe*, Oxford: Oxford University Press.

Giddens, A. (1991) *Consequences of Modernity*, Cambridge: Polity Press.

Gramsci, A. (1975) *Note sul Machiavelli, sulla politica e sullo Stato moderno*, Roma: Editori Riuniti.

Habermas, J. (1992) *The Structural Transformation of the Public Sphere: Inquiry into a Category of Bourgeois Society*, Cambridge: Polity Press.

Heinz, W. R. (2001) 'Work and the Life Course: a cosmopolitan-local perspective', in V. W. Marshall, W. R. Heinz, H. Krüger and A. Verma (eds) *Restructuring Work and the Life Course*, Toronto: University of Toronto Press, pp 3–23.

Held, D. (2006) *Models of Democracy*, Cambridge: Polity Press.

Honneth, A. (1996) *The Struggle for Recognition: Moral Grammar of Social Conflicts*, Cambridge: Cambridge University Press.

IARD (2001) *Study on the State of Young People and Youth Policy in Europe. Final report*, Milano: IARD.

Isin, E. F. and Wood, P. K. (1999) *Citizenship and Identity*, London: Sage Publications.

Jessop, R. (2002) *The Future of the Capitalist State*, Cambridge: Polity Press.

Lagrange, H. and Oberti, M. (eds) (2006) Émeutes *urbaines et protestations, une singularité française* (Urban riots and protest, a French singularity), Paris: Presses de Sciences Po.

Lapeyronnie, D. (2006) 'Révolte primitive dans les banlieues françaises, essai sur les émeutes de l'automne 2005' (Primitive rebellion in French suburbs, essay on the autumn 2005 riots), *Déviance et société*, vol 30, no 4, pp 431–48.

Lauritzen, P., Hansen, B. J., Azzopardi, A., Walther, A., Raykova, A. and Baenziger, D. (2005) *Youth Policy in the Slovak Republic*, Strasbourg: Council of Europe.

Lister, R. (2003) 'Acquiring responsibilities and citizenship: social participation and social responsibilities', in European Observatory on the Social Situation, Demography and Family (ed) *Family Forms and the Young Generation in Europe. Proceedings of the Conference Held in Milan, 20–22 September, 2001.* Vienna: ÖIF, pp 95–103.

Masschelein, J. and Quaghebeur, K. (2003) 'Participation as strategy of immunisation?' *Ästhetik & Kommunikation*, no 34, pp 73–6.

Mayer, K.-U. (1997) 'Notes on a comparative political economy of life courses', *Comparative Social Research*, vol 16, pp 203–26.

Pais, J. M. (2008) 'Young people, citizenship and leisure', in R. Bendit and M. Hahn-Bleibtreu (eds) *Youth Transitions. Processes of Social Inclusion and Patterns of Vulnerability in a Globalised World*, Opladen and Farmington Hills: Budrich, pp 227–45.

Rose, N. (2000) 'Government and control' in D. Garland and R. Sparks (eds) *Criminology and Social Theory*, Oxford: Oxford University Press, pp 183–208.

Sennett, R. (1977) *The Fall of Public Man*, New York: Knopf.

Smith, N., Lister, R., Middleton, S. and Cox, L. (2005) 'Young people as real citizens: Towards an inclusionary understanding of citizenship', *Journal of Youth Studies*, vol 8, no 4, pp 425–45.

Sörbom, A. (2010) 'It is merely changing: an analysis of the concept of individualisation in relation to contemporary political participation', in E. Amnå (ed) *New Forms of Citizen Participation: Normative Implications*, Baden-Baden: Nomos, pp 115–31.

Spannring, R., Ogris, G. and Gaiser, W. (eds) (2008) *Youth and Political Participation in Europe. Results of the Comparative Study EUYOUPART*, Opladen and Farmington Hills: Barbara Budrich.

Taylor-Gooby, P. (ed) (2004) *New Risks, New Welfare. The Transformation of the New Welfare State*, Oxford: Oxford University Press.

Van Berkel, R. and Hornemann-Møller, I. (eds) (2002) *Active Social Policies in the EU: Inclusion Through Participation?* Bristol: The Policy Press.

Walther, A. (2006) 'Regimes of youth transitions. Choice, flexibility and security in young people's experiences across different European contexts', *Young*, vol 14, no 2, pp 119–39.

Walther, A. (2011) *Regimes der Unterstützung im Lebenslauf*, Opladen and Farmington Hills: Barbara Budrich.

Walther, A., du Bois-Reymond, M. and Biggart, A. (eds) (2006) *Participation in Transition. Motivation of Young People in Europe for Learning and Working*, Frankfurt a.M.: Lang.

Dynamic *and* socially embedded: biographies of participation in youth

Gill Jones

This book has opened up the issue of participation in youth to explore what lies beneath the superficial discourse. It has examined official and unofficial constructions of participation by young people in a range of socio-political domains, explored the motivations and rationales underlying official attempts to increase participation among young people, and offered a critique of their effectiveness. This agenda was not undertaken in a vacuum. Political participation is a form of citizenship, a term which describes the complex relationship between the individual and formal society (the state): a relationship which changes not only over time but also over the life course. In this postscript, I shall briefly examine the effects of individualisation on citizenship in youth, and more broadly on young people's biographies. Then I would like to consider why it is not only policy structures which affect young people's participation, but also the beliefs and practices in their families. This leads me to question how young people can become active citizens in the manner expected of them when their economic and social dependence on their parents has been extended.

From collectivism to individualisation

The shift in post-industrial societies from modernity, with its fixed ideologies, to a more relativist middle-ground world view, demographic change, and the crisis in welfare capitalism are only some of the major social shifts in recent decades. In post-war welfare states, citizenship was thought of in terms of universal rights (to employment, to housing or to welfare) aimed at ensuring a minimum basic standard of living. There has since been a shift towards seeing citizenship in terms of individual responsibility. Welfare dependency is seen by those on the centre-right of politics as one of the main causes of social ills, generating a 'feckless' underclass culture. A blame culture has thus developed. The social glue of shared experience which held communities together is said to be under threat. We are no longer 'all in this together'; each of us stands alone. The reality is not only greater inequality, but the *individualisation* of poverty. Responsibility for escaping poverty is increasingly laid at the feet of the individual, who is *blamed* for his or her own circumstances. Structural explanations of social inequality have been disregarded by policy makers, in favour of cultural ones, which have themselves been distorted and exaggerated. The violent riots in English cities in the summer of 2011 were quickly defined by most politicians as criminally rather than politically motivated (just as similar occurrences have been in other countries), and were followed by calls to clamp down punitively on a 'feral underclass' (Kenneth Clarke, Minister for Justice, *Guardian*, 6 September 2011). The social commentator Polly Toynbee, writing in the *Guardian* newspaper (13 September, 2011), reminded us that there was also a 'feral elite'.

Oddly, the shift away from collectivism has involved an emphasis on 'the community'. Not only are poor people blamed for their circumstances, but, as Chapter 2 in this volume indicates, those who do not actively and visibly participate as citizens are blamed for wasting their social capital. In the UK, the Prime Minister, David Cameron, talks of something nebulous he describes as the 'Big Society' while dismantling the welfare state that has arguably helped hold Britain together since the 1940s. There is therefore a difference between government rhetoric and government action.

Young people as citizens

Demographic shifts have upset the dependency ratio (the ratio of contributors to dependants), putting pressure on governments worldwide, and making welfare 'reform' economically necessary, as well as (for some) politically desirable. The impact on young people has been considerable. The welfare state in Britain had been starting to recognise young people as citizens in their own right by the 1970s, but many of their welfare rights have been withdrawn or eroded since then. The role of social protection of young people has been placed instead on parents, not only on economic grounds, but also on the more dubious assumptions that increased parental responsibility would 'strengthen family life' and in particular increase parental authority over their children (Jones, 2005). While governments may wish to save the burden on the taxpayer and increase the authority and control of parents, it must be remembered that families are mediators of social inequality, capable of intergenerational processes of transmission on both advantage and disadvantage. Parents now face an unprecedented burden, which some are not prepared to take on board (Jones, 2009).

The changing relationship between state and parents in social protection has affected the citizenship of young people. Many citizenship rights are held by parents on their children's behalf – thus children and young people are 'proxy citizens' rather than full ones (Jones and Wallace, 1992). Parents are expected to act as mediators between their children and the 'outside world', in a protective role towards their children, until such time as their children can take over responsibility for themselves (and others). There is no 'moment' when this change in status occurs, and different young people become responsible at different times and in different ways. Unfortunately, policy makers need to impose a structure on the transition to responsibility/ capacity in a way which is amenable to legislation. A standardised age framework is built up which governs the ages at which young people can leave school, receive welfare and housing support, and so on. Age is thus used by policy makers as a simple proxy variable for more complex qualitative concepts such as capacity (which is harder to measure), and so age-structured policies gradually (though rather messily) phase out the role of parents, and increase the status of young people on the basis of their age alone, in a manner which is insensitive to cultural practices (Jones and Bell, 2000). As Walther suggests, policy makers can legitimise age-discriminating limits on participation by emphasising young people's lack of competence, all on the basis of some very dubious assumptions.

Young people have always been less likely than other age groups to vote in general elections, but in recent decades those who are politically motivated have turned instead to issue politics to express their political views. It seems that young people have lacked the will, or the ability, to argue for their own cause; it is perhaps remarkable that they have not been able to develop means of formal collective bargaining outside student movements. On the other hand, this may simply be a result of the diversity of experience in youth: it is the most disadvantaged who are the least represented. Phil Cohen (1997) argued that riots in Britain in the 1980s occurred *because* young people lacked any form of collective bargaining. White et al (2000), investigating reasons for political apathy in Britain, found that young people tended to view politicians as untrustworthy, self-interested, ineffective, remote and unrepresentative. While possibly confirming this image by withdrawing many of the grants and benefits which helped young people make their transitions to adulthood, politicians have talked of lowering the voting age to 16 years. It may have been naïve to think that younger people would become more involved in formal political processes while becoming more excluded from economic ones.

Official approaches to participation in youth broadly take two forms which could be characterised as cynical or idealistic. Loncle and colleagues (Chapter 2) question the motivation underlying the enthusiasm of politicians for involving young people in policy initiatives, and reveal how allowing young people in France 'a voice' becomes a means of manipulating them into legitimising government policies. Indeed, it is clear from recent history that young people have frequently been manipulated as a political resource (see Jones, 2009) – the legacies of this is still visible in Italy and Spain (Chapters 7 and 8) – begging the question why young people are so often seen as 'empty vessels' waiting to be filled with ideological beliefs (Wallace and Kovatcheva, 1998) . In contrast to this more cynical approach, advocates for the young somewhat idealistically stress that giving young people 'a voice', while valuable in itself, should be part of a bigger agenda allowing young people to become more actively involved in the development and implementation of policies affecting them, and thus enabling them to have greater control over their own lives – agency, in other words.

Citizenship processes

There is a distinction between feeling a citizen, being recognised as a citizen, and active citizenship, as Ruth Lister (2008, p 17) indicates. She quotes T. H. Marshall's (1950) description of citizenship as a status bestowed on those who *are* full members of a community. Research on membership of youth parliaments shows that those who join are already integrated and it seems that those with inherited social and cultural capital may have a head start. Some young people are likely to have been socialised into political participation by politically active parents, as Chapter 10 indicates. For some, this may take the form of student politics (a training ground for party politics), while others, in the past, particularly, may have been brought up to support the trade union movement. For those lacking the 'right sort' of social and cultural capital from their parents, it seems that secondary socialisation through education and training for citizenship may be needed. There has been a perception, going back to the 18th-century Enlightenment and indeed before, of young people as 'savages' in need of 'civilising' through education into acceptance of the prevailing values and norms of society, before they can become responsible adults (Cohen, 1997; Jones, 2009) and as this book indicates, citizenship education can be seen as part of a 'civilising agenda'.

Public and private worlds

The life course is characterised by a shifting balance of rights and responsibilities. During their childhood and youth individuals build up competences in different areas of their lives – through experience, education and training – to allow them to take on responsibility in those areas. However, as Walther argues, competence is defined by policy makers according to narrow criteria which reveal how little they understand about the competences and skills of young people. It is important to understand young people's subjective perceptions and cultural beliefs. Young people have perceptions about their own capacity to change things through their actions (competence beliefs), but these beliefs (part of their identity capital) are constructed over their early life courses around previous experience of success or failure, including the ways in which they have been labelled in schools (see Jones, 2009). These subjective constructions of their own competence become central to the 'imagined futures' of young people, constraining and shaping their identities and life plans (Thomson et al, 2004).

A Catch-22 conundrum exists whereby young people have to be recognised as citizens (by self and others) in order to want to and be able to participate but have to participate in order to claim citizenship (Lister 2008, p 11). This is because participation and non-participation are dichotomised. One to open up and expand ways of defining participation (as the book has done), and the other is to understand citizenship as a *process*. Walther (Chapter 12) in effect does both when he suggests that participation practice should be seen as part of an education process rather than as a prerequisite for citizenship.

The acquisition of citizenship status is not a one-way process, as the status (or at least the roles and actions associated with it) shifts over the life course. Many of the problems with conceptualising participation in youth also apply at other times in the life course where economic independence has been compromised, such as among older people who have retired or women who have withdrawn from the workforce to care for children. Women's citizenship is affected by their 'dependence' on their partners, when their domestic/parenting work is not recognised (Lister, 1990, 2008). As the Introduction to this book notes, atypical work arrangements adversely affect worker participation unless the concept of participation is expanded to include the practice of everyday life. The increasing privatisation of family life and the separation of the public and domestic spheres mean that many people make non-visible social contributions which, being in the private sphere, are not formally recognised. Thus, young people may have heavy domestic responsibilities, working in family businesses, or caring for their siblings or parents, for example, and have developed competences in these areas, but receive no recognition.

There is stigma and blame attached to 'dependence' in both the public *and private* sphere (Jones, 2009, c.f. Sennet, 2003). Young people who are unable to be economically independent, because there are no jobs, are blamed as layabouts and social parasites. Social respect, deriving (according to Sennett, 2003) from self-development, self-sufficiency and reciprocity, is blind to the roles and responsibilities of private family life – and the second and third of these are particularly problematic for young people who are in a process of transition to independence. In youth the balance between rights and responsibilities inevitably shifts. The emphasis on children's rights gradually gives way to an emphasis on adult responsibilities, with young people somewhere in between. Over their life course, individuals are likely to achieve a balance between dependency and contribution ('balanced reciprocity'), but it is futile to expect immediate reciprocity in youth. Nevertheless, even when – as now – youth unemployment is soaring to unprecedented levels, it is the work ethic, as formally practised in the labour market, which remains the key to social respect.

Social biographies

All these considerations suggest that a life course approach should be taken to issues of participation and citizenship. This agenda means understanding individual biographies as socially embedded, and involving both public and private relationships of dependence and obligation. Thomson et al (2004) take a biographical approach to citizenship, seeing it as an ongoing process of construction and negotiation. This allows an investigation of the ways in which structural barriers (and indeed bridges) to social membership impinge on the ways in which biographies are developed; it also challenges the notion that failure to 'engage' is an individual responsibility. A biographical approach is not individualising when the social context of the individual is taken into account. The central question is whether young people are constrained by standardised 'institutional biographies' which have been mapped out for them or more able to create personal biographical projects ('biographies of choice').

Young people's lives are constrained by legislative frameworks and their 'standardised biographical patterns' (Beck, 1992) are thus defined by institutions rather than by young people themselves. Policy makers devise age frameworks for standardising 'youth' in different ways and in different domains (Jones and Bell, 2000, show that in Britain these are arbitrary and often contradictory). These frameworks determine what young people can do and when, without regard for longer-standing 'traditional' cultural or familial patterns of biography. The models of youth which underlie them are based on normative white middle-class beliefs and practice. There are, however, social class differences in attitudes towards parental support and dependence in youth. Thus, working-class families expect young people to become economically independent at a relatively early age, and failure to do so is seen as shameful; in middle-class families it is not unusual or shameful to continue to be dependent or semi-dependent on parents for longer (Jones, 2009). This means that policies extending dependency in youth are likely to be more damaging to working-class young people and their families than to middle-class ones. Government support for young people has become increasingly conditional on 'good' behaviour (defined politically rather than culturally) and what was once seen as a framework for social protection has been reconstructed as a means of social control. Everyday cultural beliefs and practices – enacted in peer groups and in family life – may thus underlie resistance by young people or by their parents to conforming to policy expectations.

The concept of 'reflexive biographies' (Giddens, 1991) suggests that, rather than resistance, there is negotiation between the individual and others in the management of risk and opportunity. Thus, citizenship processes are negotiated 'reflexively' between self and others (for Beck, these others are institutional frameworks which are the products of decisions individuals have themselves made). Walther points out in this volume those *others* – public institutions – have become less and less clearly defined and possibilities for deliberative negotiation are decreasing. This theory is particularly problematic for young people who can claim no such ownership over formal institutions. It is clear from both Giddens and Beck that the management of reflexive biographies requires a range of external and personal resources, which most young people lack.

Economic recession disproportionately affects young people and, according to Leahy and Burgess (in this volume), exploits their powerlessness. It will be argued that, nevertheless, young people have more opportunities than ever before, and here too there is a caveat. Giddens (1994) distinguishes between choice, which he says has become obligatory, and decision making, which requires power. Young people's 'choices' are structured by others. Evans (2002) uses the concept of 'bounded agency' to describe constraints which exist even when young people feel that they have the power to choose.

However much policy makers would like to stress autonomy, freedom of choice, and rationality in youth, and however much advocates for young people would like to be able to stress the concept of agency, the reality is that agency in youth is compromised. In practice, young people have very limited power to make choices and construct their individual biographies, being constrained by structures of opportunity or disadvantage, including and especially policy legislation, over which they have no control. Participation cannot therefore be viewed as a 'magic bullet' which will change young people's relationship to the social structures that shape their lives, as long as they are prevented from achieving economic independence.

Implications

A recurrent theme of this book has been about the ability of members of youth parliaments and other initiatives to represent young people, and it has been noted that lack of participation reflects wider social inequalities. Several of the authors in this book have commented on the social divisions between young people who participate and those who do not. Youth parliaments include the most vocal and socially integrated, but not those unable to verbalise their concerns and frustrations. It is argued that processes of participation can themselves be divisive; Coussée and Jeffs, for example, suggest that youth work, as part of an educational civilisation strategy, empowers the powerful but (often unconsciously) serves to control the vulnerable.

All of this indicates to me that an emphasis on participation alone is not enough, even if it were to encompass a wider range of young people. What is really required is a framework of policy initiatives which are based on an informed understanding of the needs of young people, and which are therefore designed to enable successful transitions into independent adult life – policies which address issues concerning employment, housing, welfare, transport, childcare, etc. This is what Loncle describes as the difference between transversal policies (based on wide-ranging transition needs) and specialised youth policies (based on age status).

This policy agenda means recognising heterogeneity in youth, and realising that young people within a fairly small age range can be in a very wide range of social circumstances, as students, workers or unemployed, as living with their parents or in their own homes, as children and as parents themselves, as single or in partnerships. It means understanding the cultural patterns of belief and practice that underlie their behaviour, and the structural inequalities which impact on their ability to take advantage of opportunities and manage risks. It means understanding young people's lives not just in the context of their peer groups, but also in the context of their family lives. The main dynamic in youth is the drive towards economic independence, and even in a recession we – society – must find ways to support this if we are not to fail a generation of young people.

References

Attias-Donfut, C. and Wolff, F.-C. (2000) 'Complementarity between public and private transfers' in S. Arber and C. Attias-Donfut (eds) *The Myth of Generational Conflict: Family and State in Ageing Societies*, London: Routledge.

Beck, U. (1992) *The Risk Society: Towards a New Modernity* (trans. M. Ritter). London: Sage.

Cohen, P. (1997) *Rethinking the Youth Question: Education, Labour and Cultural Studies* (2nd edn), Basingstoke: Macmillan.

Evans, K. (2002) 'Taking control of their lives? Agency in young–adult transitions in England and the New Germany'. *Journal of Youth Studies*, vol 5, no 3, pp 245–70.

Giddens, A. (1991) *Modernity and Self-Identity: Self and Society in the Late Modern Age*. Cambridge: Polity.

Giddens, A. (1994) 'Living in a post-traditional society', in U. Beck, A. Giddens and S. Lash. *Reflexive Modernization: Politics, Tradition and Aesthetics in the Modern Social Order.* Cambridge: Polity Press.

Jones, G. (2005) 'Social protection policies for young people: a cross-national comparison', in H. Bradley and J. van Hoof (eds) *Young People in Europe: Labour Markets and Citizenship*. Bristol: The Policy Press, pp 41–62.

Jones, G. (2009) *Youth*. Cambridge: Polity Press.

Jones, G. and Bell, R. (2000) *Balancing Acts? Youth, Parenting and Public Policy*, York: York Publishing.

Jones, G. and Wallace, C. (1992) *Youth, Family and Citizenship*, Buckingham: Open University Press.

Lister, R. (1990) 'Women, economic dependency and citizenship', *Journal of Social Policy*, vol 19, no 4, pp 445–67.

Lister, R. (2008) 'Unpacking children's citizenship', in A. Invernizzi and J. Williams (eds) *Children and Citizenship*, London: Sage, pp 9–19.

Marshall, T. H. (1950) *Citizenship and Social Class and Other Essays* Cambridge: Cambridge University Press.

Sennett, R. (2003) *Respect: The Formation of Character in an Age of Inequality*, Harmondsworth: Penguin.

Thomson, R., Holland, J., McGrellis, S., Bell, R., Henderson, S. and Sharpe, S. (2004) 'Inventing adulthoods: a biographical approach to understanding youth citizenship', *Sociological Review*, vol 52, no 2, pp 218–39.

Wallace, C. and Kovatcheva, S. (1998) *Youth in Society: The Construction and Deconstruction of Youth in East and West Europe*, Basingstoke: Macmillan.

White, C., Bruce, S. and Ritchie, J. (2000) *Young People's Politics: Political Interest and Engagement Amongst 14- to 24-Year-Olds*, York: Joseph Rowntree Foundation.

Index

Note: the letter 'n' following a page number indicates an endnote and 't' a table.

Austria 230, 235t
Finland 230, 235t
France 194, 231, 235t
Ireland 117, 193t, 194
Italy 194, 232, 235t
Slovakia 194, 235t
delegates
Spain 126
mental wellbeing
Finland 175–6
and ICT 174, 176–82
study circles 62
*Study on the state of young people and
youth policy in Europe* (IARD) 26–7
subculture 148, 150
suicide: Ireland 112
Sunday Schools 63
Sweden 83, 165
Swirak, K. *see* Powell, F. et al

T

technology 111 *see also* Internet
Thomas, Nigel: *Handbook of Children
and Young People's Participation* 2, 10
Thomson, R. et al 250
Tisdall, M. 79
Tonnucci, Francesco 133
Tovey, H. 110
Toynbee, Polly 246
trade unions 9, 65
Finland 231
Trimmer, Sarah 64
Tunisia: political protest 149–50
Turkey *see* civic participation:
CivicWeb project
Twitter 146, 151

U

unemployment 11
youth
Ireland 112–13, 115
Italy 96, 104
UNICEF 131
United Kingdom
Big Society 246
citizenship models 238
civic participation 165, 195
electoral participation 247
parental responsibility 246
participation 77
riots 153, 247

welfare state 246
youth sector 34n2
Youth Service 67–8, 68–9
see also England; Wales
United Nations: International
Convention on Children's Rights
131, 189, 211
United States 39, 61, 62
Up2Youth project 12, 23, 28, 89, 119
case studies 148–9, 238–40
Italy 94
urban planning 7, 9

V

value-memes: human development
47–51, 52–3
values 42
Varadekar, Leo 110
vocational training 25
voluntary sector 32, 115, 164, 196t,
199, 232
Ireland 112
von Schwanenflügel, L. 199
voting 6, 45 *see also* elections

W

Wales 61, 62 *see also* United Kingdom
Walther, A. 24, 247, 249, 251 *see also*
Biggart, A. et al
Walther, A. et al 6
Web 2.0: and political participation
143, 144–8, 153, 169
welfare
de-legitimisation 8
dependency 245
provision 59–60
reform 246
welfare states
comparison 10–12
Finland 234
Ireland 115
Italy 93
methodisation 66–7
models 233–7
provision 228
and regulation 229
social work and 8
United Kingdom 246
and youth 24, 25, 62–3
Wenger, E. 200–1
White, C. et al 247